Apache OFBiz Cookbook

Over 60 simple but incredibly effective recipes for taking control of OFBiz

Ruth Hoffman

BIRMINGHAM - MUMBAI

Apache OFBiz Cookbook

First published: September 2010

Production Reference: 1020910

Published by Packt Publishing Ltd.
32 Lincoln Road
Olton
Birmingham, B27 6PA, UK.

ISBN 978-1-847199-18-8

www.packtpub.com

Cover Image by Harmeet Singh (singharmeet@yahoo.com)

Credits

Author

Ruth Hoffman

Reviewers

Adrian Crum

Shi Jinghai

Acquisition Editor

Chaitanya Apte

Development Editor

Rakesh Shejwal

Technical Editor

Vanjeet D'souza

Indexer

Hemangini Bari

Editorial Team Leader

Mithun Sehgal

Project Team Leader

Ashwin Shetty

Project Coordinator

Joel Goveya

Proofreader

Jonathan Todd

Graphics

Geetanjali Sawant

Production Coordinator

Arvindkumar Gupta

Cover Work

Arvindkumar Gupta

About the Author

Ruth Hoffman is an OFBiz evangelist with over 25 years of information technology experience, including stints in software design and development, training, project management, product marketing, and software sales, She has dedicated the last few years of her eventful career to furthering the OFBiz vision. Whether it be writing about OFBiz, providing implementation and OFBiz consulting services, or just "kicking the OFBiz tires" for each new release, she enjoys working with and telling the world about all that this amazing ERP software suite has to offer.

Ruth's current passion is her quest to provide high quality, cost effective OFBiz training and documentation. She has pursued this quest through multiple channels, including the OFBiz website. She invites everyone to stop by, take a gander, and give some feedback at `http://www.myofbiz.com`

As a long-standing supporter of OFBiz, she has authored several other OFBiz titles, including *OFBiz E-Commerce Out-Of-The-Box* and *The OFBiz Catalog Manager*. For more information, please see: `http://www.myofbiz.com`.

I would like to thank my partner, JC, for being so patient and understanding, my daughter for not getting too upset when I cancelled our planned Lilac Festival adventure, and my dog Sadie for sitting by me all those long hours when no one else would.

Also, my sincerest thanks go to Adrian Crum and Shi Jinghai for their dedicated efforts in providing technical reviews of this book. Thanks for keeping me honest and setting me straight on a number of occasions. Your contributions are greatly appreciated!

About the Reviewers

Adrian Crum is an IT Manager/Computer programmer for a company that builds homes. Prior to that, he owned and operated a computer retail/service/consulting business. He was Technical Editor of *Coast Compute Magazine*, and a contributing writer for *Programmer's Journal*. Adrian has been involved with the Apache OFBiz project as a contributing programmer since 2004, and he is a member of the Project Management Committee. His extensive experience in many programming languages and cross-platform development has been a key part of his contributions to the Apache OFBiz project.

Shi Jinghai graduated from Tsinghua University in 1991. In 2001, he took part in the China 2G Citizen Card Project and became an important system designer of the National Citizen Identity Information System of China. In 2004, he started his own company (Beijing Langhua Ltd.) focusing on IT services based on some excellent open source projects such as OFBiz, OpenCms, JBoss Portal, and Jasig CAS among others.

Table of Contents

Preface

This book is designed to be read in any order, and is a collection of recipes found, by experience, to be most useful for developers working with the OFBiz project. Let it be your guide to enhancing your OFBiz productivity by saving you valuable time. Written specifically to give clear and straightforward answers to the most commonly asked OFBiz questions, this compendium of OFBiz recipes will show you everything you need to know to get things done in OFBiz.

Whether you are new to OFBiz or an old pro, you are sure to find many useful hints and handy tips here. Topics range from getting started, to configuration and system setup, security and database management, through the final stages of developing and testing new OFBiz applications. We are now Open For Business.

What this book covers

Chapter 1, Getting Started: If you already know how to get started with OFBiz then you can confidently skip this chapter. If, however, you are new to OFBiz, then you may find helpful hints in here to get you started, including getting a copy of the code from the download page or from the Subversion source code repository; fixing installation-related IP port collision errors; setting JAVA_HOME; fixing Java "Class Not Found" errors; installation verification; running JUnit tests; and some basic project artifact navigation hints, including where certain special directories (folders for Windows users) and files may be found.

Chapter 2, Java Development: OFBiz Java development starts with a clear understanding of the role of the Java CLASSPATH. In this chapter, learn how the CLASSPATH enables compilation and runtime loading of OFBiz artifacts. In addition, this chapter reveals how the OFBiz Java file-naming convention is helpful in organizing and finding Java source code. Also learn how to create OFBiz Events and Services, effectively use the provided Java debugging methods, call another OFBiz Service from within a Java program, access HTTP/HTTPS request parameters, use existing tools to handle error messages, use Java properties files, send e-mail using existing OFBiz Service(s), and manipulate XML documents using provided tools.

Chapter 3, The User Interface: Users interact with OFBiz—that is, the "User Interface"—through web pages often referred to within the project as "screens" or "screen views". In this chapter, see how web pages are built from the OFBiz Screen widget, including how to add actions, HTML markup, CSS, and other widgets (Tree, Menu, and Form widgets) to a single screen view widget definition. If your tastes run more towards creating your own screen views, see how to use FreeMarker templates inside Screen widget definitions to build (HTML) web pages. Also discussed in this chapter: passing parameters from the Screen widget's runtime context to the FreeMarker rendering engine, writing JavaScript and including it in a FreeMarker template, calling OFBiz Java methods directly from the FreeMarker context, forcing FreeMarker to render content with HTML markup at runtime, and how to upload a file—that is, support multipart HTML forms—in FreeMarker.

Chapter 4, OFBiz Services: OFBiz "Services" are reusable snippets of code that represent business processing or other logic. You write an OFBiz Service one time and invoke it anytime, anywhere and as often as needed. In this chapter, discover how to manage existing Services, invoke Services from an HTML form, and implement your own Service. Learn how Services communicate and interact during runtime operations using input and output attributes and triggers called Service Event Condition Actions, or SECAs. See best practices for handling errors within a Service and/or SECA. Also discussed are tips on implementing Services in languages other than Java, and a quick introduction to special SECA for incoming e-mail and operations on specific entities.

Chapter 5, The OFBiz Entity Engine: The OFBiz Entity Engine is the magic behind the database agnostic, data-driven tour-de-force that is OFBiz. In this chapter, see how to configure and use the Entity Engine to your advantage. Specifically, see how to change from the default Derby database to another database (note: throughout the OFBiz documentation, the term "data source" is used interchangeably with "database"); how to connect to remote and multiple databases; how entity groups work to help OFBiz organize access to multiple databases; and disable some system database startup checks, map new database field types, create your own entity definition file and entity definition, modify an existing entity definition—often referred to as the entity's model—and build view-entities that represent SQL join statements.

Chapter 6, OFBiz Security: What book about enterprise software would be complete without a word concerning security? In this chapter, get a quick introduction to securing your OFBiz instance, including recipes to lock down communication ports, disable demonstration accounts, protect web pages and web applications using OFBiz Security Groups, enable support for "tarpitting", retrieve forgotten passwords, change existing passwords, handle SSL certificates, and use OFBiz single sign-on support by way of the "external login key" feature.

Chapter 7, WebTools: Often lost in the OFBiz shuffle is a discussion covering basic usage of the many and varied tools that come with the project to manage your OFBiz instance. Collectively called "WebTools", this chapter looks at several important tasks easily accomplished using WebTools, including managing the cache, configuring system and application log tool settings for debug and troubleshooting support; exporting and importing database data; managing localization labels, and accessing databases using the SQL processor tool. Also discussed are introductions to the immensely useful Entity Reference Tool, finding and viewing OFBiz usage statistics, tracing OFBiz artifact dependencies, and working with temporal expressions.

Chapter 8, Web Services: With service orientation at the core of the OFBiz architecture, OFBiz is uniquely qualified to act as both a web services client and service provider for any number of web service interactions. In this chapter, learn how to act as a web services client and request service using URL parameter passing, `HttpClient` and XML document exchanges, and XML-RPC service requests. If you wish to provide web services, see how to set up OFBiz to serve XML-RPC services, generate and serve WSDL documents, and build both SOAP-based clients and services.

Chapter 9, OFBiz Tips and Tricks: This chapter is a collection of recipes that don't fit under other topic areas. Included here are hints on what to do if you run out of memory during OFBiz execution, reloading/reinitializing the OFBiz database, creating a new administrative user login and password, and getting the OFBiz version number (from Subversion checkouts or trunk builds only). Also included here are hints on using the provided ANT build tool to build an entire OFBiz instance, build a single OFBiz Component, and create a new OFBiz Component or Application. If you are looking for tips on creating a FreeMarker transformation, preparing data using Groovy, how to pop-up a new browser window, and OFBiz visual themes, you will find useful information here.

Appendix, Entity Engine by Example: In this Appendix, see how to effectively use the OFBiz Entity Engine to bring your OFBiz data drive applications to life. From the provided example data model, learn how to create entities and view-entities (SQL join statements) to implement a data model. Also, see how to read, remove, and write data to/from the database using the Entity Engine API; and use the provided `EntityUtil` API to manipulate database result-sets, access the automatic sequence generator to create new and unique sequence values, and see at a glance valid values for use with the Entity "Operator".

What you need for this book

To run the recipes mentioned in this book, you will need the following software:

- Java Software Development Kit version 1.5 or greater
- Apache OFBiz release 9.04

Who this book is for

If you are an OFBiz user who has some familiarity with enterprise software systems and, perhaps more importantly, Internet and web exposure, you will be able to glean useful information from this book. For following some recipes, you will need only basic knowledge of modern browser behavior (for example, how to click a mouse button) while others assume only a passing familiarity with a text-editor and XML documents. If you are a software developer looking for Java and/or Groovy examples, this book also includes a chapter on Java software development.

Conventions

In this book, you will find a number of styles of text that distinguish between different kinds of information. Here are some examples of these styles, and an explanation of their meaning.

Code words in text are shown as follows: "Add one or more `delegator` elements to the `datasource` object".

A block of code is set as follows:

```
<field-type-def type="currency-amount" sql-type="NUMERIC(18,2)"
                java type="java.math.BigDecimal">
  <validate method="isSignedDouble"/>
</field-type-def>
```

When we wish to draw your attention to a particular part of a code block, the relevant lines or items are set in bold:

```
<field-type-def type="currency-amount" sql-type="NUMERIC(18,2)"
                java type="java.math.BigDecimal">
  <validate method="isSignedDouble"/>
</field-type-def>
```

Any command-line input or output is written as follows:

```
ant clean-install
```

New terms and important words are shown in bold. Words that you see on the screen, in menus or dialog boxes for example, appear in the text like this: "Use the WebTools Entity Reference - Interactive Version to see if the new view-entity was successfully created".

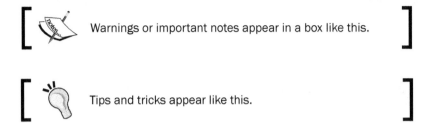

Warnings or important notes appear in a box like this.

Tips and tricks appear like this.

Reader feedback

Feedback from our readers is always welcome. Let us know what you think about this book—what you liked or may have disliked. Reader feedback is important for us to develop titles that you really get the most out of.

To send us general feedback, simply send an e-mail to feedback@packtpub.com, and mention the book title via the subject of your message.

If there is a book that you need and would like to see us publish, please send us a note in the SUGGEST A TITLE form on www.packtpub.com, or e-mail suggest@packtpub.com.

If there is a topic that you have expertise in and you are interested in either writing or contributing to a book, see our author guide on www.packtpub.com/authors.

Customer support

Now that you are the proud owner of a Packt book, we have a number of things to help you to get the most from your purchase.

Errata

Although we have taken every care to ensure the accuracy of our content, mistakes do happen. If you find a mistake in one of our books—maybe a mistake in the text or the code—we would be grateful if you would report this to us. By doing so, you can save other readers from frustration and help us improve subsequent versions of this book. If you find any errata, please report them by visiting http://www.packtpub.com/support, selecting your book, clicking on the let us know link, and entering the details of your errata. Once your errata are verified, your submission will be accepted and the errata will be uploaded on our website, or added to any list of existing errata, under the Errata section of that title. Any existing errata can be viewed by selecting your title from http://www.packtpub.com/support.

Piracy

Piracy of copyright material on the Internet is an ongoing problem across all media. At Packt, we take the protection of our copyright and licenses very seriously. If you come across any illegal copies of our works, in any form, on the Internet, please provide us with the location address or website name immediately so that we can pursue a remedy.

Please contact us at `copyright@packtpub.com` with a link to the suspected pirated material.

We appreciate your help in protecting our authors, and our ability to bring you valuable content.

Questions

You can contact us at `questions@packtpub.com` if you are having a problem with any aspect of the book, and we will do our best to address it.

1

Getting Started

The OFBiz project is a collection of hundreds of directories and files, organized to allow for easy download, start-up, customization, and enterprise deployment.

In this chapter, we shall look at a number of commonly performed tasks related to setting up and running with OFBiz, including:

- ▶ Getting the project code
- ▶ Getting code from the Apache Subversion source code repository
- ▶ Fixing IP port collision error
- ▶ Setting the JAVA_HOME environment variable
- ▶ Fixing "Class Not Found" errors
- ▶ Installation verification
- ▶ SSL operational verification
- ▶ Running JUnit tests
- ▶ Finding an OFBiz Component's top-level directory
- ▶ Locating an OFBiz Application

Introduction

OFBiz appeals to a remarkably diverse audience because of the breadth of solutions it enables. Whether you are a software developer or a business owner, you will find much to surprise, delight, and, most importantly use for your next enterprise software endeavor under the OFBiz umbrella.

In fact, there is so much to OFBiz that it is often difficult to know where to start. Unlike learning HTML or Java, OFBiz has no specification or authoritative source acting as the final arbiter of what works or is "correct". Rather, OFBiz is a well organized collection of "artifacts" that may, at the user's discretion, be mixed, matched, reorganized, and augmented with new artifacts to arrive at just about any business solution imaginable.

Just imagine an open source software project that includes:

- ▶ Its own database schema and seed data already loaded and ready to run.
- ▶ An event-driven Service engine that enables code reusability across the entire instance. Services may be written in Java or any supported language, including Groovy, Bean Shell, JPython, and more.
- ▶ Hundreds of business logic workflow implementations ranging from a complete e-commerce Application to manufacturing and MRP, content management, user authentication, and authorization support all out-of-the-box and ready to use.
- ▶ Everything you need to serve up complete browser compliant **User Interfaces** (**UI**).
- ▶ And much more!

With all the possibilities that OFBiz brings to the table, where does one begin? From experience, the best way to get up and running quickly is to download the project code and start kicking the "tires". Use some of the suggestions in this book to help quickly experience some of the state-of-the-art tools, utilities, and complete Applications that are part of OFBiz out-of-the-box.

Always remember: there is no "right" or "wrong" way to doing anything with OFBiz.

Everything you need to get up and running quickly and with minimum fuss is packaged with the OFBiz distribution. That includes an integrated database, a ready to use web server, and all the network and communications infrastructure necessary to be up and running in minutes. All you need to do before you download OFBiz is:

- ▶ Ensure that the prerequisite **Java Software Development Kit** (SDK) is installed. Please see the following table.
- ▶ Access to a reliable Internet connection.
- ▶ A modern browser handy to do some installation verification.

How do you know which version of Java to install? The following table summarizes available download options and necessary Java prerequisites:

Download title	Recommended usage	Minimum Java version	OFBiz version
`apache-ofbiz-09.04.zip`	Recommended for new users and those looking for the most stable project package.	Java 1.5	*
`apache-ofbiz-4.0.zip`	Legacy release. Not recommended for new users.	Java 1.4 or Java 1.5	
"Nightly Trunk Builds" `ofbiz-trunk-current.zip`	Project committers or users needing latest code. May not be stable or thoroughly tested! These files are available on the "snapshots" download page.	Java 1.6 * *	Nightly trunk builds do not have release numbers.

* Nightly builds and version numbers represent bug fixes only.

* * "trunk" versions before January 2010, Java 1.5

Once OFBiz is downloaded and available locally on your hard drive, install it by "unpacking" it with your operating system's "unzip" tool.

Once unzipped, OFBiz is ready to run.

Looking for the Java SDK?

Most Java SDKs are available from Sun Microsystems at:

`http://www.java.com/`

MAC users will need to contact Apple directly or use the **Software Update** feature available on the Apple menu.

Getting the project code

Because OFBiz is more than just a few randomly organized files and directories, the collective and organized resources that go into making OFBiz, including the Apache infrastructure and software developers, are often called the "Project". The OFBiz project generates OFBiz code that is stored in a Subversion source code repository. It is a release and version of this code, extracted from the source code repository, built, and packaged using a "zip" archive tool, that we download as an OFBiz user.

Getting ready

Decide which version to download. It is recommended that new users download OFBiz Release 9.04. Experienced users and those wishing to contribute back to the project should consider starting with the latest version of the OFBiz source code "trunk". This code may be found on the Apache OFBiz "snapshot" web page.

Ensure you have the following necessary prerequisites in place:

▸ A computer with a **Java Virtual Machine** (**JVM**) installed. If you are unsure of the version, please refer to the table provided in the introduction to this chapter.

▸ A modern browser (Internet Explorer, Firefox, Safari, Opera or the like).

▸ Internet connection with HTTP access to the OFBiz download website.

How to do it...

Apache OFBiz can be downloaded as shown in the following steps:

1. Using your browser, navigate to the Apache OFBiz download site (`http://ofbiz.apache.org/download.html`) to reveal the **Download Apache OFBiz** web page as shown:

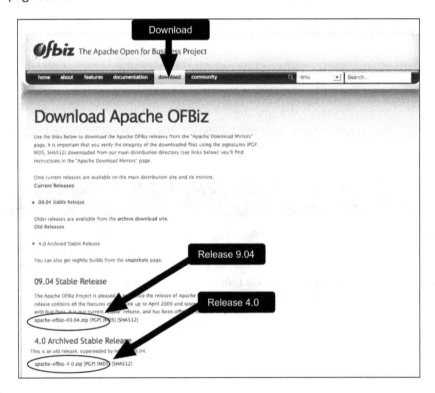

2. Use your browser to select the desired OFBiz release. New users are urged to download the release represented by the `apache-ofbiz-09.04.zip` file. At any point in time, this download represents the most stable release of OFBiz.

3. Commence the download by clicking on the file link provided.

 Note: The official OFBiz download website is often in a state of flux. At times, you may be directed to a mirror site before you are allowed to download any code. On other occasions, clicking the OFBiz download file will directly initiate the download. If you find this all very confusing, you are not alone. Feel free to comment on the official OFBiz mailing list and voice your opinion. More information about the OFBiz user mailing lists may be found here: `https://cwiki.apache.org/confluence/display/OFBADMIN/Mailing+Lists`

4. Once the download has completed, unpack OFBiz by running your operating system's `unzip` or equivalent command against the download file.

5. Change directories to the OFBiz install directory and run the following ANT command to build the distribution and load the database: `ant run-install`

6. After the ANT build script has completed, from the install directory run the appropriate OFBiz startup script provided for your operating system.

7. Optionally, run tests to verify that everything is working

How it works...

OFBiz is packaged to include everything you need to run right out-of-the-box. Once your download is on your desktop, all you need do is unbundle it, build the distribution using the provided ANT tool, and start it up. No other configuration steps are necessary.

There's more...

There are a number of ways to start up OFBiz. Depending on your operating system environment and your proclivities towards working on the command line, you may:

▸ Use one of the provided start up scripts

▸ Invoke OFBiz from the command line directly or use the ANT build tool as shown here:

Windows	Unix	Command line
startofbiz.bat	startofbiz.sh	java -Xmx256M -jar ofbiz.jar
		ant run

OFBiz runs inside and depends on a JVM. Before OFBiz can even start up, the JVM must be operational. The distribution provides all the tools necessary in the form of startup scripts to get the JVM up and running without any further work on your part.

For the curious, the following summarizes the OFBiz start-up sequence. This information is useful if you ever want to integrate third-party code or add your own Java programs to the OFBiz mix:

1. The Java Virtual Machine (JVM) is started from one of the available startup scripts or the command line.

2. The OFBiz startup program (`ofbiz.jar`) is invoked as part of the JVM initialization.

3. OFBiz loads all `Components`, builds the Java `classpath`, initializes communications, and verifies connections to one or more configured databases. While the OFBiz distribution includes the embedded Derby database, any number and combination of other databases may be configured.

4. The embedded Tomcat http/https listener is started.

5. OFBiz is up and running!

See also

For more information on prerequisites, getting the OFBiz code, and downloading and starting OFBiz up, please visit the **What Do I Get?** section on the following OFBiz web page: `http://ci.apache.org/projects/ofbiz/snapshots/`

 Note: Be careful not to use the **DOWNLOAD OFBIZ** button on the snapshots download web page. Unless you want to download the latest OFBiz trunk nightly build, this button should not be confused with the **DOWNLOAD OFBIZ** button found on the official OFBiz loading web page: `http://ofbiz.apache.org`

Getting code from the Subversion repository

If you are planning to contribute back to the project or are just curious about downloading from the OFBiz source code control system, you may download a complete OFBiz package from the Subversion source code repository using the following procedure.

You will need a Subversion client, or an IDE with a Subversion client installed in order to access and download from Subversion.

Getting ready

Before you can download directly from the OFBiz Subversion repository, you must first have a Subversion client installed locally. Subversion clients come in several forms. The Subversion software comes with a command-line client and a command-line tool that facilitates checkout and download from a Subversion repository. This command is the `co` command.

Some users prefer to use built-in IDE (Integrated Development Environment) Subversion clients. One such client, Subclipse (`http://subclpse.tigris.org`), allows the user to checkout and install OFBiz from within the IDE using IDE-specific commands.

It goes without saying: you must also have an Internet connection with access to the OFBiz Subversion repository.

How to do it...

OFBiz source code can be downloaded from the Subversion repository by the following steps:

1. From a command-line window, type the following Subversion command:

   ```
   svn co http://svn.apache.org/repos/asf/ofbiz/trunk ofbiz
   ```

2. Navigate to the install directory. If you used the above command, navigate to the `ofbiz` directory. For UNIX users, a command similar to the following is suggested:

   ```
   cd ofbiz
   ```

3. Run the build script provided:

   ```
   ant run-install
   ```

How it works...

OFBiz project source code is saved in a repository managed by the Subversion source code control system. Subversion uses a tree-like structure to organize and group together project artifacts, including source code. Each time a project developer commits an artifact to the repository, a new OFBiz version number is created, similar to a leaf on a tree. The project has had thousands of commits over its lifetime, hence the current version number is well on its way towards one million.

To request a version of OFBiz from the repository, a user issues a Subversion checkout command, `co`. A Subversion checkout fetches by default the latest leaf or version of the project from the Subversion code tree.

The OFBiz source code repository contains all previous versions of OFBiz. You may checkout any version at any time. Additionally, you may checkout "releases" of OFBiz where a "release" is a "branch" of the source code tree, by indicating your desire using the `co` command options.

Once the fetch from the repository is complete, you must run the OFBiz build script to build the project before running the OFBiz startup scripts. The build script rebuilds all included Java programs, rebuilds the runtime CLASSPATH, and checks and loads the database with seed and demonstration data.

See also

For more information on using Eclipse with the OFBiz Subversion repository, please refer to the following OFBiz Wiki page:

```
http://cwiki.apache.org/confluence/display/OFBIZ/Running+and+Debuggin
g+OFBiz+in+Eclipse
```

For more information on Subversion, please refer to the Subversion website located at:

```
http://subversion.tigris.org
```

Fixing IP port collision errors

One of the most common OFBiz startup errors involves IP port collisions. OFBiz requires several **Internet Protocol** (**IP**) ports to run. All OFBiz downloads have these ports set to default values so that you may start up OFBiz without further configuration.

Occasionally, these default values are in conflict with IP ports used by other software already running on your system. If OFBiz cannot acquire the ports it needs to run, it will immediately shutdown and you will receive an error similar to the following on the command line (from which you started OFBiz):

```
(main)  [ Http11Protocol.java:178:ERROR]
Error initializing endpoint java.net.BindException: Address already in
use: 8080
```

Getting ready

To remedy IP port conflicts, you may either turn off the software using the ports OFBiz needs or you can change the OFBiz configuration so that it uses ports not used by other software.

How to do it...

To change the OFBiz IP port configuration, perform the following:

1. Determine the port(s) that is/are in conflict by observing the console or command line window. Alternatively, you may view the primary OFBiz log file located in `~/runtime/logs/ofbiz.log`

2. Locate the OFBiz configuration file where the port is set.

3. Edit the OFBiz configuration by changing the port number to a non-conflicting value.

4. Restart OFBiz.

How it works...

For example, to fix collisions on port 8080, the IP port that OFBiz listens on for HTTP requests, navigate to the `ofbiz-containers.xml` file as shown in the following figure and change the value for port 8080 to another port not in use.

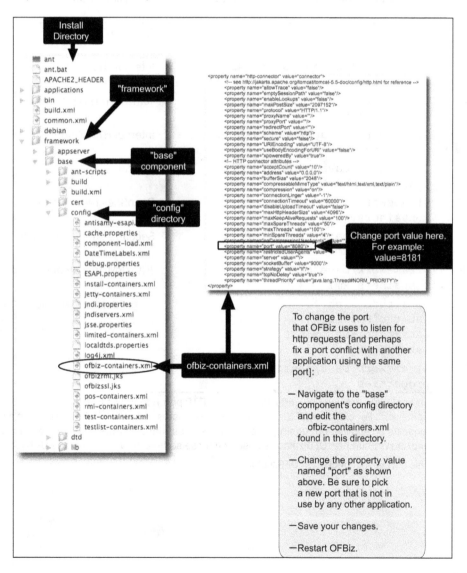

Note: Setting the HTTP port to a value between 1-1024 may require operating system administrative privileges in order to start up OFBiz. This is a constraint placed on these ports outside the control of OFBiz.

There's more...

The following is a list of IP port configuration file locators for reference:

Port #	Configuration file location relative to install directory	Port usage note
8080	~framework/base/config/ofbiz-containers.xml	Tomcat HTTP listener
	~framework/webapp/config/url.properties	Internal HTTP port *
8443	~framework/base/config/ofbiz-containers.xml	Tomcat HTTPS listener
	~framework/webapp/config/url.properties	Internal HTTPS port *
8009	~framework/base/config/ofbiz-containers.xml	AJP connector
9990	~framework/base/config/ofbiz-containers.xml	BeanShell remote telnet port
9991	~framework/base/config/ofbiz-containers.xml	Second, required telnet port
1099	~framework/base/config/rmi-containers.xml	JNDI/RMI dispatcher
10523	~startofbiz.sh ~startofbiz.bat ~startofbizNoLog.bat ~stopofbiz.sh	Admin port to start/stop OFBiz
389	~framework/base/config/jndiLdap.properties	LDAP port**

*   Internal ports are used by OFBiz to translate HTTP port references internal to the framework. For example, OFBiz automatically translates between HTTP and HTTPS if a user requests an Application running on a secure port, but the user enters the wrong protocol and/or port number; OFBiz knows based on these settings how to correct the URL request.

**   This port is not checked at OFBiz start-up.

The JAVA_HOME setting

OFBiz startup scripts must invoke the Java executable as part of its initiation process. If you are using one of the provided startup scripts and you can't start up OFBiz because the Java executable cannot be found (you will get an immediate error to this effect), you can easily add the necessary statement to the script to indicate the location of the Java executable.

Note: The scripts as they are distributed today assume that you have previously set the JAVA_HOME environment variable using your computer's environment variable setting tools to the location of the Java runtime executable. This setting should be in the environment prior to invoking the OFBiz startup script. If this location has not been set or has been set incorrectly, you will not be able to start up OFBiz.

Getting ready

To set up JAVA_HOME, you need to first perform the following steps:

1. Determine the location of the appropriate version of Java given the release of OFBiz installed.

2. Navigate to the install directory where the startup scripts are located.

3. Open up the appropriate startup script (startofbiz.bat for Windows or startofbiz.sh for Unix).

How to do it...

JAVA_HOME can be set up in the following way:

1. Add a line similar to the following prior to the comment line "location of java executables" as shown in the following snippet from the Unix startofbiz.sh startup script shown here:

```
# This is an example of setting the JAVA_HOME variable in the
# UNIX startofbiz.sh script:

JAVA_HOME=/bin/java
export JAVA_HOME

# location of java executables
if [ -f "$JAVA_HOME/bin/java" ]; then
  JAVA="$JAVA_HOME/bin/java"
else
  JAVA=java
fi
```

2. Save your changes.

3. Restart OFBiz using the modified startup script.

How it works...

The JAVA_HOME environment variable sets the location of the Java executable relative to the hard drive and the file system of the host operating system so that the startup scripts know where to find it. In this way, you could have many Java versions installed on your computer and still tell OFBiz which installed version to use at any point in time.

Out-of-the-box OFBiz assumes that the JAVA_HOME variable has been set prior to the invocation of the startup script. As an alternative to modifying startup scripts, you may also set JAVA_HOME from the command line prior to invoking the startup script.

There's more...

If you are starting up OFBiz from the command line and not using the startup scripts, you should set your JAVA_HOME prior to invoking OFBiz. For example, if your Java executable is located in the /opt/java directory (folder for Windows readers), and you are running a Unix system, then set the JAVA_HOME environment variable as follows:

```
JAVA_HOME=/opt/java
export $JAVA_HOME
java -jar ofbiz.jar
```

"Class Not Found" errors

Another startup error that you may encounter is a "Class Not Found" error. This is usually indicative of incompatibilities between the Java runtime in use and the version of OFBiz. These errors will show up in the console window and in the OFBiz log file (~runtime/logs/ofbiz.log), and occasionally as a web page error during normal OFBiz operations.

Getting ready

Tracking down the source of "Class Not Found" errors may involve some detective work. In some cases, these errors are not immediately fatal. If the error is causing OFBiz to immediately shutdown, then you most probably have an incompatibility between the OFBiz runtime and the version of the JVM in use.

To fix OFBiz startup "Class Not Found" errors, you must first determine the version of Java being invoked from the startup script or the command line. The following section shows how this can be determined.

How to do it...

To find out which version of the Java JVM OFBiz is running in and where your JAVA_HOME environment variable is pointing, perform the following:

1. Navigate to the OFBiz install directory.
2. As the user invoking the startup script or command line Java execute statement, type in the following Java command:

    ```
    java -version
    ```

If the information returned does not say 1.5 or 1.6, then you will need to install the Java 1.5 or 1.6 SDK. You may also need to modify the JAVA_HOME variable as shown previously.

How it works...

The Java runtime executable may be invoked with the -version parameter to return the version of the JVM being called. When executed this way, the JVM is started, the version number is checked, and then the JVM is shutdown.

Running this command as the same user who invokes the OFBiz startup scripts ensures that you pass to the JVM the same environment settings, including the JAVA_HOME setting that will be available when the startup script is invoked. In this way, you may quickly determine which version of Java you are running when you start up OFBiz.

If the version number returned is not compatible with the OFBiz release you are running, then you will need to either set your JAVA_HOME variable as shown previously to the appropriate version of Java or install the necessary Java SDK. The following table summarizes OFBiz Java dependencies:

Release	Java version
OFBiz 9.04	1.5
OFBiz 4.0	1.5
OFBiz trunk	1.6

There's more...

There is no recommended Java reference platform for OFBiz. Known implementations of the Java SDK that have successfully built OFBiz include the Sun and Mac Java SDKs.

Installation verification

To quickly ascertain if OFBiz has installed correctly and is ready for use, you may use your browser to view various OFBiz Application features, including the built-in e-commerce demonstration store.

Getting ready

Once OFBiz is unpacked and, if downloaded from the Subversion repository, built using the `ant` run-install command, you are ready to start the installation verification by observing the OFBiz e-commerce demonstration store.

How to do it...

To view the e-commerce demonstration store, follow these steps:

1. Change to the OFBiz install directory.
2. Start OFBiz using one of the startup scripts provided or directly from the command line.
3. Open a web browser and enter the URL of the OFBiz e-commerce Application demonstration website: `http://localhost:8080/ecommerce`
4. Observe the OFBiz e-commerce demonstration store's main web page. It should look something like the following:

5. If the web page displays correctly, then you may be confident that at least the OFBiz database and web server software are operating correctly.

How it works...

A quick and easy way to verify that your OFBiz download is working correctly is to start an instance and observe that one of the non-password protected Applications is operational. The OFBiz e-commerce Application, a fully-featured e-commerce website store, is a robust and demanding OFBiz Application. Running the e-commerce Application demonstrates and exercises many core OFBiz features including, but not limited to, successful operations of the following:

- OFBiz Entity engine
- OFBiz Service engine
- Integrated web server (Apache Tomcat)
- Integrated Java servlet container (Apache Catalina/Tomcat)
- Network connectivity
- Web browser UI compliance

There's more...

If the main e-commerce web page is displayed and looks similar to that shown above then you may be confident that at least part of OFBiz is working correctly. This, however, should be considered simply the starting point.

SSL verification

It is entirely possible that the HTTP listener may be working, but secure URLs using the HTTPS protocol may not be. To verify that the **Secure Sockets Layer** (**SSL**) encryption works and that OFBiz is listening for web requests on the secure HTTPS configured port, navigate to the OFBiz WebTools main landing page and attempt to access any of the menu selections provided.

Getting ready

Aside from starting up an instance of OFBiz, there are no special prerequisites necessary to test OFBiz SSL support.

How to do it...

OFBiz SSL support can be tested by following these steps:

1. From any compliant web browser, enter the URL of an OFBiz password-protected Application. For example, enter the URL of the WebTools Application: `http://localhost:8080/webtools`

2. The WebTools Application has a main landing web page as shown below. This web page is not password-protected. In order to access the protected WebTools applications, you must select the **Login** link on this main landing page as shown in the following:

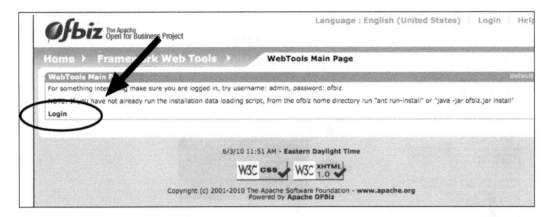

3. When presented with the WebTools login screen, login using the default username of **admin** and default password of **ofbiz**. This HTML login form should look something like the following:

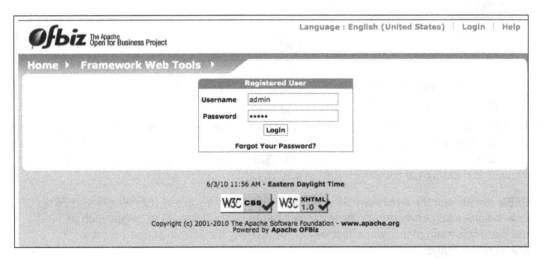

4. Successful login will bring up the protected portion of the WebTools Application UI. Observe that you are able to see the main web page as shown here:

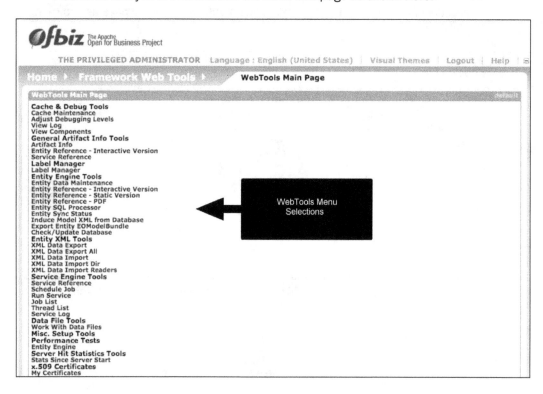

How it works...

The SSL protocol implementation is an integral part of the OFBiz project. Out-of-the-box, OFBiz is configured to use the HTTPS protocol running on port 8443 to support SSL. All password-protected portions of the project use SSL keys and encryption to secure the transfer and storage of sensitive information.

OFBiz comes with the necessary SSL certificate installed to support a generic web browser to web server SSL environment. By accessing password-protected web pages such as the WebTools main menu, you effectively are exercising the built-in support for the SSL implementation.

Note: HTTPS, SSL and SSL encryption are no substitutes for a firewall and a well thought-out security policy.

There's more...

WebTools, like all OFBiz backend Applications, has been configured to require authentication prior to access. The default OFBiz authentication process forces the user to access any SSL-secured URL through the HTTPS port. The astute observer may have noticed that WebTools was initially accessed using the HTTP protocol on port 8080. If OFBiz is working correctly, it will automatically make the translation from HTTP port 8080 to HTTPS port 8443.

See also

For more on security, refer to *Chapter 7, OFBiz Security*.

Running JUnit tests

Beyond simple "is it running ok?" types of tests, OFBiz comes with many JUnit tests that you can run. JUnit exercises very specific processing logic within OFBiz, and success or failure of any particular JUnit test is not an indication of OFBiz overall health.

Getting ready

The following must be performed first of all:

1. If OFBiz is running, shut it down by running the shutdown script provided or by killing the Java process from the command line.
2. Navigate to the OFBiz install directory.

How to do it...

JUnit tests can be run in the following way:

1. Open a command line in the OFBiz install directory.
2. Run the following ANT command to start all available JUnit tests, `ant run-tests`
3. Observe the results by reviewing the OFBiz `ofbiz.log` logfile located in the `~runtime/logs` directory or the output on the command line from which the JUnit test command was invoked.

How it works...

Out-of-the-box OFBiz comes complete with many JUnit test scenarios embedded within the code base. The provided ANT target directives, when invoked, run through all available tests, redirecting results to the primary OFBiz logfile located in the ~runtime/logs/ofbiz.log file.

There's more...

JUnit test results are intermixed with standard logfile text. A sample of what you may expect to see after running all tests from the command line is extracted from the OFBiz logfile (~runtime/logs/ofbiz.log) and shown here:

```
[Java] 2010-02-02 12:45:11,552 (main) [  TestRunContainer.java:144:INFO ] [JUNIT] Pass: true I # Tests: 20 I # Failed: 0 # Errors: 0
[Java] 2010-02-02 12:45:11,552 (main) [  TestRunContainer.java:147:INFO ] [JUNIT] ---------------------------- ERRORS ---------------------------- [JUNIT]
[Java] 2010-02-02 12:45:11,552 (main) [  TestRunContainer.java:150:INFO ] None
[Java] 2010-02-02 12:45:11,552 (main) [  TestRunContainer.java:160:INFO ] [JUNIT] ---------------------------------------------------------------- [JUNIT]
[Java] 2010-02-02 12:45:11,553 (main) [  TestRunContainer.java:161:INFO ] [JUNIT] ------------------------- FAILURES ------------------------- [JUNIT]
[Java] 2010-02-02 12:45:11,553 (main) [  TestRunContainer.java:164:INFO ] None
[Java] 2010-02-02 12:45:11,553 (main) [  TestRunContainer.java:174:INFO ] [JUNIT] ---------------------------------------------------------------- [JUNIT]
```

Locating an OFBiz Component

The OFBiz project is organized into groups of directories and files where some directories have a special meaning and are called "Components". To find an OFBiz Component is to find the top-level directory where the Component begins and to locate the configuration file ofbiz-component.xml used to configure that Component.

Note: OFBiz is flexible enough to support an unlimited number of Components. To enable this feature, OFBiz has its own Component configuration files starting with the file located in ~framework/base/config/component-load.xml. This recipe assumes you are looking for and wish to navigate to the top-level location of an existing Component as configured in this and other OFBiz Component configuration settings files.

Getting ready

Before the Component can be located, the following prerequisites should be met:

1. Determine the name of the Component you are searching for.
2. Make sure you have the Component name and not the Application name.

3. If you know which parent grouping the Component falls into, make note of this directory name. The basic OFBiz directory layout is shown here:

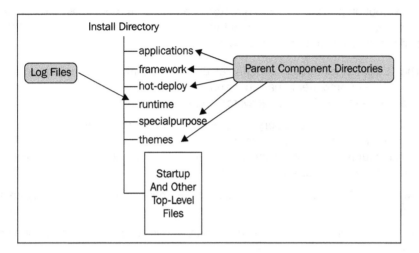

How to do it...

To locate the Component, perform the following:

1. Navigate to the OFBiz install directory.
2. If you know the parent directory name for this Component, navigate to that directory.
3. If you do not know the name of the parent Component directory, search each of the OFBiz Component parent directories for the directory with the same name as the Component name you are looking for.
4. When you find a match, you will have located your Component.

Note: This technique only works if you have not altered any of the Component configuration files discussed later. Because OFBiz may be configured to support any number of Components located anywhere within the code base, a Component's name and a Component's location are only guaranteed to be the same out-of-the-box. This guarantee is predicated on nothing more than best practices. Take note that under normal circumstances, the Component's name and top-level directory name most probably will be the same.

How it works...

The OFBiz distribution is organized into directories and files. At the highest level is the installation or `install` directory. This directory contains all the files needed by OFBiz to start up and run. It also contains the five parent Component directories:

- ▶ The `framework` directory contains all the Components necessary to run OFBiz. Many of the other Components have dependencies on Components in this directory. This directory is loaded first during system initialization.

- ▶ The `applications` directory contains Components that represent many of the business related Applications packaged with OFBiz. For example, you will find the manufacturing, content management, and order management Components and associated Applications in this directory.

- ▶ The `specialpurpose` directory contains yet more OFBiz packaged Applications and Components.

- ▶ The `themes` directory contains the resources necessary to implement one or more OFBiz themes.

- ▶ The `hot-deploy` directory is intended for the placement of new Components and Applications. Out-of-the-box it is empty, containing no OFBiz artifacts.

These parent directories are not Components in and of themselves, but rather are directories that group similar Components. Organizing Components this way makes it easier for humans to find specific Components. It also allows OFBiz to load Components in a pre-set order.

A master list of all Components within an OFBiz installation is found in the `~framework/base/config/component-load.xml` file. This file informs OFBiz which parent Component directories should be searched for the parent Component directory configuration file: `component-load.xml`. Within each `component-load.xml` file are found directives instructing OFBiz on which Components to load per parent Component directory.

There's more...

You may exclude an entire parent Component directory and all its contained Components from being loaded by commenting out directives in the `~framework/base/config/component-load.xml`. You may also exclude individual Components from loading by commenting the appropriate `component-load.xml` for each individual parent Component.

Locating an OFBiz Application

An OFBiz "Application" is a set of directories and files that are located within a Component. Referred to as "webapps", an OFBiz Application may contain all the artifacts necessary to deliver a web browser-compliant UI. As a testament to its flexibility, an OFBiz instance and any OFBiz Component may include an unlimited number of webapps.

An OFBiz Application is defined by the presence of the `webapp` directory located just beneath a containing Component's top-level directory, and may include one or more of the following files and directories:

- A single `WEB-INF` directory

- Beneath the `WEB-INF` directory, find a `web.xml` deployment descriptor file

- Also beneath the `WEB-INF` directory, a `controller.xml` controller servlet configuration file may be present

- Many other resources may be present depending on the needs of the Application

Getting ready

To locate an Application, firstly the following should be taken care of:

1. Determine the name of the Application you are searching for.

2. Try to ascertain the Component in which this Application is located An OFBiz Component may have one or more OFBiz Applications within it.

How to do it...

To locate the Application, perform the following:

1. Navigate to the OFBiz install directory.

2. If you know the name of the Component in which this Application is located, navigate to that Component's top-level directory.

3. Open the `ofbiz-component.xml` file in the top-level Component directory. In this file, locate any XML elements starting with a `webapp` tag. There may be many of these declarations within a single `ofbiz-component.xml` file. Each declaration represents the configuration of a single OFBiz web Application. For example, the following is taken from the OFBiz e-commerce Component. Two OFBiz Applications, the `"eccomerce"` and the `"ecomclone"`, are configured. The top-level directory location of each Component is given by the `location` attribute value for the `webapp` element:

```
<webapp name="ecommerce"
        title="eCommerce"
        server="default-server"
        location="webapp/ecommerce"
        mount-point="/"
        app-bar-display="false"/>
<webapp name="ecomclone"
```

```
title="eCommerce Clone"
server="default-server"
location="webapp/ecomclone"
mount-point="/ecomclone"
app-bar-display="false"/>
```

How it works...

OFBiz Applications are configured for each Component using the `ofbiz-component.xml` file. If one or more `webapp` elements are present in an `ofbiz-component.xml` file, this is a trigger to OFBiz that there are Applications for this Component. OFBiz will attempt to load all Component applications in the order defined in the `ofbiz-component.xml` file at system startup.

There's more...

To mount an Application as the "root" Application, set the `mount-point` attribute value to `"/"` as shown earlier. This will change the default URL for this webapp from `http://localhost:8080/name` to `http://localhost:8080/`. Only one webapp may be set to the root mount-point per OFBiz instance.

2
Java Development

In this chapter, we will cover

- ► CLASSPATH basics
- ► Java file naming conventions
- ► Creating OFBiz Java Events
- ► Creating OFBiz Java Services
- ► Debugging
- ► Calling an OFBiz Service from a Java program
- ► Java programs and request parameters
- ► Error messages: best practices
- ► Using properties files
- ► Sending e-mail
- ► Manipulating XML files

Note: This chapter is not intended to instruct Java developers planning to commit code back to the OFBiz project. Such code is subject to the **OFBiz Contributors Best Practices** document found at:
`http://cwiki.apache.org/confluence/x/JIB2`

Introduction

Before you can write effective OFBiz Java code, you need to understand some basics about the environment in which OFBiz operates. In *the previous chapter,* we learned that OFBiz executes within a JVM. That JVM, in turn, hosts a Java servlet container. The servlet container provides all the basic programming infrastructure necessary to build and run OFBiz web applications (sometimes referred to as "webapps").

 Out-of-the-box, bundled with the distribution, OFBiz embeds the Tomcat servlet container, `http://apache.tomcat.org`. It is possible to implement other servlet containers as well as run OFBiz within a Java application server such as JBoss, WebSphere®, or WebLogic®.

In this book, we first describe what it takes to develop OFBiz webapps. Traditionally, writing Java web applications has meant writing entire servlets. When writing OFBiz webapps, you typically do not write an entire servlet. Instead, you create one or more Java methods that are invoked by the OFBiz controller servlet either directly as an "Event" or "Service", or indirectly by another Java program.

Running inside a servlet container means that your OFBiz Java code will have access to all the resources necessary to communicate with client browsers; any other OFBiz Service, tool, or artifact on the runtime CLASSPATH; and effectively and efficiently interact with the database.

Beyond writing OFBiz Java-based Events and Services, it is also possible to write entirely new Java classes that may be placed on the CLASSPATH as desired. If placed on the CLASSPATH before OFBiz is restarted, these classes will automatically be loaded and available for use.

Java runtime CLASSPATH

The Java CLASSPATH is an environment variable containing a list of resources (for example: Java class files, JAR and ZIP archive files) used during program execution. Within the OFBiz environment, the CLASSPATH may become quite complex with hundreds of entries. Therefore, it is comforting to know that OFBiz makes it easy for us to manipulate the CLASSPATH and add new resources.

How to do it...

Resources can be added to the runtime CLASSPATH by following these steps:

1. Put that resource in any directory that is already listed in the CLASSPATH. Examples of default CLASSPATH directory locations include:

   `~framework/base/lib`

   or

   `~framework/webapp/lib`

   (Where "~" represents the fully qualified directory path of the OFBiz installation root location.)

2. Restart OFBiz.

How it works...

OFBiz bootstraps itself by loading Java class files for execution based on initial CLASSPATH entries. As it starts up, it traverses each Component, building out the CLASSPATH and dynamically loading necessary class files based on the established Component directory layout and on each Component's `ofbiz-component.xml` file. By placing a new class or JAR file in an existing CLASSPATH directory, OFBiz will find and load the resource automatically as part of the normal startup process.

Java compile time CLASSPATH

The Java compiler uses information on the CLASSPATH to resolve references to Java classes that are present within your OFBiz program. Since there may be many class references within your Java code, OFBiz makes it easy to add classes and JAR files to the compile time CLASSPATH by providing the ANT tool.

Getting ready

Open the `build.xml` file in the Component that contains your Java source.

How to do it...

To add classes and JAR files to the compile time CLASSPATH, do as follows:

1. Locate the section within the `build.xml` file named `local.class.path`

2. Add your new JAR file or Java class file location within the path directive as shown in the following:

```
<path id="local.class.path">
    <fileset dir="../../framework/base/lib" includes="*.jar"/>
    <fileset dir="../../framework/base/lib/commons" includes="*.jar"/>
    <fileset dir="../../framework/base/lib/j2eespecs" includes="*.jar"/>
    <fileset dir="../../framework/base/build/lib" includes="*.jar"/>
    <fileset dir="../../framework/entity/lib" includes="*.jar"/>
    <fileset dir="../../framework/entity/build/lib" includes="*.jar"/>
    <fileset dir="../../framework/security/build/lib" includes="*.jar"/>
    <fileset dir="../../framework/service/lib" includes="*.jar"/>
    <fileset dir="../../framework/service/build/lib" includes="*.jar"/>
    <fileset dir="../../framework/minilang/build/lib" includes="*.jar"/>
    <fileset dir="../../framework/webapp/lib" includes="*.jar"/>
    <fileset dir="../../framework/webapp/build/lib" includes="*.jar"/>
    <fileset dir="../../framework/common/build/lib" includes="*.jar"/>
    <fileset dir="../party/build/lib" includes="*.jar"/>
    <fileset dir="../product/build/lib" includes="*.jar"/>
    <fileset dir="../marketing/build/lib" includes="*.jar"/>
    <fileset dir="../order/build/lib" includes="*.jar"/>
    <!-- <fileset dir="lib/worldpay" includes="*.jar"/> -->
    <!-- <fileset dir="lib/cybersource" includes="*.jar"/> -->
    <fileset dir="lib" includes="*.jar"/>
</path>
```

> To add to the compile time CLASSPATH, create one or more ANT fileset entries and place them within the ANT path directive as shown here. The format for an entry is shown here as the directory location and the files to include.

3. Save and close the file.

4. Invoke ANT to build your program with the new CLASSPATH entries.

How it works...

OFBiz provides a convenient tool in a pre-configured ANT `build.xml` file to manage the OFBiz compile time CLASSPATH. To add new compile time entries, simply modify the ANT `build.xml` file.

Naming conventions

Just as there are OFBiz conventions that cover Component and Application, directory and file layout, Java file-naming best practices have been established to help organize and locate resources.

How to do it...

The following are the OFBiz naming conventions:

▶ Use Java CamelCase when picking a name for your Java class file or your method. CamelCase names are names in which compound words, such as "My Application", are joined together without spaces to form "MyApplication".

▶ Class files that contain OFBiz Services have a suffix of "`Services.java`". For example, a Java class file containing Services could be called "`MyServices.java`". Only place OFBiz Services inside a file with the "`Services.java`" suffix.

▸ Class files that contain OFBiz Events have a suffix of "Events.java". Only place OFBiz Events inside a file with the "Events.java" suffix.

▸ Other Java class files that you may see have suffixes such as "Worker.java" or "Helper.Java". These files should not contain OFBiz Events or Services.

▸ All OFBiz class files have packaging notation that maps to the directory hierarchy relative to the src directory in the containing Component.

Writing OFBiz Java Events

Writing an OFBiz Java Event is as simple as writing a Java method and then configuring OFBiz to be able to find the Event on the Java CLASSPATH. When would you want to write a Java Event? Any time you want to process input from a web application, such as the submission of an HTML form entry or as a result of a URL request, an Event may be coded to accept the HTTP/HTTPS request and return a response object to the browser.

When writing your first Event, it is often easier to add your Event's method to an existing Java class file. Any existing class file will work. Remember that the OFBiz convention is to add an "Events.java" suffix to class files containing Events.

Getting ready

To start writing Events, the following have to be taken care of:

1. Decide which Component you want your OFBiz Event to run in.
2. Check for Java build/compile dependencies in the build.xml file for every Component you selected in step 1.
3. Create your controller.xml file request-mapping entry.
4. Create your href or HTML form to call your Event.
5. Navigate to the OFBiz Component's source directory src where you wish to run your new Event.

How to do it...

Now, you can write new Events by following these steps:

1. Open the Java class file using a text editor of your choosing.
2. Create the OFBiz Java Event method as shown

```
public static String myEvent(HttpServletRequest request,
HttpServletResponse response)
{
        // method body goes here
        return "request-map response name value";
}
```

3. Add code to the body of the method.

4. Save the class file.

5. Navigate to the root directory in which your Event source code is located.

6. Run the Component's ANT build script from the command line.

7. Observe that there are no build or compile errors. If there are, return to step 1.

8. Restart OFBiz.

9. Test by invoking the URL or form from a web page.

How it works...

The following figure depicts an OFBiz Java Event:

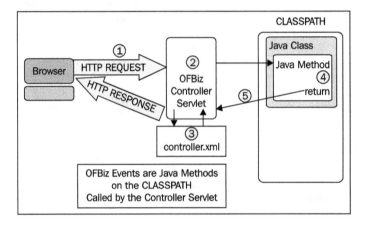

Referring to the figure, an OFBiz Event gets invoked as follows:

1. A **Browser** or other requestor initiates an HTTP or HTTPS request message.

2. The **Controller Servlet** intercepts that request.

3. The **Controller Servlet** determines processing control based on the request-map entry in the **controller.xml** file.

4. Program control is passed to the Event where it executes its program logic.

5. The Event returns program control to OFBiz and either directly passes the response object to the browser or allows OFBiz to build the response, including any HTML web page rendering as configured in the **controller.xml** file.

There's more...

An OFBiz Event must have the following Java method modifiers:

Java method modifiers	"public", "static"
Return type	`String`
Method name	Identical to the Event name as called in the `controller.xml` file *
Parameter list	`HttpServletRequest request, HttpServletResponse response` **

* For example, if the method name is "`myEvent`" (as shown previously) and this method is in the `org.ofbiz.MyEvents` package, then the `controller.xml` request-map entry would look something like the following:

```
<request-map uri="myEventURI">
    <event type="java" path="org.ofbiz.MyEvents"
            invoke="myEvent" />
    <!--Other attributes removed for readability -->
</request-map>
```

** The `HttpServletRequest` and `HttpServletResponse` variable may be named anything. Convention has them labeled as "request" and "response" respectively.

An OFBiz Event may have many return values, where each value represents a directive instructing the **Controller Servlet** on what to do upon method return. For example, if we had a method with the following code:

```
return "success";
return "error";
return "nice_try";
```

Then we might have a `controller.xml` file with the following response names configured:

```
<response-name="success" type="view" value="some_view" />
<response-name="error" type="view" value="some_view_error_page" />
<response-name="nice_try" type="request-redirect"
                          value="myEventURI" />
<response-name="redo" type="view-last" value="myEventURI" />
```

There may be many OFBiz Events with the same method name and package declaration on the CLASSPATH. In that case, OFBiz will use the last one found and pass control to that method. You may also have many request-maps defined with the same URI and different Event mappings. In that case, OFBiz will use the last URI found (as it sequentially parses the `controller.xml` file from top to bottom) as the target mapping.

Changes to the `controller.xml` file are immediate and do not require the OFBiz instance to be restarted.

When an OFBiz Event returns from processing, it passes execution control back to OFBiz, which then uses the response-map name/value pairs in `controller.xml` to determine what to do next. Usually a "view" or web page is the next step in processing. Views are built dynamically by OFBiz based on view-mapping settings in the `controller.xml` file.

Sometimes, the next processing step is not to create a view, but rather to perform some other OFBiz Event processing. The following table shows response type values and how they may be used to control processing flow:

Response type	Usage
none	Allow the Event to process the return view. This is really useful when you want to stream content directly to the browser.
request	Forward control to another request-map defined in the `controller.xml` file.
request-redirect	A servlet redirect to pass control to another request-map defined in the `controller.xml` file.
view	Create the view (web page) as defined by this view-mapping and return control to the browser.
view-last	Create the `view-last` web page and return control to the browser. If the last viewed web page has been set in the session attributes (`_LAST_VIEW_NAME_`) then this view will return to the browser.
view-home	Create the `view_home` view and return control to the browser.

You may override the response mapping at any time by placing the URL of the desired target override on the calling URL. For example, if you wish to override the configured behavior for the following URL to always invoke the `newRequest` request-map, write the following:

```
<a href="<@ofbizUrl>callEvent/newRequest</@ofbizUrl>">
  Click Here to Call Me!
</a>
```

Writing OFBiz Java Services

OFBiz "Services" are reusable code snippets implemented as Java methods. What makes using OFBiz Services so compelling? Unlike OFBiz Events or servlets, the Service context is controlled by OFBiz, thus relieving the programmer from having to do such mundane tasks as managing transactions, handling retries, and validating input and output values. Once written, a Service may be invoked as many times and by as many Service consumers as required.

Getting ready

To start writing Services, we must first perform the following:

1. Navigate to the Component's source directory containing the Java class file to be used for the new Service method.
2. Check for any Java class or JAR file dependencies in the `build.xml` file.
3. To test your Service, create a web page with a form to call the new Service.
4. Create an entry in the `controller.xml` file to allow access to your Service.
5. Navigate to the OFBiz Component where the Java class file containing the source for your Event exists.
6. Open the Java class file using a text editor of your choosing.

How to do it...

Creating a Service can be done by performing the following simple steps:

1. Create the OFBiz Java Service method declaration.
2. Add the required code and save the file.
3. Run the Component's ANT build script.
4. Create the Service definition.
5. Start up OFBiz. (Restart if already running).
6. Test by invoking the URL from a web page or calling from another Service or Event.

How it works...

Services are Java methods that are invoked by the **OFBiz Service Engine** as shown. Consumers of OFBiz Services may be web browsers, other OFBiz Events or Services, and even remote systems (for example SOAP-based messaging requests).

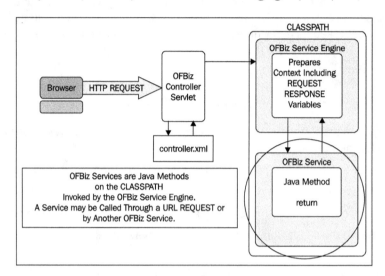

There's more...

For a Java method to be an OFBiz Service, it must have a method declaration as follows:

```
public static Map myService(DispatchContext dctx, Map context){
    // The method's body contains the logic that
    // makes up a Service's processing. This is the most
    // simple method you could devise. While a valid OFBiz Service
    // this method does nothing.
    Map result = ServiceUtil.returnSuccess();
    return result;
}
```

Where the method declaration has the following required modifiers:

Java method modifiers	"public", "static"
Return type	Map
Method name	Identical to the Service name as configured in the Service's configuration file
Parameter list	DispatchContext dctx, Map context *

* The DispatchContext and context objects may be named anything. Convention has them named as dctx and context respectively.

For a Service to be consumed, it must be "registered" with OFBiz and have a "Service definition". An example Service definition might look like the following:

```
<service name="myService"  engine="java"
         location="org.ofbiz.myServices" invoke="myService">
    <description>
       A Service that does nothing. It takes no inputs and returns
       nothing
    </description>
</service>
```

To "register" a Service, OFBiz must be made aware of the Service definition. Service definitions are entries in an OFBiz XML file designated as containing one or more Service definitions. OFBiz is alerted to the existence of all Service definition files by one or more entries in an `ofbiz-component.xml` file as shown:

```
<service-resource type="model" loader="main"
                  location="servicedef/myServices.xml"/>
```

While there is only one `ofbiz-component.xml` file per Component, any single OFBiz Component may have any number of files containing Service definitions. There is no limit to the number of Service or Service definitions any single instance of OFBiz can support.

For a quick test of an OFBiz Service, call the Service directly from a web page. To make a test invocation of an OFBiz Service from a web page:

1. Create a `controller.xml` request-map entry for the Service.

    For example, to call a Service called `myService`, the `controller.xml` file may have an entry such as:

    ```
    <request-map uri="myService">
        <security https="false" auth="false"/>
        <!-- invoke points to the Service name as defined in the
             Service Definition -->
        <event type="service" invoke="myService"/>
        <response name="success" type="view" value="main"/>
        <response name="error" type="view" value="error"/>
    </request-map>
    ```

2. Create an HTML `form` or `href` request for the Service's URI as configured in the `controller.xml`, as follows:

    ```
    <form action ="<@ofbizUrl>myService</@ofbizUrl>" method="post">
        <input type="hidden" name="param1" value="I_am_hidden">
    </form>
    <a href="<@ofbizUrl>myService&param1=I_am_hidden</@ofbizUrl>
    ```

3. Invoke the HTML `form` or `href` link from the web page and observe the results. By putting debug statements in your Service, you should see them log to the console window if your Service logic is being executed.

See also

For more information on the syntax of a Service definition and individual Service definition elements, please see the official OFBiz **Service Engine Guide** on the OFBiz Wiki:

```
https://cwiki.apache.org/confluence/display/OFBTECH/
Service+Engine+Guide
```

Debugging using the logfile

A handy debugging technique available to any OFBiz Java programmer at any time is to write messages to the OFBiz console log from within your program.

Getting ready

Firstly, ensure the following:

1. Make sure to import the OFBiz `org.ofbiz.base.util.Debug` utility into your Java program.

2. To ensure that your logfile entry is properly marked with the class name and line number from where it was called, check that the Java constant named `module` is defined within your class file as shown below:

```
public static final String module = MyClass.class.getName();
```

3. If you have turned off console window logging (the default out-of-the-box setting), make sure to return the startup file to its original setting to allow logging to the console window.

How to do it...

To always write to the console window, call the OFBiz Debug utility as shown:

```
import org.ofbiz.base.util.Debug;
// Code intentionally left out
Debug.log("This is an error message", module);
//Or, if you don't want to write to using the Logger
System.out.println("This is an error message");
```

How it works...

A call to the `org.ofbiz.base.util.Debug` method as shown earlier will always write a message to both the error logfile, `ofbiz.log` and the console window, if it is open.

To write log messages under other conditions, consult the log4J settings and pick the appropriate `Debug` utility method. For example, to write to the logfile and/or console window only when "Fatal" messages are turned on, you might have a statement such as the following in your code:

```
Debug.logFatal("Some message", module);
```

The OFBiz logging facility is an integration of the Apache log4J Java program logging toolkit: `http://logging.apache.org/log4j/`.

Toggling log settings, that is turning them on or off, is easily accomplished using the WebTools **Logging** tab, **Log Configuration** utility.

Calling OFBiz Services from a Java program

Calling an existing OFBiz Service from another OFBiz method is very simple.

Getting ready

Prepare any necessary context parameters. To call an OFBiz Service, you may need to pass one or more parameters (called "IN" or "INOUT" parameters) using a Java Map structure. Consult the WebTools **Service List** for more information on any particular Service's required and optional input and/or output parameters.

How to do it...

The following code snippet highlights the necessary Java code to call Services synchronously, asynchronously, and as scheduled processes:

Note: Only enough code necessary to illustrate Service invocation is shown.

```
import org.ofbiz.service.DispatchContext;
import org.ofbiz.service.GenericServiceException;
import org.ofbiz.service.LocalDispatcher;
import org.ofbiz.service.ServiceUtil;
// For an OFBiz Service, get the service dispatcher as follows
LocalDispatcher dispatcher = dctx.getDispatcher();
// For an OFBiz Event, get the service dispatcher as follows
LocalDispatcher dispatcher =
        (LocalDispatcher) request.getAttribute("dispatcher");

int param1 = 0;
```

```
    String param2 = "Param 2";
    Map input = UtilMisc.toMap("param1", new Integer(param1),
                               "param2", param2);
    try {
        // Example of a synchronous Service call. Returns immediately,
        // and the Service is invoked and runs in parallel
        // with the calling program
        Map syncResults = dispatcher.runSync("someService", input);
        // Example of an asynchronous Service call. Returns immediately,
        // but the Service may not be run until some time in the future
        Map asyncResults = dispatcher.runAsync("someService", input);
        // Example of calling a Service to run synchronously and ignore
        // the result.
        Map syncResultsIgnore = dispatcher.runSyncIgnore("someService",
                                                        input);
        // You may use the dispatcher to schedule a Service
        long startTime = (new Date()).getTime();
        dispatcher.schedule("someService", input, startTime);
    }
    catch (GenericServiceException e) {
        Debug.logError(e, module);
        return ServiceUtil.returnError(e.getMessage());
    }
```

How it works...

To set your program up to call an OFBiz Service, you must first instantiate a
`LocalDispatcher` object. This Java object will provide all the necessary environmental
information required to invoke a Service.

When you invoke one of the `LocalDispatcher` object's Service invocation methods, you
are telling the `LocalDispatcher` to pass program control to the OFBiz "Service dispatcher",
which in turn passes control to the OFBiz "Service engine" configured in the Service definition
for the target Service. The Service engine invokes the target Service and passes context
information, including all configured `IN` parameters, to the Service. When the target Service
finishes processing, or has been scheduled to run, in the case of scheduled and asynchronous
requests, control is passed back to the calling program.

If an error occurs during the Service's processing or during the passing of context information
(for example, on parameter validation), a `GenericServiceException` is thrown by the
Service engine and control returns to the `catch` block of the calling program.

There's more...

You can use the `ModelService` object to make your job easier when calling Services. For example, if you have many parameters to pass to a Service and they are already in a **Java Map** (perhaps they were passed in from another Service), instead of moving them one-by-one to the required Service input Map structure, you can use knowledge of the Service's model to do this all in one statement.

```
// You first need to get the Service's model
ModelService modelService = null;
try {
    modelService =
        dispatcher.getDispatchContext().getModelService("myService");
}
catch (GenericServiceException e) {
    // Error process left out
}
Map persistMap = modelService.makeValid(paramMap,
                                     ModelService.IN_PARAM);
persistMap.put("userLogin", userLogin);
// Add another parameter to the Map
try {
    // Now call the new Service with the persistMap created above
    Map persistResult = dispatcher.runSync("myService1", persistMap);
```

As OFBiz manages Service transaction needs, the calling program may pass transaction timeout indicators. Similarly, the calling program may instruct the Service engine to wrap the target Service in a separate transaction.

```
// Transaction timeout is in milliseconds
// true = wrap this Service invocation in a separate transaction
Map result = dispatcher.runSync("myService", contextMap, 1000, true);
```

Getting and validating request parameters (Events)

Very often, you write OFBiz Events so as to have complete control over HTTP/HTTPS request parameters. Getting those parameters out of the `HttpServletRequest` object and into your program is simplified when using OFBiz tools.

How to do it...

The following code snippet demonstrates taking `HttpServletRequest` object request parameters from the request and placing them in local variables for processing:

```java
import javax.servlet.http.HttpServletRequest;
import javax.servlet.http.HttpServletResponse;
import org.ofbiz.base.util.UtilHttp;
import org.ofbiz.base.util.UtilValidate

public static String myEvent(HttpServletRequest request,
                             HttpServletResponse response) {
    // Some code up here
    Map httpParams = UtilHttp.getParameterMap(request);
    // use the OFBiz utility to make this easy
    String param1 = (String) httpParams.get("param1");
    // Some Validation Examples follow
    if(UtilValidate.isEmpty((String) httpParams.get("param2")) {
        return "error";
    }
    if(UtilValidate.isNotEmpty((String) httpParams.get("param3")) {
        return "error";
    }
    if(UtilValidate.isEmail((String) httpParams.get("param4")) {
        String emailAddr = (String) httpParams.get("param4"));
        // do some processing here
    }
    return "success";
}
```

How it works...

The `HttpServletRequest` object is passed to the OFBiz Event (Java method) as an input parameter where it may be retrieved directly using `HttpServletRequest` object API calls. To make the programmer's job even easier, OFBiz provides a utility that allows for moving all the request parameters into a local Java Map structure as shown earlier.

There's more...

For a full accounting of the `HttpServletRequest` object, please see the Java servlet API:

```
http://java.sun.com/j2ee/1.4/docs/api/javax/servlet/http/
HttpServletRequest.html
```

For more information on available `org.ofbiz.util.UtilValidate` methods, please see the OFBiz Javadocs available online at:

`http://ci.apache.org/projects/ofbiz/site/javadocs/`

Getting and validating request parameters (Services)

The following Java code snippet demonstrates first retrieving two request parameters (`param1` and `param2`) from the `context` Map passed to every OFBiz Service. Note that all request parameters start out life as strings of characters. The OFBiz Service engine will automatically convert request values to the appropriate type based on Service definition configuration.

How to do it...

The following code shows you how to retrieve parameters:

```
import java.util.*;
import org.ofbiz.service.ServiceUtil;
import org.ofbiz.base.util.UtilHttp;
import org.ofbiz.base.util.UtilValidate

public static Map myService(DispatchContext dctx, Map context){
    // Some code here
    // First, just get a request parameter from the context
    // Note: this must already be configured as part of the
    // Service definitions INPUT parameters
    String param1 = (String) context.get("param1");
    Integer param2 = (Integer) context.get("param2");

    // You may use the UtilValidate methods to validate these.
    if(UtilValidate.isNotEmpty(param1)) {
        return ServiceUtil.returnError("ERROR Message here!");
        // Use OFBiz
    }
    Map result = ServiceUtil.returnSuccess();
    result.put("value1", "this is a value");
    return result;
}
```

How it works...

For OFBiz Services, the context in which the Service operates is controlled by OFBiz. The only HTTP/HTTPS request parameters available to the Service are those that have been defined as IN parameters within the Service definition. To access any values that have been defined in Service definition, including request parameters, retrieve the value from the context Map as shown earlier.

Note: Request parameters are ignored and not passed to a Service if the Service definition does not include an attribute entry with the request parameter's name and request parameter's mode="IN" or mode="INOUT".

Regardless of the contents of the map passed when a Service returns from execution, Service parameters not defined as mode="OUT" or mode="INOUT" are not made available to subsequent Service context consumers. In other words, if you have values that you would want returned to the context as a result of your Service's processing, declare them as mode="OUT" or mode="INOUT" in the Service definition.

Managing error messages

HttpServletRequest object's attributes are used to pass error messages from Java programs to other OFBiz resources, including web pages. By convention, error messages are passed as either a single HttpServletRequest attribute name/value pair (where the name is _ERROR_MESSAGE_) or as a list of messages (where the name of the list is _ERROR_MESSAGE_LIST_). All HttpServletRequest object attributes are assumed to be Java Strings.

How to do it...

While you may pass error messages in any fashion you like, the consolidation of error messages and message lists for consumption by other OFBiz resources is made easier if you follow some simple rules:

1. From within an Event, set the appropriate HttpServletRequest attribute as shown:

```
request.setAttribute("_ERROR_MESSAGE_",
                     "Error: This is an error message");
// Or pass a list of error messages
List myErrors = UtilMisc.toList("This is an error message",
                                "This is another error message");
request.setAttribute("_ERROR_MESSAGE_LIST_", myErrors);
```

2. From within a Service, you have several options. Best practices suggest never to place the error messages within the `HttpServletRequest` object directly. Rather, call the appropriate `org.ofbiz.Service.ServiceUtil` method as shown below:

```
// Don't forget to import org.ofbiz.service.ServiceUtil
// For a successful return from a Service
// with no error messages to report
return ServiceUtil.returnSuccess();
// For error messages that have not be localized
// or that you want passed as is:
ServiceUtil.returnError("This is an error");
// For a list of error messages that you want passed as is
// back to the context
List myErrorList = UtilMisc.toList("This is an error message",
                            "This is another error message");
ServiceUtil.returnError(myErrorList);
// For error messages that have been localized:
ServiceUtil.returnError(UtilProperties.getMessage(resource_error,
                            "SomeErrorMessage",locale));
// For error messages from an OFBiz exception objects,
// in this case "e"
return ServiceUtil.returnError(e.getMessage());
```

3. To access error messages as a result of a call to an OFBiz Service:

```
import org.ofbiz.service.ModelService;
import org.ofbiz.service.ServiceUtil;
Map result = dispatcher.runSync("someService", inputParameterMap);
// Service recalls return response messages.
// A response message in turn may contain an error message.
// To get the error message from the results of a Service call:
if (ModelService.RESPOND_ERROR.equals(
        (String) result.get(ModelService.RESPONSE_MESSAGE))) {
        Map<String, Object> messageMap =
                        UtilMisc.toMap("errorMessage",
                            result.get(ModelService.ERROR_MESSAGE));
}
```

There's more...

If you are wondering how errors reported by Java programs and set in the `HttpServletRequest` object make their way to web pages where they are consumed by browsers and others, then a review of the following FreeMarker template might be in order:

```
<#if requestAttributes.errorMessageList?has_content>
    <#assign errorMessageList=requestAttributes.errorMessageList>
```

```
</#if>
<#if requestAttributes.eventMessageList?has_content>
  <#assign eventMessageList=requestAttributes.eventMessageList>
</#if>
<#if requestAttributes.serviceValidationException?exists>
  <#assign serviceValidationException =
          requestAttributes.serviceValidationException>
</#if>
<#if requestAttributes.uiLabelMap?has_content>
  <#assign uiLabelMap = requestAttributes.uiLabelMap>
</#if>
```

Using Java properties files

Java properties files are a native Java mechanism for maintaining a set of persistent values, called "properties", across invocations of the JVM. They are typically files that are persistent to the local file system.

Properties files consist of one or more key/value pairs, very much like a Java Map structure.

How to do it...

The following code snippet demonstrates finding the value for the `CommonDatabaseProblem` key from the `CommonUiLabels` Java property file:

```
import org.ofbiz.base.util.UtilProperties;
errMsg = UtilProperties.getMessage("CommonUiLabels",
        "CommonDatabaseProblem", messageMap, locale);
```

How it works...

OFBiz makes using Java properties files convenient and easy by loading them as resources on the Java CLASSPATH and providing several utility methods to access file contents.

See also

Please see the OFBiz `UtilProperties` API:

http://ci.apache.org/projects/ofbiz/site/javadocs/

Sending e-mail from an OFBiz Event or Service

If you ever need to send an e-mail programmatically, OFBiz provides a number of Services that simplify the process. In this section, we look at an example of using the basic OFBiz `sendMail` Service.

Getting ready

Using the OFBiz WebTools **Service Manager** utility, we can see at a glance that there are many input and output parameters that the `sendMail` Service may take. The only required input parameters, however, are:

Parameter name	Notes
body	This is the content of the e-mail (not an attachment).
sendTo	Valid e-mail address. This is the recipient of this e-mail.
subject	E-mail header subject.

How to do it...

The follow example demonstrates calling the `sendMail` Service from an OFBiz Event. Calling the `sendMail` Service from another Java program such as a servlet or Service works the same way.

Note: The following program is for demonstration purposes only. It will compile and run within an OFBiz instance. However, much of the logic is hardcoded. This is intentional. Only enough code is shown to highlight the topic. You will need to add the proper import statements as they have been removed to conserve space.

```
public static String exampleSendEmail(HttpServletRequest request,
        HttpServletResponse response) {
    // Get the local Service dispatcher from the context
    // Note: Dont forget to import the org.ofbiz.service.* classes
    LocalDispatcher dispatcher =
            (LocalDispatcher) request.getAttribute("dispatcher");
    String errMsg = null;
    // The following are hardcoded as an example only
    // Your program would set these up from the context or from
    // database lookups
    String mailBody = "This is the body of my email";
    Map sendMailContext = new HashMap();
```

```
sendMailContext.put("sendTo", "me@ofbiz.org");
sendMailContext.put("sendCC", "cc@ofbiz.org");
sendMailContext.put("sendBcc","you@ofbiz.org" );
sendMailContext.put("sendFrom", "info@ofbiz.org");
sendMailContext.put("subject",
                    "Testing emails sent from an OFBiz Event");
sendMailContext.put("body", mailBody);
try {
    // Call the sendMail Service and pass the sendMailContext
    // Map object.
    // Set timeout to 360 and wrap with a new transaction
    Map<String, Object> result =
        dispatcher.runSync("sendMail", sendMailContext,360, true);
    // Note easy way to get errors when they are returned
    // from another Service
    if (ModelService.RESPOND_ERROR.equals((String)
        result.get(ModelService.RESPONSE_MESSAGE))) {
            Map<String, Object> messageMap =
                UtilMisc.toMap("errorMessage",
                    result.get(ModelService.ERROR_MESSAGE));
            errMsg = "Problem sending this email";
            request.setAttribute("_ERROR_MESSAGE_", errMsg);
            return "error";
        }
    }
catch (GenericServiceException e) {
    // For Events error messages are passed back
    Debug.logWarning(e, "", module);
    // as Request Attributes
    errMsg = "Problem with the sendMail Service call";
    request.setAttribute("_ERROR_MESSAGE_", errMsg);
    return "error";
}
return "success";
}
```

How it works...

The OFBiz framework includes an integration of the **JavaMail** framework. Building on top of these facilities, OFBiz provides a number of Services, of which the `sendMail` Service is the most basic, to send (and receive) e-mail messages.

`sendMail`, as shown earlier, is an OFBiz Service. It is always available (on the CLASSPATH) to use at runtime. To access this Service at runtime, get the `LocalDispatcher` from the context and use that object to call the OFBiz Service dispatcher service.

There's more...

Out-of-the-box OFBiz provides a number of Services that ultimately result in a call to the `sendMail` Service and e-mail being sent. The following is a list of several available Services:

Service	Usage
sendCommEventAsEmail	Send the e-mail and record a record in the database with the resultant status.
sendEmailToContactList	Send this e-mail to all recipients on a contact list. The contact list is a list of e-mail recipients taken from the database.
sendMailFromScreen	Creates the body content from a Screen widget. Needs the web store/website ID in order to work.
sendMailFromUrl	Takes the URL of the calling HTTP request and stuffs that into the body of the e-mail. Useful if you want to track which web page the e-mail request (if you have many) came from.
sendMailMultiPart	Send an e-mail that has multiple MIME parts.
sendEmailDated	Checks for e-mails that may have failed and resends.

See also

For the complete list, please see the WebTools **Service List** tool.

Handling XML files

If you ever have a requirement to manipulate XML files, whether it be as a result of an incoming XML-RPC or a need to process a local file system XML document, OFBiz has a number of tools that you may find useful. The following program demonstrates just some of the many options available.

Getting ready

To use the OFBiz XML utilities, import the `org.ofbiz.base.util*` package.

How to do it...

The following program demonstrates creating, writing to, and reading from an XML document using OFBiz utilities.

Note: The following program is for demonstration purposes only. It will compile and run within an OFBiz instance. However, much of the logic is hardcoded. This is intentional. Only enough code is shown to illustrate the handling of XML files.

```java
/* Don't forget to
    import org.w3c.dom.Document;
    import org.w3c.dom.Element;
    import org.xml.sax.SAXException;
    import org.ofbiz.base.util.*;
*/
public static String basicXmlExamples(HttpServletRequest
        request, HttpServletResponse response) {
    Document testDocument = null;
    // First, demonstrate making an XML document
    try {
        testDocument =
                UtilXml.makeEmptyXmlDocument("testDocumentName");
        Element testElem = testDocument.getDocumentElement();
        UtilXml.addChildElement(testElem, "FirstElement",
                                        testDocument);
        UtilXml.addChildElementValue(testElem,
                        "FirstElement","someValue", testDocument);
    }
    catch (Exception e) {
        return "error";
    }
    String stringWithXml = null;
    // Now use OFBiz utils to make a String out of this XML Document
    try {
        stringWithXml = UtilXml.writeXmlDocument(testDocument);
    }
    catch (IOException e) {
        // Error processing removed.
        return "error";
    }
    try {
        testDocument = UtilXml.readXmlDocument(stringWithXml, false);
        // Read an XML document from String
    }
    catch (SAXException e2) {
        // Error processing removed.
        return "error";
```

```
    }
    catch (ParserConfigurationException e2) {
        // Error processing removed in the interest of space
        return "error";
    }
    catch (IOException e2) {
        // Error processing removed in the interest of space
        return "error";
    }
    // Use some other OFBiz XML File Utilities
    // Transverses the XML document and extract values
    List<Object> errorList = FastList.newInstance();
    Element firstElement = testDocument.getDocumentElement();
    String firstElementValue =
            UtilXml.childElementValue(firstElement,"FirstElement");
    // Get child element values
    return "success";
}
```

How it works...

OFBiz includes a number of tools and utilities to help in managing XML documents. As long as the tool package is on the compile time CLASSPATH, it will be available to use in processing XML documents.

3
The User Interface

In this chapter, we shall examine the following User Interface topics:

- ▶ Building HTML web pages using the OFBiz Screen widget tool
- ▶ Adding actions to Screen widget definitions
- ▶ Adding HTML (and CSS) markup within Screen widget definitions
- ▶ Platform-specific, Tree, Menu, and Form widgets
- ▶ Creating HTML using FreeMarker
- ▶ Passing parameters from the Screen widget to FreeMarker
- ▶ Writing JavaScript to pop-up a new browser window in FreeMarker
- ▶ Calling Java methods using FreeMarker directives
- ▶ Forcing FreeMarker to render HTML markup
- ▶ Uploading files from FreeMarker

Introduction

Users communicate with OFBiz webapps using an off-the-shelf web browser. To build a User Interface (UI) for an OFBiz webapp is to build one or more HTML web pages destined for consumption by a web browser. While OFBiz provides several mechanisms for building HTML web pages, the suggested best practice is to use the OFBiz Screen widget tool to create OFBiz "screens". This tool takes an OFBiz Screen widget configuration as input and creates HTML web pages referred to as "screens" as output.

How does OFBiz know which screen's Screen widget definition to use when building an HTML web page? By using the controller's `controller.xml` view-mapping(s), OFBiz translates a browser URL request to a specific screen's definition as shown:

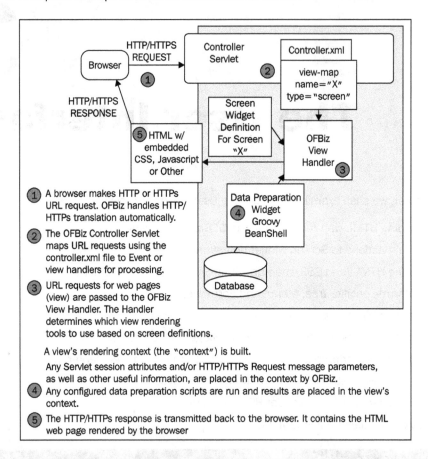

① A browser makes HTTP or HTTPs URL request. OFBiz handles HTTP/HTTPs translation automatically.

② The OFBiz Controller Servlet maps URL requests using the controller.xml file to Event or view handlers for processing.

③ URL requests for web pages (view) are passed to the OFBiz View Handler. The Handler determines which view rendering tools to use based on screen definitions.

A view's rendering context (the "context") is built.

Any Servlet session attributes and/or HTTP/HTTPs Request message parameters, as well as other useful information, are placed in the context by OFBiz.

④ Any configured data preparation scripts are run and results are placed in the view's context.

⑤ The HTTP/HTTPs response is transmitted back to the browser. It contains the HTML web page rendered by the browser

Creating HTML web pages

Creating a new web page begins with defining an OFBiz "screen". Web page screens are built by creating one or more Screen widget definitions used by the OFBiz screen handler to generate HTML.

Getting ready

Ensure you have the "screen handler" defined in the `controller.xml` file for your webapp as shown here:

```
<handler name="screen" type="view"
        class="org.ofbiz.widget.screen.ScreenWidgetViewHandler"/>
```

To create a new OFBiz screen, it is often easiest to add a Screen widget definition to an existing Screen widget definition file. These files are XML documents, usually located under the `widgets` directory within a containing Component.

If you want to create a new Screen widget definition file, copy an existing file and remove all the Screen widget definitions. Make sure you retain the XML document XSD as shown:

```
<screens xmlns:xsi="http://www.w3.org/2001/XMLSchema-instance"
        xsi:noNamespaceSchemaLocation=
                "http://ofbiz.apache.org/dtds/widget-screen.xsd">
```

How to do it...

HTML web page screens can be created by the following steps:

1. Open a Screen widget definition file.
2. Create the Screen widget definition by adding a `screen` element.
3. Add any Screen widget `actions` elements. Close the `actions` element with an end tag (`</actions>`).
4. Add any Screen widget `widgets` elements. Close the `widgets` element with an end tag (`</widgets>`).
5. Save the new screen definition.
6. Add one or more `controller.xml` view-map entries that point to the Screen widget definition.

> Note: Screen definitions are effective immediately. You do not need to restart OFBiz.

How it works...

The OFBiz screen handler takes Screen widget definitions (as pointed to using `controller.xml` view-map entries) and creates HTML documents or OFBiz "screens". Screen widget definitions are instructions to the screen handler on how to build screens by merging the specified `actions` with HTML.

Note: Screen actions are run from the "inside" out. As you may have any number of actions defined, so you may have any number of action declarations embedded within other action declarations. Embedded declarations are resolved from the deepest nested level outwards.

Screen widget definitions are contained in XML documents that, by convention, have their own directory called the `widget` directory within a containing Component.

 Note: Screen widget definition files may be located anywhere within the OFBiz installation. `controller.xml` view-mappings uniquely identify these files for the screen handler. Once defined, a screen's definition is available for all OFBiz webapps regardless of the definition file's location.

Each Screen widget "definition" document has one or more Screen widget "definitions". A definition is nothing more than an XML element with child elements and attributes that describe how a screen is to be constructed. Each definition starts with a `screen` element that has a `name` attribute. Following the `screen` element are one or more `section` elements. Within `section` elements, there may be one or more `widgets` and/or `actions` elements as shown:

 Note: As with any well-formed XML document, comments are indicated using the following XML comment notation: `<!-- -->`. Comments are not interpreted by the screen handler.

```xml
<screen name="my_screen">
<section>
        <actions>
                <!--Pointer to any data preparation scripts
                    go here -->
                <!--Set any context variables here -->
        </actions>
        <widgets>
                <!--Add any pointers to widgets here -->
                <!--Add any pointers to FreeMarker template files
                    here -->
        </widgets>
</section>
</screen>
```

Any widget element may contain any number of nested elements within it, including file location pointers to other Screen, Form, Menu, and Tree widget definitions as shown:

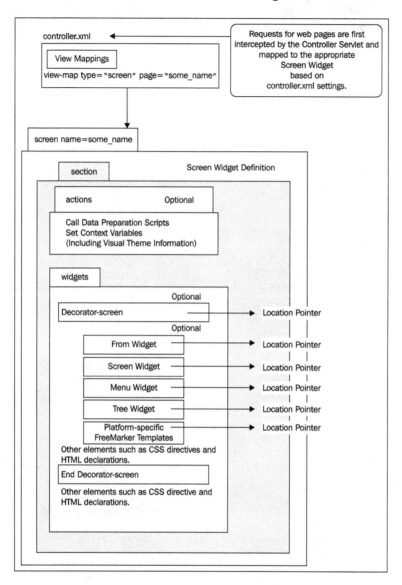

There's more...

Sometimes, when you have a webapp that has more than one web page, it makes sense to use multiple screens like building blocks by embedding one inside the other. This is the idea behind the "decorator-screen" widget. The decorator-screen is a special `widgets` element type that allows for the embedding of one or more Screen widget definitions within it.

For example, many times there will be multiple web pages that have the same or very similar HTML head elements. Using a `decorator-screen`, you may define a single screen to act as the "decorator" or wrapper for screens where the content may change from screen to screen. For example, the following OFBiz screen definition uses the `myDecorator` decorator-screen to wrap the `main` screen with a header and footer as shown:

```
<screen name="main">
  <section>
    <widgets>
      <!--Use this Decorator-Screen to wrap the screen named "main"
          screen -->
      <!--Since "myDecorator" is in the same file, we don't need to
          give it the full Component location -->
      <decorator-screen name="myDecorator">
        <decorator-section name="body">
          <platform-specific>
            <html>
              <html-template location=
                  "component://myComponent/webapp/myWebapp/main.ftl"/>
            </html>
          </platform-specific>
        </decorator-section>
      </decorator-screen>
    </widgets>
  </section>
</screen>

<!--Heres the Screen-Decorator for the screen named "main" -->
<screen name="myDecorator">
  <section>
    <widgets>
      <platform-specific>
        <html>
          <html-template location=
              "component://myComponent/webapp/myWebapp/header.ftl"/>
        </html>
      </platform-specific>
      <!--=========== Insert The Screen Named "main" Here ======== -->
      <decorator-section-include name="body" />
      <!--================= End of Body Insertion ================ -->
      <platform-specific>
        <html>
          <html-template location=
              "component://myComponent/webapp/myWebapp/footer.ftl"/>
        </html>
      </platform-specific>
    </widgets>
  </section>
</screen>
```

Out-of-the-box, many OFBiz decorator-screen locations are pre-set and passed to Screen widgets as web application context parameters similar to the following:

```
<decorator-screen
    name="main-decorator"
    location="${parameters.mainDecoratorLocation}">
```

> Note: `mainDecoratorLocation` is defined in the servlet's deployment descriptor file, `web.xml`, for this webapp as shown:
>
> ```
> <context-param>
>   <param-name>mainDecoratorLocation</param-name>
>   <param-value>
>   component://product/widget/catalog/CommonScreens.xml
>   </param-value>
>   <description>
>     The location of the main-decorator screen to use
>     for this webapp; referred to as a context
>     variable in screen def XML files
>   </description>
> </context-param>
> ```

"Decorator-screens" give the web screen builder a flexible way to reuse screen building blocks. They are not required, and you may build a fully functional OFBiz webapp with nothing more than a single Screen widget.

Adding actions to Screen widgets

Using data from a database or other source to build portions of your web page dynamically enables efficient and effective web page creation by freeing the screen's author from hardcoding values. To give widgets access to data sources and allow data preparation tools to fetch required input data, widget definitions include an `actions` element. Within the `actions` element, you may include directives to:

- Read and set context variables
- Make database calls directly
- Call scripting languages such as BeanShell or Groovy
- Call other OFBiz Services

Getting ready

Some initial preparation has to be done to add new actions, as follows:

1. Open a Screen widget definition file and select a screen to add an action to.
2. If your Screen widget definition does not have an `actions` element defined, add one.

How to do it...

Actions can be added by the following steps:

1. Add one more `actions` element. Each action is either a directive instructing OFBiz to gather data directly and place that data in the screen's context, or a file location pointer to a script file.
2. Close the `actions` element with an end tag (`</actions>`).
3. Save the file.

 Note: The addition of `actions` to a screen definition is immediate. You do not need to restart OFBiz.

How it works...

The OFBiz screen handler invokes the `actions` declarations (in the order presented) to prepare data for merger with `widgets` declarations.

There's more...

To get Java properties file resources, add a directive similar to the following within the `actions` element of your widget definition:

```
<property-map  resource="CommonUiLabels"  map-name="uiLabelMap"
               global="true"/>
```

To call a Groovy script, add an `actions` directive similar to the following:

```
<script location=
"component://myComponent/webapp/WEB-INF/actions/aGroovyScript.groovy"
/>
```

To make database calls directly from within a Screen widget's `actions` element, use the following `actions` element example—taken from the content Component's Screen widget definition for the `Showforum` screen—as your guide:

```
<actions>
  <entity-condition list="forumMessages"
                    entity-name="ContentAssocViewTo">
    <condition-list combine="and">
      <condition-expr field-name="contentIdStart"
                      from-field="parameters.forumId"/>
      <condition-list combine="or">
        <condition-expr field-name="caContentAssocTypeId"
                        value="PUBLISH_LINK"/>
        <condition-expr field-name="caContentAssocTypeId"
                        value="RESPONSE"/>
      </condition-list>
    </condition-list>
    <order-by field-name="createdDate"/>
  </entity-condition>
</actions>
```

You may even call an OFBiz Service from within an OFBiz widget. For example, the following XML snippet taken from a Screen widget definition (available out-of-the-box) calls a Service to assemble resources for a web page:

```
<actions>
  <service service-name="getVisualThemeResources">
    <field-map field-name="visualThemeId"/>
    <field-map field-name="themeResources"
               from-field="layoutSettings"/>
  </service>
</actions>
```

HTML markup in Screen widgets

The `widgets` element within a Screen widget definition may contain one or more XML statements defining an HTML markup tag. In the cases where it isn't practical to call another widget or a FreeMarker template, you may want to insert one or more HTML directives within the Screen widget definition.

How to do it...

Adding HTML markup is as simple as the following:

1. Within any `widgets` element, add one or more XML statements with HTML markup. Example XML HTML markup elements include: `label`, `container`, and `link`.

2. Close all HTML markup elements with respective end tags.

3. Save and close the file.

 Note: The addition of HTML markup to a widget is immediate. You do not need to restart OFBiz.

How it works..

HTML markup statements are interpreted inline (and in the order in which they are written) as the screen handler parses the screen's definition. There is a one-to-one translation between the XML-wrapped HTML markup and the target HTML output.

There's more...

The following table lists some commonly used HTML and the equivalent XML statements:

Types	HTML	XML
Plain text	`Here IS Some Text`	`<label text="Here IS Some Text"/>`
Markup tags	`<h1></h1>`	`<label style="h1"></label>`
	`<p></p>`	`<label style="p"> </label>`
DIVs	`<div> </div>`	`<container></container>`
HTML hyperlink	`<a href= "a URL"> Click Me!</a>`	`<link target="a URL" text="Click Me!"/>`

CSS styling in Screen widgets

You may add CSS styling markup (`div` and `class` directives) directly to widget XML statements by using the HTML markup tags as described.

How to do it...

CSS styling markup can be added simply by following these steps:

1. Within any `widgets` element, add one or more XML statements with HTML and CSS markup.
2. Close all HTML markup elements with appropriate end tags.
3. Save and close the file.

How it works...

HTML CSS directives placed within the `widgets` element of a screen definition are translated into HTML based on conversions built-in to the OFBiz screen handler and Screen widget screen generation tool. Several common HTML elements may be specified directly within the Screen widget definition or on a screenlet's element in this way.

There's more...

To instruct the Screen widget to create a web page with the following HTML and CSS markup:

```
<div id="idA" class="classA">
  <h1>This is an image </h1>
  <img src="/images/img.png" height=40 width=40 />
</div>
```

Add the following within the `widgets` element of a screen definition:

```
<widgets>
  <container style="classA" id="idA">
    <label style="h1">This is an image</label>
    <image src="/images/img.png"
           height="40" width="40" url-mode="content"/>
  </container>
</widgets>
```

Note: The XML `container` element creates a `div`. The XML `style` attribute is equivalent to the HTML CSS `class` attribute. The XML `id` attribute is equivalent to the CSS `id` attribute. Attribute values are names of CSS styles as found defined either locally within a FreeMarker template or in an external CSS stylesheet file.

OFBiz also allows for portions of a Screen widget, called a "screenlet", to be defined. Screenlets may have HTML and CSS attributes added directly to the element as shown:

```
<screenlet style="classA" id="idA" >
  <platform-specific>
    <html>
      <html-template location="mywebpage.ftl"/>
    </html>
  </platform-specific>
</screenlet>
```

Platform-specific widgets

Platform-specific widgets are used to specify HTML templates. Currently, the only HTML template type supported are FreeMarker templates. There are two types of FreeMarker templates supported: HTML and XSL Formatting Objects (or XSL-FO) templates with markup to generate PDFs.

How to do it...

HTML platform-specific templates can be specified by following these steps:

1. Open a Screen widget definition file.

2. Locate a screen definition within the Screen widget definition file.

3. Create a `platform-specific` element within the `widgets` element. If a `widgets` element does not exist, create one.

4. To add an HTML FreeMarker file, create an `html` element.

5. To specify a FreeMarker template with XSL-FO markup, add an `xsl-fo` element beneath the `platform-specific` element.

6. Close all elements with end tags.

7. Save and close the file.

8. Test as appropriate.

How it works...

Platform-specific widgets point to FreeMarker template files. Since any widget may be located anywhere within an OFBiz instance, the `location` attribute specifies a path location relative to an OFBiz Component. For example, the following platform-specific widget points to a FreeMarker file located in the common Component:

```
<platform-specific>
  <html>
    <html-templatelocation="component://common/webcommon/login.ftl"/>
  </html>
</platform-specific>
```

There's more...

To instruct OFBiz to invoke the **Apache Formatting Objects Processor** (FOP) tool, and take one or more FreeMarker files with XSL-FO content and transform some data, you might write a widget specification as follows:

```
<xsl-fo>
  <html-template location=
      "component://common/webcommon/includes/fo/start.fo.ftl"/>
  <html-template location=
      "component://common/webcommon/includes/fo/basic-header.fo.ftl"/>
  <html-template location=
      "component://common/webcommon/includes/fo/basic-footer.fo.ftl"/>
</xsl-fo>
```

OFBiz Tree widgets

OFBiz Tree widgets are widgets that automatically generate HTML unordered lists (HTML `ul` and `li` markup tags) from the specified database content and/or other XML declarations.

Tree widgets are defined in Tree widget definition files that have an XML XSD declaration as follows. Tree widget definition files may be located anywhere within an OFBiz install:

```
<trees xmlns:xsi="http://www.w3.org/2001/XMLSchema-instance"
       xsi:noNamespaceSchemaLocation=
           "http://ofbiz.apache.org/dtds/widget-tree.xsd">
</trees>
```

How to do it...

Tree widgets can be added by the following steps:

1. Create a Tree widget definition within an existing Tree widget definition file. Start with a `tree name` and a `root-node-name` attribute. The `root-node-name` is a trigger to OFBiz to create an HTML `ul` markup tag.

2. Create one or more "nodes". A tree node is created when you specify a `node` element.

3. Create one or more "sub-nodes".

4. Close all `node` and `sub-node` elements.

5. Save the file.

6. Add the Tree widget to an existing Screen widget definition. For example,
   `<include-tree name="MyTree" />`

How it works...

Tree widgets create HTML by taking the XML widget declarations and merging those declarations with any specified database values to create the corresponding HTML. Tree widgets build one or more HTML unordered lists (`ul`) with associated list tags, HTML styling, and hyperlinks. For example:

Basic tree	

XML	`<tree name="mytree" root-node-name="first-node" >`
	    `<node name="first-node">`
	    `</node>`
	`</tree>`

HTML	`<ul class="basic-tree">`
	    `<li>`
	        `<a class="leafnode"> </a>`
	    `</li>`
	`</ul>`

There's more...

For example, the following screenshot shows a browser web page built from a single OFBiz Screen widget, decorator-screen, a single embedded Tree widget, and a single embedded FreeMarker template:

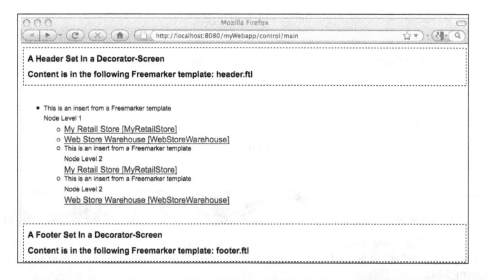

OFBiz Menu widgets

OFBiz Menu widgets are widgets that automatically generate HTML unordered list elements (HTML ul and li markup tags) from lists of database content or other sources. For example, Menu widgets figure prominently in the Accounting Manager Application by generating menu options for the main web page.

OFBiz Menu widgets are defined in XML document files containing the following XSD:

```
<menus xmlns:xsi="http://www.w3.org/2001/XMLSchema-instance"
       xsi:noNamespaceSchemaLocation=
          "http://ofbiz.apache.org/dtds/widget-menu.xsd">
```

How to do it...

Menu widgets can be added by following these steps:

1. Create a Menu widget definition within an existing Menu widget definition file.

2. Give the Menu widget a name.

3. Add one or more menu-item elements as shown:
   ```
   <menu name="MyMenu" title="Menu">
     <menu-item name="myMenuItem1"
                 title="Menu Items 'R Us"><link="someLink2" />
     </menu-item>
     <menu-item name="myMenuItem2"
                 title="Menu Items 'R Us"><link="someLink2" />
     </menu-item>
   </menu>
   ```

4. Make sure to close all elements with end tags.

5. Save and close the definition file.

6. Add the Menu widget to an existing Screen widget definition.
   For example: `<include-menu name="MyMenu" />`

How it works...

Similar to the Tree widget, the Menu widget creates a list of HTML unordered list elements and associated HTML hyperlink markup based on configured XML declarations.

OFBiz Form widgets

OFBiz Form widgets are widgets that create HTML forms based on XML declarations found in a Form widget definition file. A Form widget definition file is any XML document that has the following XSD:

```
<forms xmlns:xsi="http://www.w3.org/2001/XMLSchema-instance"
       xsi:noNamespaceSchemaLocation=
           "http://ofbiz.apache.org/dtds/widget-form.xsd">
```

How to do it...

Form widgets can be added by following these simple steps:

1. Create a Form widget definition within an existing Form widget definition file.

2. Give the Form widget a name.

3. Add one or more `field` elements. Be sure to close all elements with end tags.

4. A simple Form widget definition that creates a single HTML form with a single HTML form `<INPUT type="text">` element may be defined as follows:

```
<form name="MyForm" target="someTargetURL" title="MyForm" >
  <field name="Field 1"><text /> </field>
</form>
```

5. Add the Form widget to an existing Screen widget definition. For example:
   `<include-form name="MyForm" />`

How it works...

Similar to other OFBiz widgets, the OFBiz screen handler takes Form widget XML directives and creates HTML forms.

There's more..

HTML forms have many variations. The following lists some `FORM` widget field elements with equivalent HTML renderings. The same Screen widget (the `main` screen), decorator-screen, and FreeMarker files were used. This demonstrates the flexibility of using widgets within an OFBiz webapp UI:

- ▶ Form widget `field` attribute to display an `INPUT TEXT` box:

```
<field name="PlainOldTextInput">
    <text/>
</field>
```

- ▶ Form widget `field` attribute to display an HTML `SELECT` box (drop-down menu) w/ static SELECT OPTION(s):

```
<field name="DropDownExample">
  <drop-down allow-empty="false">
    <option key="_NA_" description="No Description"/>
    <option key="key1" description="First Option"/>
    <option key="key2" description="Second Option"/>
    <option key="key3" description="3rd Option" />
  </drop-down>
</field>
```

- ▶ Form widget `field` element to upload a file:

```
<field name="UploadImageData">
    <file />
</field>
```

- ▶ Form widget field attribute to display an HTML TEXTAREA and a SUBMIT button:

```
<field name="Field3" title="A Text Area">
    <textarea rows="5" cols="30" />
</field>
```

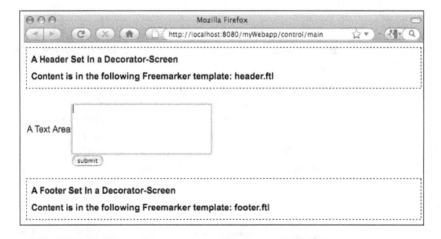

Creating web pages using FreeMarker

Some people find writing XML code to create HTML counterintuitive. For those who choose not to use OFBiz widgets but would rather write HTML directly using FreeMarker, this section is for you.

Getting ready

The following prerequisites are needed to be taken care of:

1. At a minimum, you will need to define a Screen widget with a `widgets` element declaration pointing to your FreeMarker template file.

2. For any required data preparation, add declarations to the `actions` portion of the Screen widget definition.

3. If needed, create any Groovy or BeanShell scripts in preparation for screen rendering.

4. Open an existing FreeMarker file or create a new one.

How to do it...

Add HTML and/or FreeMarker directives to your file. For example, a simple web page that displays "Hello World" might have the following content:

```
<html xmls="http://www.w3.org/1999/xhtml">
  <head>
    <link rel="stylesheet"
    href="<@ofbizContentUrl>/images/default.css</@ofbizContentUrl>"
    type="text/css"/>
  </head>
  <body>
    <h1>Hello World </h1>
  </body>
</html>
```

Where `~/images/default.css` is an external style sheet that contains styles for this HTML document.

How it works...

While OFBiz widgets are designed to prepare data and create HTML within the context of a single widget definition, FreeMarker provides a much cleaner separation of data preparation from HTML authoring. The OFBiz screen handler merges data from Screen widget `actions` into HTML using FreeMarker template directives.

FreeMarker templates consist of a procedural-oriented declaratives (`if/then/else`) mixed with HTML that allow for considerable control over how HTML web pages will be rendered. Many times when building OFBiz webapps using FreeMarker, you will need access to information about the execution context or current user session. The following tips show how to access context information while working within a FreeMarker file:

To access HTTP/HTTPS request attributes set from the Screen widget, OFBiz Services, OFBiz Events, or any other process:

```
<#assign x = requestAttributes._SOME_REQUEST_
ATTRIBUTE_?has_content/>
```

To access HTTP/HTTPS request parameters from a URL, HTML form:

```
<#assign y = requestParameters.SOME_REQUEST_
PARAMETER?has_content/>
```

Servlet context session attributes as set from another web page, OFBiz Screen widget, OFBiz Service, OFBiz Event, or other:

```
<#assign z = sessionAttributes.SOME_SESSION_
ATTRIBUTE?has_content/>
```

Note: Context information passed from the Screen widget and from backend applications, for example error messages, are usually passed as HTTP/HTTPS request attributes.

There's more

FreeMarker transformations are similar to macros in that they are shortcuts that convert wrapped values in some predetermined fashion. The OFBiz folks have pre-built and supply with the distribution a number of useful FreeMarker transformations.

For example, to easily build the HTML hyperlink for an image, external CSS file, or JavaScript file, wrap the hyperlink URL within the following transformation tags:

```
<@ofbizContentUrl></@ofbizContentUrl>
```

This transform creates a link based on URLs relative to the entire OFBiz instance.

To create a navigation hyperlink to a URL relative to a runtime instance of an OFBiz webapp, enclose the URL in the following transformation directives:

```
<@ofbizUrl></@ofbizUrl>
```

Using this transform not only relieves the author from knowing where URLs are relative to the framework and/or currently executing web application, but they also perform any necessary SSL translations automatically.

See also

For more information about FreeMarker, please see the FreeMarker manual located at:

```
http://FreeMarker.sourceforge.net/docs/index.html
```

Passing Screen widget parameters to FreeMarker

It is possible to pass context information, such as the name of a screen, to a FreeMarker template and/or a Groovy script directly from the Screen widget definition.

How to do it...

Context information can be passed to FreeMarker in the following way:

1. Under the `actions` element within a Screen widget definition, add one/more `set` elements with the `field` attribute set to the name of the variable and the `value` attribute set to the value of the variable.

2. Retrieve this variable using the name specified in step 1.

How it works

Setting `field` values using the earlier method places the named variable with its value within the execution context. Once in the context, the FreeMarker rendering engine and any other screen rendering artifact, including any OFBiz widget, has access to it.

There's more

For example, to add an action to set a context variable named `myScreenVariable`, you might code something like the following:

```
<actions>
    <set field="myScreenVariable" value="aValue">
</actions>
```

Within FreeMarker, you may access this value as follows:

```
<#assign localVariable = myScreenVariable>
```

To retrieve this value using Groovy:

```
localScreenName = context.myScreenVariable;
```

Calling Java methods from FreeMarker

Many times, it is convenient to call an OFBiz Java utility or tool directly from within FreeMarker. The OFBiz FreeMarker implementation allows for calling Java methods (utilities and tools) directly from within FreeMarker directives.

How to do it...

Java methods may be called from FreeMarker in the following way:

1. Open the FreeMarker template file.
2. To call an OFBiz Java method, use the FreeMarker `assign` directive and be sure to use the full Java packaging notation for the method as shown here:

    ```
    <#assign value =
         Static["org.ofbiz.base.util.UtilProperties"].
            getPropertyValue("general.properties", defaultUrl)>
    ```

3. Close the file.

 Note: Changes to FreeMarker files are immediate. You do not need to restart OFBiz.

How it works...

The FreeMarker program is a Java Application (not to be confused with an OFBiz web application) that takes FreeMarker directives, HTML markup, and prepared data and creates HTML destined for a browser. FreeMarker runs within the same JVM as OFBiz and therefore has access to all the runtime tools and utilities on the CLASSPATH.

There's more...

To call an OFBiz Service (and use the `UtilMisc.toMap` utility) from within a FreeMarker file, use the following:

```
<#assign result =
    dispatcher.runSync("aService",
        Static["org.ofbiz.base.util.UtilMisc"].toMap("contextValue1",
        someValue, "userLogin", userLogin))/>
```

Forcing FreeMarker to render HTML markup

Prepared data input to FreeMarker templates is assumed to be free of any HTML tags. Any HTML markup tags embedded within prepared data will be ignored, and the data will be rendered as is.

There are cases where prepared data contains HTML markup that you want FreeMarker to render as markup. For example, you may have content stored within the database that has HTML markup tags included. In this scenario, you will need to force FreeMarker to read HTML as markup and render accordingly.

How to do it...

Within the FreeMarker template file, wrap the prepared data in the following OFBiz provided utility:

```
${StringUtil.wrapString(textData)}
```

How it works

FreeMarker is a templating engine that merges prepared data with FreeMarker templating instructions to output HTML (and other) document type(s). The data that is fed into a FreeMarker template is assumed to be free of any HTML tags as the template itself typically contains all the HTML markup necessary to render the final document.

When data containing HTML markup is passed as prepared data to a FreeMarker template, any embedded HTML tags are rendered as character equivalents and not HTML markup. For example, if prepared data contains the character sequence <p> then the final HTML document will display the character sequence <p>. That's fine if you want <p> displayed. But what if you really want <p> to be HTML markup for the beginning of a paragraph?

To force the FreeMarker engine to view prepared data with an eye towards using embedded HTML markup as HTML markup, you will need to wrap the prepared data as shown earlier.

Uploading files in FreeMarker forms

To upload files from within FreeMarker templates, use the standard HTML `form "file"` type attribute.

Getting ready

Firstly ensure the following:

1. Make sure you have a backend OFBiz Event or Service configured to accept the uploaded file.

2. Configure the `controller.xml` request-map to designate the backend Event or Service to call when the `form` is submitted.

How to do it...

Files can be uploaded in forms by following these steps:

1. Within a new or existing FreeMarker file, create or modify an HTML `form`. Be sure to include the `form` attribute `enctype` as `"multipart/form-data"`.

2. Add an input type of `"file"` as shown here:

```
<form action="<@ofbizUrl>myFileUpload</@ofbizUrl>"
      name="addContentForm" method="post"
      enctype="multipart/form-data">
  <#-- Add the rest of the Form's elements -->
  <input type="file" name="uploadedFile" size="25"
         id="uploadedFile" />
</form>
```

How it works...

FreeMarker supports all the standard HTML `form` input types, including the `file` type. Remember, to upload a file you will need an OFBiz Event or Service to accept that file, on the backend.

There 's more...

In support of the OFBiz Content Management Application, there are a number of file upload Services available to use within your webapp. While a detailed discussion of how the Content Manager works is beyond the scope of this book, you can use any of these existing OFBiz Services to help you learn not only how file uploading may be accomplished on the backend, but also how the OFBiz Content Manager Application works.

For example, using the `createContentFromUploadedFile` Service within your own webapp allows for a file upload from a browser to the local server hard drive without regards to the file type. This Service will copy any type of file (plain-text, PDF, MSWord, any image format, and others) using binary data transfers to the local OFBiz install sub-directory location `~/runtime/uploads/`.

Without any further work by you, beyond:

- ▶ Creating a `controller.xml` request-map entry to direct requests to the `createContentFromUploadedFile` Service.

- ▶ Creating an HTML `form` that includes, at a minimum, a `contentId` and a `dataResourceId` as shown here:

```
<form action="<@ofbizUrl>createContentFromUploadedFile</@
ofbizUrl>"
        name="aForm" method="post" enctype="multipart/form-data">
    <input type="hidden" name="dataResourceId" value="DR_01" />
    <input type="hidden" name="contentId" value="CT_01" />
    <label>Upload File</label>
    <input type="file" name="uploadedFile"    size="30">
    <input type="submit" class="button" value="submit" />
</form>
```

You may easily handle a file upload within your OFBiz web application.

It is left as an exercise to the reader to learn what the `dataResourceId` and `contentId` values are and what they are used for.

4
OFBiz Services

In this chapter, we explore the following OFBiz Service topics:

- Managing OFBiz Services
- Calling asynchronous, synchronous, and recurring Services from an HTML form
- Creating a Service definition file
- Creating a Service definition
- Service implementation
- Defining Service input and output attributes
- Service Event Condition Actions (SECAs)
- Service groups
- Handling Service errors
- Implementing Groovy Services
- Mail Event Condition Actions (MECAs)
- Entity Event Condition Actions (EECAs)

Introduction

OFBiz has been characterized as having an "event-driven, service-oriented architecture". Long before it was fashionable to build complex enterprise computer systems using service-oriented techniques, OFBiz implemented a number of architectural features enabling a service-oriented design. These features include:

- A context-aware Service Engine available for use across the entire framework or, if configured, externally through supported network interfaces. OFBiz Service consumers need not concern themselves with the location of the called Service nor with a Service's implementation details. OFBiz handles all that transparently to both the service provider and consumer.

- Multiple invocation methods including: **inline** or synchronous with the calling program; **out-of-band** or asynchronous from the caller's processing logic and/or as a scheduled job for recurring execution. OFBiz handles all input, output, and context parameter transfers seamlessly to both Service provider and Service caller.

- Chaining of Services for a true, event-driven Service platform and implementation of complex workflows. Services may be configured to be invoked based on external events or triggers. Once triggered, an OFBiz Service may call other Service(s) based on additional triggering Events and/or conditions. Any combination of Services may be chained together to form **Service Event Condition Action(s) or SECAs**.

- A fully integrated job scheduler for recurring and single use asynchronous job scheduling. The OFBiz job scheduler handles all the mundane coordination tasks associated with job scheduling, including calendar lookups, frequency, and interval timing.

- Service creation and implementation tools, including selectable input and output validations based on configured parameter types; authentication and authorization checks integrated with OFBiz user login processing, and even localization preservation across Service calls.

The heart of the OFBiz service-oriented implementation is the Service Engine factory. Using a factory pattern, OFBiz provides an easily extendable Service management and invocation tool supporting any number of concurrent Services and any number of third-party execution engines including, but not limited to: Java, Groovy, Javascript, JPython, and the OFBiz "simple" Service (based on the OFBiz Mini-Language.) By offloading Service implementation to programming language-specific engines, OFBiz Services may be written and implemented in any language that suits the developer's fancy.

The Service Engine factory may be called from anywhere in the framework to handle the details of Service invocation, as shown in the following diagram:

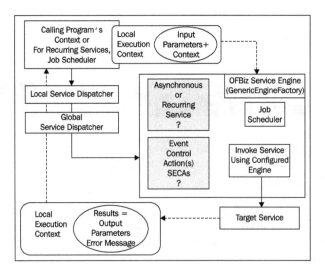

Managing existing OFBiz Services

Out-of-the-box OFBiz comes with many hundreds of Services. To find and otherwise manage OFBiz Services, a fully featured Service management dashboard is provided. Privileged users may conveniently handle all Service related tasks using the OFBiz WebTools toolkit as described.

How to do it...

To access the OFBiz Service management main web page, navigate to the following WebTools URL:

```
https://localhost:8443/webtools/control/ServiceList
```

When prompted for a username and password, login as the administrative user (username "admin", password "ofbiz").

How it works...

WebTools provides a dashboard-like UI to view, manage, run, and support OFBiz Services. The main web page for OFBiz Service support is found at:

```
https://localhost:8443/webtools/ServiceList
```

(Note the use of case-sensitive addressing). This web page is shown in the following figure:

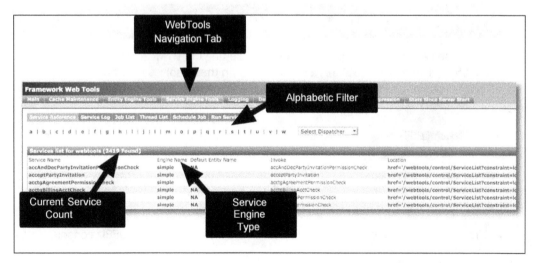

There's more...

Asynchronous and scheduled Service requests are managed by the OFBiz job scheduler. The job scheduler consists of multiple execution threads as configured in the `~framework/service/config/serviceengine.xml` file. Threads run from one or more thread "pools". From the OFBiz **Thread List** web page, you may see at a glance the configuration of the OFBiz job scheduler as well as thread and thread pool usage as shown here:

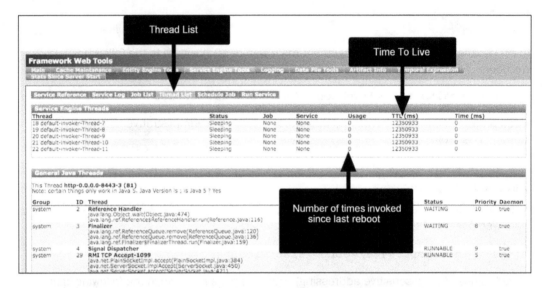

Calling a Service from an HTML form

Services may be called directly from HTML forms by setting the HTML form's `action` element to point to the URL of a `controller.xml` request-map that resolves to either an OFBiz Event that calls a Service or directly to a Service. To demonstrate this, the following section uses the WebTool's **Run Service** HTML form to invoke a Service.

Getting ready

For the purposes of this recipe, we shall use an existing Service called `testScv` and invoke it from the WebTools UI. In this example, we will not be creating an HTML form nor creating a Service, but rather using an existing form and Service:

- To view the results of the `testScv` Service's execution, open an OFBiz console window from the command line
- Alternatively, to view the results of the execution, run the Unix `tail` command `tail -f ofbiz.log` on the `ofbiz.log` file `~runtime/ofbiz.log` while performing this recipe

How to do it...

Services may be called directly from HTML forms by following these steps:

1. Navigate directly to the **Run Service** WebTools web page by selecting the **Run Service** URL: ~webtools/control/runService.

2. From the **Run Service** form, enter in **testScv** in the field labeled **Service**.

3. Leave the field labeled **Pool** as is.

4. Hit the **Submit** button to bring up the **Schedule Job** web page.

5. On the **Schedule Job** web page, enter in any values for the requested form fields. These fields correspond to any Service INPUT parameters as configured in the Service definition for testScv.

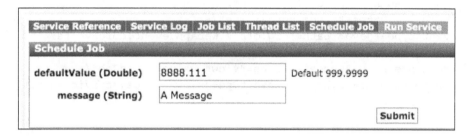

| Service Reference | Service Log | Job List | Thread List | Schedule Job | Run Service |

Schedule Job

defaultValue (Double)	8888.111	Default 999.9999
message (String)	A Message	
		Submit

6. Hit the **Submit** button. The testScv has been called by using an HTML form.

7. To verify that the input parameters entered in step 6 earlier are processed by the testScv, inspect the ofbiz.log file as shown:

```
---- SVC-CONTEXT: defaultValue => 8888.111
---- SVC-CONTEXT: message => A Message
---- SVC-CONTEXT: timeZone => sun.util.calendar.ZoneInfo[id="America/New_York",offset=-18000000,dstSavings=36000
ava.util.SimpleTimeZone[id=America/New_York,offset=-18000000,dstSavings=3600000,useDaylight=true,startYear=0,sta
k=1,startTime=7200000,startTimeMode=0,endMode=3,endMonth=10,endDay=1,endDayOfWeek=1,endTime=7200000,endTimeMode=
---- SVC-CONTEXT: userLogin => [GenericEntity:UserLogin][createdStamp,2010-03-08 16:09:14.761(java.sql.Timestamp
.sql.Timestamp)][currentPassword,(SHA)47ca69ebb4bdc9ae0adec130880165d2cc05db1a(java.lang.String)][disabledDateTi
gedOut,null()][isSystem,null()][lastCurrencyUom,null()][lastLocale,null()][lastTimeZone,null()][lastUpdatedStamp
lastUpdatedTxStamp,2010-03-17 14:52:38.618(java.sql.Timestamp)][partyId,admin(java.lang.String)][passwordHint,nu
FailedLogins,0(java.lang.Long)][userLdapDn,null()][userLoginId,admin(java.lang.String)]
---- SVC-CONTEXT: locale => en_US
-----SERVICE TEST----- : A Message
```

How it works...

Any OFBiz Service may be called from an OFBiz webapp HTML form simply by:

1. Creating an HTML form with an action attribute URL for the target Service.

2. Creating a `controller.xml` entry with a request-map for the target Service that matches the HTML form's `action` URL. For example, the HTML form for the **Run Service** tool has an `action` value as shown in the following code snippet:

```
<form name= "scheduleForm" method= "POST"
     action= "/webtools/control/scheduleService" />
   <input type="text" name="testScv" />
   <!-- Stuff Intentionally Removed >
 </form>
```

When the form is submitted, the URL set within the form's `action` (webtools/control/scheduledService) is intercepted by the WebTools controller servlet, which consults its `controller.xml` file to determine how to handle this request. The `controller.xml` entry for this URL is shown here:

```
<request-map uri="scheduleService">
  <security https="true" auth="true"/>
  event type="java" path="org.ofbiz.webapp.event.CoreEvents"
        invoke="scheduleService"/>
  <response name="success" type="view" value="FindJob"/>
  <response name="sync_success" type="view" value="serviceResult"/>
  <response name="error" type="view" value="scheduleJob"/>
</request-map>
```

The URL request is mapped to an OFBiz Event called `scheduleService`. Inside the `scheduleService` Event, a call is made to the Service Engine to invoke `testScv` using the Java Service implementation engine as shown in the `testScv` Service definition file:

```
<service name="testScv" engine="java" export="true"
         validate="false" require-new-transaction="true"
         location="org.ofbiz.common.CommonServices" invoke="testScv">
  <description>Test service</description>
  <attribute name="defaultValue" type="Double"
             mode="IN" default-value="999.9999"/>
  <attribute name="message" type="String" mode="IN" optional="true"/>
  <attribute name="resp" type="String" mode="OUT"/>
</service>
```

After `testScv` has been executed, processing control returns to the OFBiz request handler (part of the controller servlet) and then back to the calling webapp as configured in the `controller.xml` file.

Calling asynchronous Services from HTML forms

You can use WebTools and HTML forms to run a Service asynchronously either one time or on a recurring basis. The following demonstrates the steps necessary to schedule `testScv` to be executed one time, asynchronously, as a scheduled job.

Getting ready

Navigate directly to the **Schedule Job** web page.

`~https://localhost:8443/webtools/control/scheduleJob`

How to do it...

To execute `testScv` asynchronously follow, these steps:

1. In the **Service** form field, enter in **testScv** as shown in the screenshot.
2. Leave the **Job** field empty. OFBiz will pick a unique name automatically.
3. Use the calendar pop-up icon directly next to the **Start Date/Time** field to select any date and time after the current wall clock time.

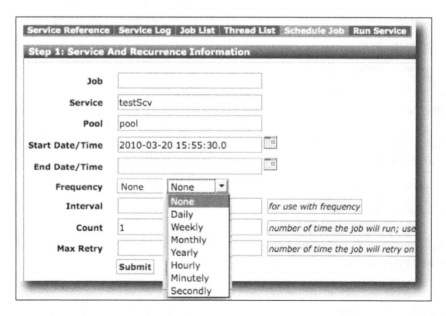

Field	Usage
Pool	By default, only one thread pool, called **pool**, is configured. To add more thread pools, see the `serviceengine.xml` file.
Frequency	A frequency of **None** tells OFBiz to run this Service once.
Interval	Interval is used with frequency to indicate how many times to invoke the Service.
Count	-1 indicates forever. Any valid integer is acceptable here.

4. Submit this form by clicking the **Submit** button to bring up the **Service Parameters** form, which allows the caller to provide alternative input parameters to the Service.

5. Add INPUT parameters as shown:

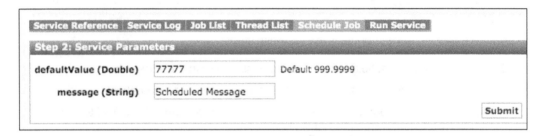

6. Submit the **Service Parameters** form. testScv will be scheduled to run at the specified time.

How it works...

Scheduled Services are run asynchronously from the calling program. As such, requests for scheduling are handled by the OFBiz job scheduler. Each scheduled Service is assigned a unique job identifier (jobId) and execution pool by the job scheduler. After the Service is scheduled for execution, control returns to the calling program.

There's more...

Using the OFBiz job scheduler **Job List** web page, you may find all scheduled jobs. In the following screenshot, testScv is shown as scheduled for execution on the **Job List Search Results** web page as specified in the recipe:

Because the `testScv` only writes output to the logfile, we may verify successful execution and scheduling by observing the `ofbiz.log` runtime logfile as shown:

```
2010-03-20 15:55:33,558 (default-invoker-Thread-7) [     ServiceEcaRule.java:133:INFO ] For Service ECA [testScv] on [invoke] go†
e][equals][auto][true][String]
---- SVC-CONTEXT: locale => en_US
---- SVC-CONTEXT: timeZone => sun.util.calendar.ZoneInfo[id="America/New_York",offset=-18000000,dstSavings=3600000,useDaylight=tr
ava.util.SimpleTimeZone[id=America/New_York,offset=-18000000,dstSavings=3600000,useDaylight=true,startYear=0,startMode=3,startMon
k=1,startTime=7200000,startTimeMode=0,endMode=3,endMonth=10,endDay=1,endDayOfWeek=1,endTime=7200000,endTimeMode=0]]
---- SVC-CONTEXT: defaultValue => 77777.0
---- SVC-CONTEXT: message => Scheduled Message
---- SVC-CONTEXT: userLogin => [GenericEntity:UserLogin][createdStamp,2010-03-08 16:09:14.761(java.sql.Timestamp)][createdTxStamp
.sql.Timestamp)][currentPassword,(SHA)47ca69ebb4bdc9ae0adec130880165d2cc05db1a(java.lang.String)][enabled,Y(java.lang.String)][l
52:38.619(java.sql.Timestamp)][lastUpdatedTxStamp,2010-03-17 14:52:38.618(java.sql.Timestamp)][partyId,admin(java.lang.String)][
lang.Long)][userLoginId,admin(java.lang.String)]
-----SERVICE TEST----- : Scheduled Message
```

Calling a Service many times from an HTML form

It is possible to call a Service multiple times from a single HTML form (for example, one time for each row in the form) by placing a line similar to the following with a `service-multi` event type defined for the `controller.xml` request-map entry of the target Service.

How to do it...

Follow these steps to call a Service multiple times:

1. Use the event type `service-multi` within the `controller.xml` request-map entry as shown here:

```
<request-map uri="someService" />
  <event type="service-multi" invoke="someService"/>
  <!-- Other request-map statements intentionally left out -->
</request-map>
```

2. If using an OFBiz Form Widget, add a line similar to the following to the Form Widget definition. Note, the `list-name` is the name of the list that is generating multiple rows for the HTML form:

```
<form name="someFormName" type="multi" use-row-submit="true"
      list-name="someList" target="someServiceName"      /
         <!-- Form fields removed for reading clarity -->
</form>
```

3. If using a FreeMarker template, add lines similar to the following:

```
<form name="mostrecent" mode="POST"
      action="<@ofbizUrl>someService</@ofbizUrl>"/>
  <#assign row=0/>
  <#list someList as listItem>
```

```
<#-- HTML removed for reading clarity.
     Each row has a unique input name associated with it
     allowing this single Form to be submitted to the
     "someServiceName" Service from each row -->
<input type="radio" name="someFormField_o_${row}"
       value="someValue" checked/>
<input type="radio" name="someFormField_o_${row}"
       value="someValue"/>
</#list>
</form>
```

How it works...

The Event type `service-multi` provides a convenient shortcut for coding HTML forms that are embedded within lists. Each list item is automatically converted to a unique `form` field so that a single Service may be called from any row within the list.

Creating a new Service definition file

Services are defined in Service definition XML document files. By convention, Service definition files are located in a containing Component's `servicedef` directory. This may be changed by editing the Component's `ofbiz-component.xml` file.

How to do it...

To define a new Service definition file, follow these few steps:

1. Check the `ofbiz-component.xml` file to make sure there is a location pointer to the Service definition file. For example:

   ```
   <!-- For Service Definition files, use the following -->
   <service-resource type="model" loader="main"
                   location="servicedef/Services.xml"/>

   <!-- For Service Event Control Action files, use the following -->
   <service-resource type="eca" loader="main"
                   location="servicedef/secas.xml"/>

   <!-- For Service Group Definition files, use the following -->
   <service-resource type="group" loader="main"
                   location="servicedef/groups.xml"/>
   ```

2. Using your favorite operating system editor or IDE tool, add Service definition files in the directory locations specified in the `ofbiz-component.xml` file shown earlier. Make sure each file has the appropriate XML version and XSD declarations in the beginning of the file, as follows:

```
<?xml version="1.0" encoding="UTF-8"?>
<services xmlns:xsi="http://www.w3.org/2001/XMLSchema-instance"
          xsi:noNamespaceSchemaLocation=
                    "http://ofbiz.apache.org/dtds/services.xsd">
```

3. Make sure the new Service definition file has a closing `</services>` tag.

4. Insert as many Service definitions within this file as needed.

5. Save and close the file.

6. Restart OFBiz to make any changes to the `ofbiz-component.xml` file effective.

How it works...

OFBiz is made aware of Service definition files by placing one or more declarations about the definition files within a Component's `ofbiz-component.xml` file. There is one such declaration for each Service definition file located within the containing Component. Each declaration instructs OFBiz as to what types of definitions are found in the file and the location of the file relative to the Component's root. There is no limit to the number of Service definition file declarations that may be included in a single `ofbiz-component.xml` file.

Creating a new Service definition

OFBiz is made aware of a Service by the presence of a Service definition within a Service definition file. Each OFBiz Service has a Service definition that configures the Service with a name, location information, Service implementation engine type, and other optional parameters.

How to do it...

To create a new Service definition, follow these steps:

1. Find an existing Service definition file or create a new one.

2. Add one or more `service` element XML declarations. For example:

```
<service name="someName" engine="one_of_the_available_engines"
         location="component_or_CLASSPATH_location"
<!-- Add any INPUT/OUTPUT attribute elements here -->
<!-- Add a PERMISSION-SERVICE element -->
<!-- For Simple Services, add any AUTO-ATTRIBUTE elements -->
</service>
```

3. Make sure the new Service definition element has a closing `</services>` tag.

4. Save and close the file.

5. Restart OFBiz.

How it works...

Using Service definitions, OFBiz removes Service location and implementation details from the Service and "injects" these values at runtime. This enables the Service developer to concentrate on implementing business logic and the Service consumer to call the Service without regard for location or implementation details.

When a Service is called, OFBiz automatically locates the Service on the CLASSPATH by consulting the Service's Service definition, manages all defined context parameters and passes control to the appropriate Service implementation engine.

See also

All supported Service definition configurations are documented in the Service definition file XML schema located at:

`~framework/service/dtd/services.xsd`

Implementing Services

Services may be implemented—that is, developed in any language—for which there is a corresponding Service implementation engine. As of this writing, Service Engines supported include, but are not limited to: Java, Groovy, BeanShell, Mini-Language, Jacl, Javascript, JPython.

Getting ready

Before starting work on any new Service, you must first decide which tool to use to develop your Service. For simple database read, write, and update processing, you may want to use the OFBiz Mini-Language tool to develop "simple Services". Simple Services consist of one or more XML declarations instructing OFBiz on how to handle business processing tasks.

For those who prefer to use procedural languages such as Java or Groovy, these options are available as well.

How to do it...

To implement a Service definition, follow these steps:

1. Create a new Service definition.
2. Create the Service implementation using a tool of choice (Java, Mini-Language, Groovy).
3. For Java Services, you must rebuild the component containing the Java code. For Mini-Language and other scripting tools such as Groovy, there is no need to rebuild the Component.
4. Restart OFBiz.
5. Test the Service definition.

How it works...

A Service's Service definition describes to OFBiz how a Service is implemented and where it is located on the runtime CLASSPATH. To create a new Service requires only an implementation of the Service (using a supported programming tool) and a proper Service definition entry in a valid Service definition file.

There's more...

Service Engines are configured in the following file:

`~framework/config/service/serviceengine.xml`

Defining Service attributes (INPUT/OUTPUT)

Service input and output parameters are defined within the Service's definition using XML declaration statements with an element tag of `attribute`. Each XML `attribute` element declaration represents either an input parameter (`INPUT`), an output parameter (`OUTPUT`), or a parameter that is passed as both input and output (`INOUT`). The participation of each parameter as an input or output value may be made optional by adding an `optional` attribute to the declaration. By default, the `optional` value is `false`, and all parameters that are defined are required to be passed. This means that the Service will fail if one or more of the configured (non-optional) parameters are not passed.

> Note: If an `INPUT` parameter is not defined for a Service, then that value will not be passed into the Service's execution context regardless of the values that are sent by the calling program. Similarly, if an `OUT` or `INOUT` parameter is not defined for a value, then that value will not be passed back to the calling program.

How to do it...

Add one or more `attribute` elements within the Service definition. For example:

```
<service name="myService" engine="SupportedEngine"
         location="somewhere.on.the.classpath" invoke="myService">
  <attribute name="attribute1" type="String" mode="IN"
             optional="true"/>
  <attribute name="attribute2" type="String" mode="IN"
             optional="false"/>
  <attribute name="attribute3" type="String" mode="INOUT"/>
</service>
```

How it works...

The OFBiz Service Engine handles the passing of input, output, and context parameters automatically based on the Service's Service definition. Only parameters configured for the Service (and several OFBiz managed context parameters such as the `userLogin` `GenericValue`, `locale`, `timeZone`, `errorMessage`, and `errorMessageList`) will be passed as input or as output.

By default, OFBiz automatically validates, at runtime, all incoming and outgoing parameters against the defined `type` attribute as configured. Validation failures will cause the Service to fail and control will be passed back to the calling program.

Service Event Condition Actions

Service Event Condition Actions (SECAs) are a powerful tool used to build complex business processing solutions out of one or more OFBiz Service(s). With SECAs, you may associate one or more Services together to form a chain of processing logic based on defined triggering events and conditions.

There are no limits on the number of SECAs supported by OFBiz, or in the number of Services that may participate within a single SECA.

Getting ready

Writing SECAs is simple. To write a SECA, you will need one or more Services to participate as either the `action` Service and/or the `target` Service. Once you have your Services defined:

1. Find or create a new SECA definition XML document. The SECA definition document must have the following XML line at the top of the file:

   ```
   <?xml version="1.0" encoding="UTF-8" ?>
   ```

2. Followed by the SECA XML schema declaration:

```
<service-eca xmlns:xsi="http://www.w3.org/2001/XMLSchema-instance"
          xsi:noNamespaceSchemaLocation=
                  "http://ofbiz.apache.org/dtds/service-eca.xsd">
```

How to do it...

Once the groundwork is laid, you can write SECAs by following these steps:

1. Create an ECA definition within a SECA definition file by adding an `eca` element with a `service` attribute similar to the following (Note: the following XML declarations are for illustration purposes only. Please substitute real values where appropriate):

```
<eca service="eca_service_name" event="required_some_event_name"
     run-on-failure="optional_true_or_false"
     run-on-error="optional_true_or_false"
     type="optional_some_type" format="optional_some_format" >
```

2. Optionally, add one ore more `condition` elements:

```
<condition field-name="some_name" operator="operator_values"
           value="some_value" type="supported_types" />
```

3. Optionally, add on or more `set` elements as input parameters or to format an existing parameter:

```
<set field-name="some_field" value="some_value"
     format="some_format" />
```

4. Add one or more `action` declarations. Each `action` declaration calls a Service to perform some action as shown below. The Service called may have the same name as the ECA:

```
<action service="some_service_to_call" mode="some_mode"
        run-as-user="optionally_set_to_a_user" />
```

5. Don't forget to close the `eca service` element with an end tag.

6. Close and save the file.

7. Restart OFBiz to make the SECA(s) configuration effective.

How it works...

When a Service is called, the first thing the OFBiz Service Engine does, even before assigning a Service implementation engine, is to check for any defined ECAs. If one or more ECAs exists for a Service, each ECA is processed before the initial target Service is invoked.

Note: Some ECAs perform actions on the output of a Service. In such cases, while the ECA itself is processed before the call to the Service, actions defined within the ECA may be invoked after the target Service is run.

In this way, it is possible to combine together any number of Services using any combination of conditions and Events, and thus solve complex business problems using one or more discrete OFBiz Services.

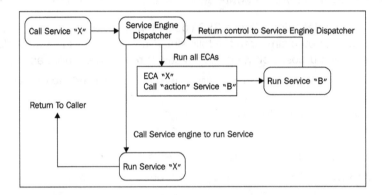

There's more...

There is no limit to the possible combinations when building SECAs. This makes the tool extremely powerful and potentially dangerous. It is possible, for example, to call Services within Services in a never-ending chain.

Service groups

Service "groups" are a technique for grouping together Services where there is a need to run all the Services together.

Getting ready

Create or find an existing Service group definition XML document. This XML document will have an XML version declaration as follows:

```
<?xml version="1.0" encoding="UTF-8" ?>
```

And a Service group XML schema declaration as shown:

```
<service-group xmlns:xsi="http://www.w3.org/2001/XMLSchema-instance"
               xsi:noNamespaceSchemaLocation=
                   "http://ofbiz.apache.org/dtds/service-group.xsd">
```

If creating a new Service group definition XML document, ensure that this document is configured in the containing Component's `ofbiz-component.xml` file. For example, if creating a Service group definition XML document in the `servicedef` directory, add a line similar to the following to the `ofbiz-component.xml` file:

```
<service-resource type="group" loader="main"
                  location="servicedef/groups.xml"/>
```

How to do it...

To group Services together, follow these steps:

1. Add one or more `group` elements as shown here. Each `group` element defines a Service group:

   ```
   <group name="updateCreditCardAndAddress" send-mode="all"> </group>
   ```

2. Within each `group` element, add one or more `invoke` declaration(s). Each `invoke` declaration points to a Service:

   ```
   <invoke name="createPostalAddress" mode="sync"
           result-to-context="true"/>
   <invoke name="createCreditCard" mode="sync"/>
   <invoke name="createPartyContactMech" mode="sync"/>
   ```

3. Close each element with an end tag.
4. Save the file.
5. Restart OFBiz to make Service group definitions effective.

How it works...

Service groups are a set of Services that should all run as a result of the initial Service call. Unlike SECAs, where conditions and triggers determine which Services will be run during any particular invocation, Service groups are used to indicate that all Services within the group should be run. Note, it is possible to have Service groups with participating Services that have SECAs defined.

The following table provides some of the more often used Service group configuration elements. Attribute values include:

group tag		
Attribute name	**Required?**	**Description**
name	Yes	The name of the Service this action will invoke.
send-mode	No	The mode in which the Service(s) should be invoked.
		Valid values: "none", "all", "first-available", "random", "round-robin".
		The default is "all".

To configure one or more Services within a `group` element declaration, add `invoke` elements configured as follows:

invoke tag		
Attribute name	**Required?**	**Description**
name	No	The name of the Service this `action` will invoke.
mode	Yes	The mode in which this Service should be invoked. Can be `sync` or `async`. Note that async actions will not update the context even when set to true.
result-to-context	No	Should the results of the action Service update the main Service's context. Valid values: "true", "false".
		Default is "false".

See also

Please refer to the Service group XML XSD schema file located at:

```
~framework/service/dtd/service-group.xsd
```

Handling Service errors

OFBiz Services may complete successfully or return to the caller with one or more errors. Upon successful completion of a Service, OFBiz automatically commits any database transactions and maps the return parameters to the context before returning control to the caller.

If a Service encounters an error and returns to the caller through an error processing path, OFBiz will automatically rollback all transactions initiated for the Service and/or SECAs regardless of the Service definition settings. To manage error processing from within a Service implementation, use the OFBiz-provided Service utility API as shown in this recipe.

Getting ready

The following examples assume a Service implemented in Java. Other Service Engine supported languages will behave in a similar fashion, although utility usage (API) details may vary.

For Java and Groovy programs, be sure to include the OFBiz Service utility program with a Java package import statement:

```
import org.ofbiz.service.ServiceUtil;
```

How to do it...

From within the Service's implementation, use the provided OFBiz utilities to control error message handling, including transaction rollback:

- To return an error message and have OFBiz manage transaction rollback from within a Java Service, add one or more lines similar to the following where appropriate:

```
org.ofbiz.service.ServiceUtil.returnError(
                         "An Error Message Here");
```

- To return a list of error messages and have OFBiz manage transaction rollback from within a Java Service, add one or more lines similar to the following:

```
// Don't forget to include imports for FastList
List<Object> errMsgList = FastList.newInstance();

// Add error messages to the errMsgList () for example
errMsgList.add("A new error message");
return ServiceUtil.returnError(errMsgList);
```

- To return an error message and have the error message localized based on the value of the `locale` context variable, add code similar to the following:

```
// Note, don't forget to import Map, UtilMisc, and
// UtilProperties to use this snippet
Map messageMap = UtilMisc.toMap("errMessage", e.getMessage());
errMsg = UtilProperties.getMessage("CommonUiLabels",
              "CommonDatabaseProblem", messageMap, locale);
return ServiceUtil.returnError(errMsg)
```

- To return an error and instruct OFBiz to **NOT** rollback transactions, add one or more lines similar to the following:

```
org.ofbiz.service.ServiceUtil.returnFailure(
      "Some error message, but don't roll back transactions");
```

▸ To pass Service errors from one Service call to another, simply use the `ServiceUtil.returnError` methods and include the error message or list of messages as method parameters.

▸ To easily retrieve an error message from the results of a Service call:

```
Map results = dispatcher.runSync("SomeService", inputMap);
String errMsg = ServiceUtil.getErrorMessage(results);
```

▸ To check if the results from a Service call contain any errors:

```
if(ServiceUtil.isError(someResult) ||
                    ServiceUtil.isFailure(someResult))
{
    return someValue;}
```

How it works...

The OFBiz best practice and convention for passing error messages from Services (and OFBiz Events) to calling programs is to use the following request attributes:

▸ `_ERROR_MESSAGE_` for a single error message

▸ `_ERROR_MESSAGE_LIST_` for a list of error messages where the list consists of one or more Java strings and each string contains an error message

When using the `ServiceUtil` error processing utilities to return from Service when an error is encountered, OFBiz will automatically map error messages and lists of error messages to the proper HTTP/HTTPS request object attribute(s).

See also

Please see the `ServiceUtil` API Javadocs:

```
http://ci.apache.org/projects/ofbiz/site/javadocs/
```

Writing Groovy Services

While Groovy is normally used for data preparation, this and other integrated scripting languages may be used to implement OFBiz Services. Using a scripting language to implement a Service has the advantage that the Service does not need to be compiled nor the containing Component rebuilt prior to use.

Getting ready

Make sure you have a "local dispatcher" and "local delegator" (if you want to use database Services) defined in the `web.xml` file, then follow these steps:

1. Check the `web.xml` file and make sure there is a local dispatcher and local delegator defined for the Component from which you will be calling the Service. For example:

```
<context-param>
  <param-name>localDispatcherName</param-name>
  <param-value>example</param-value>
  <description>
    A unique name used to identify the local dispatcher for the
    Service Engine
  </description>
</context-param>

<context-param>
  <param-name>entityDelegatorName</param-name>
  <param-value>default</param-value>
  <description>
    The Name of the Entity Delegator to use,
    defined in entityengine.xml
  </description>
</context-param>
```

2. Create the Service definition within an existing Service definition file. Note, any changes to the Service definition such as adding or removing input and/or output parameters require an OFBiz restart to become effective:

```
<service name="myGroovyService" engine="groovy"
    location="component://myComponent/script/myGroovyService.groovy"
    invoke="">
</service>
```

3. Restart OFBiz to ensure the Service's configuration (definition) is read and reloaded.

4. To test this Service from a web page, create a `controller.xml` request-map to call and test this Service from a webapp web page. For example, to call the Service in step 2:

```
<!-- ======= Testing a groovy Service ===== -->
<request-map uri="testGroovyService">
  <security https="false" auth="false"/>
  <event type="service" invoke="myGroovyService"/>
  <response name="success" type="view" value="main"/>
  <response name="error" type="view" value="main"/>
</request-map>
```

5. To test this Service from a web page, create a HTML form or link. For example, to call the Service with a request-map set to `testGroovyService` as shown in step 3, you might write something like the following:

```
<a href="<@ofbizUrl>testGroovyService</@ofbizUrl>">
  test groovy Service
</a>
```

How to do it...

Implement your Service by writing the Groovy script and saving it in the location and file specified in the Service's definition location attribute value. Note, to tell OFBiz to execute the Groovy script from top to bottom, leave the `invoke` parameter empty.

Unlike Java-based Services, there is no need to compile or restart OFBiz to make a Groovy Service immediately effective. Remember, however, that Service definition changes do require an OFBiz restart.

How it works...

Use of OFBiz Service implementation engines such as the Groovy engine make OFBiz Services implementation agnostic. Callers do not need to know that the Service is written in Groovy, and Groovy programmers do not need to concern themselves with the details of calling programs.

To make OFBiz aware that a Service is available and written in Groovy, simply indicate that the Service is to use the Groovy Service Engine by setting the `service` element's `engine` attribute value to `groovy`. OFBiz takes care of the rest.

Mail Event Condition Actions

To handle incoming e-mail automatically through the Service Engine interface, use **Mail Event Condition Actions** (MECAs).

Note: The OFBiz processes for handling incoming e-mail are not the same as those for sending e-mail. To configure OFBiz to send e-mail, please see the `~framework/common/config/general.properties` file.

Getting ready

A few steps to ensure before we can use Services to handle e-mail:

1. To trigger one or more Services based on the receipt of incoming e-mail, you will need to enable the OFBiz inbound e-mail listener by removing the appropriate comments from the `JavaMail Listener Container` entry in `~framework/base/config/ofbiz-containers.xml`.

2. Implement one or more Services using a Service implementation language of your choice to handle processing based on the occurrence of a mail Event.

How to do it...

Configure the MECA as shown in the following steps:

1. If one does not already exist, add a declaration to an `ofbiz-component.xml` file with a location pointer to the MECA definition file, as shown:

   ```
   <service-resource type="mca" loader="main"
                     location="servicedef/mca.xml"/>
   ```

2. Create a new MECA definition file or use an existing one. A valid MECA definition file will have the XML version declaration and a `service-mca` XML schema declaration element, as shown:

   ```
   <?xml version="1.0" encoding="UTF-8"?>
   <service-mca xmlns:xsi="http://www.w3.org/2001/XMLSchema-instance"
           xsi:noNamespaceSchemaLocation=
                   "http://ofbiz.apache.org/dtds/service-mca.xsd">
   ```

3. Add one or more `mca` elements as needed. Each MCA `action` element locates one or more Services:

   ```
   <mca mail-rule-name="processIncomingEmail">
     <action service="storeIncomingEmail" mode="sync"/>
   </mca>
   ```

4. Close all elements with closing tags.

5. Save and close the file.

6. Restart OFBiz to make the MCAs effective.

How it works...

The OFBiz e-mail listener process has been implemented to trigger any defined MECAs when an incoming e-mail is detected.

mca tag (required)		
Attribute name	**Required?**	**Description**
`mail-rule-name`	Yes	Name of the Service this action will invoke.

To set the conditions under which the MECA should fire, add one or more `condition-field` elements with configuration settings, as shown here:

condition-field tag (optional)		
Set conditions on e-mail header fields to invoke actions for specific events. For example, to always run a Service when the "to" e-mail header value is not equal to "me@me.com" set, write a condition rule similar to the following: `<condition-field field-name="to" operator="not-equals" value="me@me.com" />`		
Attribute name	**Required?**	**Description**
`field-name`	No	E-mail header field name.
`operator`	Yes	Valid values: `equals`, `not-equals`, `empty`, `not-empty`, `matches`, `not-matches`.
`value`	Yes	Value to compare the field-name value to.

See also

See the MECA schema definition file in `~framework/service/dtd/service-mca.xsd`.

Entity Event Condition Actions

It is possible to write ECAs for specific entities using an **Entity Event Condition Action** (EECA). For example, to trigger an Event, say a notification Service, when a field in an entity changes, you could write an EECA as we shall see in this recipe.

How to do it...

Triggering a notification Service using EECA can be done by following these steps:

1. If one does not already exist, add an entry in the `ofbiz-component.xml` file to identify the EECA definition file location as shown:

    ```
    <entity-resource type="eca" reader-name="main" loader="main"
                      location="entitydef/eecas.xml"/>
    ```

2. Create or add an EECA definition file with an XML version declaration and an XML XSD schema declaration, as shown here:

    ```
    <?xml version="1.0" encoding="UTF-8"?>
    <entity-eca xmlns:xsi="http://www.w3.org/2001/XMLSchema-instance"
            xsi:noNamespaceSchemaLocation=
                    "http://ofbiz.apache.org/dtds/entity-eca.xsd">
    ```

3. Add one or more EECA definitions to the EECA definition file. Don't forget to close each `eca` element declaration with a closing tag (`</eca>`).

    ```
    <!-- To maintain FinAccount.actualBalance and
                              FinAccount.availableBalance -->
    <eca entity="FinAccountTrans" operation="create-store"
        event="return">
      <action service="updateFinAccountBalancesFromTrans"
            mode="sync"/>
    </eca>
    ```

4. Be sure to close all XML element tags.

5. Save and close the EECA definition file.

6. Restart OFBiz to make the changes effective.

How it works...

EECA rules are checked before and/or after a call to access the database. Services defined by the `action` element are invoked when the configured entity is accessed by way of the `operation` attribute setting.

There's more...

Commonly used EECA attribute values are shown in the following table:

eca tag (Required)		
Attribute name	**Required?**	**Description**
`entity`	Yes	The name of the entity on which this operation and Event are to be applied to.
`operation`	Yes	Valid values: `create`, `store`, `remove`, `find`, `create-store`, `create-remove`, `store-remove`, `create-store-remove`, `any`.
`event`	Yes	Valid Values: `validate`, `return`, `run`, `cache-check`, `cache-put`, `cache-clear`.

To configure `action` elements for an EECA, the following configuration attribute values are supported:

action tag (Required)		
Attribute name	**Required?**	**Description**
`service`	Yes	The name of the Service to call if this operation is encountered.
`mode`	Yes	Valid values: `sync`, `async`.
`value-attr`	No	Values to pass to the Service being called as a result of this ECA.

To add one or more triggering conditions, add `condition` element declarations with the appropriate settings:

condition Tag (optional)		
Used to trigger actions based on one or more Entity fields meeting the specified conditions.		
Attribute name	**Required?**	**Description**
`field-name`	Yes	The name entity field.
`operator`	Yes	Valid values: `less`, `greater`, `less-equals`, `greater-equals`, `equals`, `not-equals`, `is-empty`, `is-not-empty`, `contains`.
`type`	No	Valid values: `PlainString`, `BigDecimal`, `Double`, `Float`, `Long`, `Integer`, `Date`, `Time`, `Timestamp`, `Boolean`, `Object`. Default: `String`.

`set` elements are used to equate entity field(s) or context variables to values. `set` declarations may be configured as shown:

set Tag (optional)		
Use the `set` declaration to establish or set the ECA on a specific field within an entity.		
Attribute name	**Required?**	**Description**
`field-name`	Yes	Indicates the value is an entity field.
`value`	No	The name of the field.

See also

Please see the EECA XSD located at `~framework/entity/dtd/entity-eca.xsd`.

5

The OFBiz Entity Engine

In this chapter, we shall examine the following Entity Engine data management topics:

- ▶ Changing the default database from Derby to another data source
- ▶ Connecting to a remote database
- ▶ Connecting to multiple databases
- ▶ Creating entity groups
- ▶ Disabling automatic database checks on OFBiz startup
- ▶ Mapping database data types
- ▶ Creating a new entity definition file
- ▶ Creating a new entity model
- ▶ Modifying an existing entity model
- ▶ Building a view-entity

Introduction

Secure and reliable data storage is the key business driver behind any data management strategy. That OFBiz takes data management seriously and does not leave all the tedious and error-prone data management tasks to the application developer or the integrator is evident from the visionary design and implementation of the Entity Engine.

The Entity Engine is a database agnostic application development and deployment framework seamlessly integrated into the OFBiz project code. It handles all the day-to-day data management tasks necessary to securely and reliably operate an enterprise. These tasks include, but are not limited to support for:

- Simultaneously connecting to an unlimited number of databases
- Managing an unlimited number of database connection pools
- Overseeing database transactions
- Handling database error conditions

The true power of the Entity Engine is that it provides OFBiz Applications with all the tools, utilities, and an Application Programming Interface (API) necessary to easily read and write data to all configured data sources in a consistent and predictable manner without concern for database connections, the physical location of the data, or the underlying data type.

To best understand how to effectively use the Entity Engine to meet all your data storage needs, a quick review of **Relational Database Management Systems (RDBMS)** is in order:

- RDBMS **tables** are the basic organizational structure of a relational database. An OFBiz **entity** is a model of a database table. As a model, entities describe a table's structure, content format, and any applicable associations a table may have with other tables.

- Database tables are further broken down into one or more **columns**. Table columns have data type and format characteristics constrained by the underlying RDBMS and assigned to them as part of a table's definition. The entity model describes a mapping of table columns to entity **fields**.

- Physically, data is stored in tables as one or more **rows**. A **record** is a unique instance of the content within a table's row. Users access table records by reading and writing one or more rows as mapped by an entity's model. In OFBiz, records are called **entity values**.

- **Keys** are a special type of field. Although there are several types of keys, OFBiz is primarily concerned with **primary keys** and **foreign keys**. A table's primary key is a column or group of columns that uniquely identifies a row within a table. The value of the primary key uniquely identifies a table's row throughout the entire database.

- A foreign key is a key used in one table to represent the value of a primary key in a related table. Foreign keys are used to establish unique and referentially correct relationships between one or more tables.

- **Relationships** are any associations that tables may have with one another.

- **Views** are "virtual" tables composed of columns from one or more tables in the database. OFBiz has a similar construct (although it differs from the traditional RDBMS definition of a "view") in the **view-entity**.

Note: while this discussion has focused on RDMS, there is nothing to preclude you from using the Entity Engine in conjunction with any other types of data source(s).

The Entity Engine provides all the tools and utilities necessary to effectively and securely access an unlimited number of databases regardless of the physical location of the data source, as shown in the following figure:

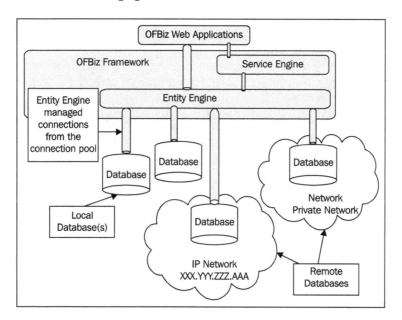

Changing the default database

Out-of-the-box, OFBiz is integrated with the Apache Derby database system (http:// db.apache.org/derby). While Derby is sufficient to handle OFBiz during software development, evaluation, and functional testing, it is not recommended for environments that experience high transaction volumes. In particular, it is not recommended for use in production environments.

Getting ready

Before configuring an external database, the following few steps have to be ensured:

1. Before changing the OFBiz Entity Engine configuration to use a remote data source, you must first create the remote database; the remote database must exist.

Note: if you are not going to install the OFBiz schema and/or seed data on the remote database, but rather intend to use it as is, you will not need to create a database. You will need, however, to define entities for each remote database table you wish to access, and assign those entities to one or more entity groups.

1. Add a user/owner for the remote database. OFBiz will access the database as this user. Make sure the user has all necessary privileges to create and remove database tables.

2. Add a user/owner password (if desired or necessary) to the remote database.

3. Ensure that the IP port the database is listening on for remote connections is open and clear of any firewall obstructions (for example, by default, PostgreSQL listens for connections on port 5432).

4. Add the appropriate database driver to the `~framework/entity/lib/jdbc` directory.

 For example, if you are using PostgreSQL version 8.3, download the `postgresql-8.3-605.jdbc2.jar` driver from the PostgreSQL website (`http://jdbc.postgresql.org/download.html`).

How to do it...

To configure another external database, follow these few steps:

1. Open the Entity Engine's configuration file located at:

   `~framework/entity/config/entityengine.xml`

2. Within the `entityengine.xml` file, configure the remote database's usage settings. A suggested method for doing this is to take an existing `datasource` element entry and modify that to reflect the necessary settings for a remote database. There are examples provided for most of the commonly used databases.

   For example, to configure a remote PostgreSQL database with the name of `myofbiz_db`, with a username `ofbiz` and password of `ofbiz`, edit the `localpostnew` configuration entry as shown here:

```
<datasource name="localpostnew"
           helper-class=
                   "org.ofbiz.entity.datasource.GenericHelperDAO"
           schema-name="public"
           field-type-name="postnew"
           check-on-start="true"
           add-missing-on-start="true"
```

```
                 use-fk-initially-deferred="false"
                 alias-view-columns="false"
                 join-style="ansi"
                 result-fetch-size="50"
                 use-binary-type-for-blob="true">
     <read-data reader-name="seed"/>
     <read-data reader-name="seed-initial"/>
     <read-data reader-name="demo"/>
     <read-data reader-name="ext"/>
     <inline-jdbc jdbc-driver="org.postgresql.Driver"
                  jdbc-uri="jdbc:postgresql://127.0.0.1/myofbiz_db"
                  jdbc-username="ofbiz"
                  jdbc-password="ofbiz"
                  isolation-level="ReadCommitted"
                  pool-minsize="2"
                  pool-maxsize="250"/>
 </datasource>
```

3. Configure the default `delegator` for this data source:

```
<delegator name="default" entity-model-reader="main"
           entity-group-reader="main" entity-eca-reader="main"
           distributed-cache-clear-enabled="false">
  <group-map group-name="org.ofbiz"
             datasource-name="localpostnew"/>
  <group-map group-name="org.ofbiz.olap"
             datasource-name="localderbyolap"/>
</delegator>
```

4. Save and close the `entityengine.xml` file.

5. From the OFBiz install directory, rebuild OFBiz by running the `ant run-install` command.

6. Start OFBiz.

7. Test by observing that the database was created and populated. You may use the WebTools entity reference page (`https://localhost:8443/webtools/control/entityref`) to search for your newly created entities, or a third-party tool designed to work with your specific database.

How it works...

The Entity Engine is configured using the `entityengine.xml` file. Whenever OFBiz is restarted, the Entity Engine initializes itself by first referencing this file, and then building and testing all the designated database connections. In this way, an unlimited number of data source connections, database types, and even low-level driver combinations may be applied at runtime without affecting the higher-level database access logic.

By abstracting the connection using one or more delegators, OFBiz further offloads low-level database connection management from the developer, and handles all connection maintenance, data mappings, and the default transaction configuration for an unlimited number of target databases.

To configure one or more database connections, add `datasource` element declarations with settings as shown here:

datasource element	
This element defines one or more database connections.	
(Note: some settings are database-specific. Shown here are the default settings for `localpostnew`, the recommended definition to use for new installations of PostgreSQL).	
Configuration setting	**Usage**
`helper-class= org.ofbiz.entity.datasource. GenericHelperDAO`	The OFBiz utility program (Java class) that performs conversions and other helper functions on behalf of the Entity Engine for this particular database.
`field-type-name="postnew"`	Pointer to the field type definition XML document that describes the field type mappings for this database. Field type files are found in the `~framework/ entity/fieldtype` directory. Each file's name is derived by adding the value in this field to a prefix of `fieldtype`. For example, field type definitions for `localpostnew`, where the `field-type-name ="postnew"` are found in: `~framework/entity/fieldtype/ fieldtypepostnew.xml`
`schema-name="public"`	Default schema name for PostgreSQL database schemas. Other databases may not require a default schema name. Configure accordingly.
`check-on-start="true"`	Instructs OFBiz to check the database against the configured data model (that is, against the configured entities for a data source) for missing entities and/ or tables.

Configuration setting	Usage
`add-missing-on-start="true"`	Instructs OFBiz to add any missing tables and keys to the database based on the defined data model. Set this to `false` if you do NOT want OFBiz to modify the target database.
`use-fk-initially-deferred= "false"`	Used to specify whether or not to set the "INITIALLY DEFERRED" option available in many databases when creating foreign keys. (Note: not all databases support this option). When enabled and supported, the foreign keys will not be checked until a transaction is committed.
	Defaults to "true".
`alias-view-columns="false"`	This value is used to compensate for a variation seen in some JDBC drivers where column names returned for aliased fields may be either the alias name or the full text of what makes up that alias name. See your database vendor's documentation for more information on settings per your target database.
	Defaults to "true".
`join-style="ansi"`	Used to specify the syntax to use when doing table joins in view-entity operations. Many databases are adopting the ANSI JOIN standard, but before that was introduced, theta joins were much more common. Two theta join styles are supported: Oracle and MS SQL. Valid values: `ansi`, `ansi-no-parenthesis`, `theta-oracle` or `theta-mssql`.
	Defaults to `ansi`.
`result-fetch-size="50"`	Used by OFBiz with the list iterator to determine default result set size.
`use-binary-type-for-blob= "true"`	Instructs OFBiz on how to map database fields typed as Binary Large Objects (BLOBs).

To specify that the Entity Engine should be connected to a database using a JDBC driver and to configure the specific connection parameters to pass, set the `inline-jdbc` element attributes as detailed here:

Connection Configuration (inline-jdbc element)	
This element configures the database connection.	
`jdbc-driver`	Java class file name of the driver to use when accessing the database. This class file must be on the OFBiz CLASSPATH.
`jdbc-uri`	Network-based location of the database. The syntax for database connection URI(s) vary from database to database. Please refer to your vendor's documentation for the appropriate syntax. For PostgreSQL, the following syntax is used: `jdbc:postgresql://{IP Address}/{Database Name}`
`jdbc-username`	The plain text username as established on the remote database for OFBiz to use to access the database.
`jdbc-password`	The plain text password as established on the remote database for OFBiz to use when connecting to the database.
`isolation-level`	Transaction isolation levels determine how insulated concurrently active transactions are from one another. This attribute establishes the default row-level locking behavior for this database connection. While details of database transaction theory are beyond the scope of this book, it is recommended that most applications should use `ReadCommitted` or `ReadUncommitted` isolation levels. Note: transactions discussed within the context of the Entity Engine's configuration are not the same transactions as configured for the Service Engine.
`pool-size`	Used to configure database connection pooling. The provided values are those found by experience to be most useful for the configured data source. The Entity Engine handles all connection acquisition and closure automatically (unless you otherwise instruct it).
`pool-maxsize`	Used to configure database connection pooling (Minerva). The provided values are those found by experience to be most useful for the configured data source.

See also

Visit `http://ofbiz.apache.org/docs/entityconfig.html` for more information.

See also your vendor's database documentation.

Connecting to a remote database

A "remote" database is any data source that is not the default Derby database. A remote database may be network connected and/or installed on the local server. The Entity Engine supports simultaneous connections to an unlimited number of remote databases in addition to, or as a replacement for, the default instance of Derby.

Each remote database connection requires a `datasource` element entry in the `entityengine.xml` file. Adding and removing database connections may be performed at any time; however, `entityengine.xml` file changes are only effective upon OFBiz restart.

Getting ready

Collect all the necessary information required to connect to the remote database. In particular, you will need, at a minimum, the following information:

- Database name.
- Username and password for OFBiz to pass when negotiating connections to the remote database. In some cases, passwords are not required. Check your remote database setup for more information.
- Database schema name, if appropriate. See the `entityengine.xml` file for examples.
- Connection location information, including the IP address and port number to connect on (for IP-based network connections).

How to do it...

Once the initial information (as stated earlier) is collected, a remote database can be connected to by following these steps:

1. Edit the `entityengine.xml` file. Add one or more `datasource` elements, one for each target database. Add one or more `delegator` elements with entity group configuration information telling the Entity Engine which entities are to be found on which target databases.
2. Add or modify any field type definitions in the appropriate field type definition file for the target remote database.
3. Add all necessary entity definitions to one or more entity definition file(s). Each table on the remote database requires an entity definition before it may be accessed through the Entity Engine.

4. If necessary, add any entity group definitions to an entity group definition file.

5. Make sure that any new entity group definition file is defined in the `ofbiz-component.xml` file.

6. To make any Entity Engine configuration changes effective, restart OFBiz.

How it works...

Entity engine database connections and entity models are built whenever OFBiz is restarted as part of its initialization process. To manage database connections, connection pooling across all defined databases, data transfer, and data source transaction specifics, OFBiz consults the `entityengine.xml` file and automatically builds the internal control settings each time it is restarted.

Connecting to multiple databases

The OFBiz Entity Engine may service an unlimited number of database connections in addition to, or as a replacement for, the default embedded Derby database.

Getting ready

The following steps should be ensured:

1. If the databases do not already exist, be sure to create them prior to editing the `entityengine.xml` file. Collect necessary connection information per database, including database location information (IP address and port), database name, username, and password if necessary.

2. Create one or more entity group definition(s) that assign a connection label using the `delegator` declaration to an Entity Engine reader. If you wish to create a new entity group definition file for the new entity model's group definitions, do so now. (Note: you can use an existing entity group definition file such as the one found in `~framework/entity/entitydef/entitygroup.xml`).

3. If the entity model definitions do not exist for the target database tables, create one entity definition for each target database table and assign that entity(s) to the appropriate entity group.

How to do it...

To add one or more databases to the Entity Engine configuration, edit the `~framework/entity/config/entityengine.xml` file as shown here:

1. Open the `entityengine.xml` file using a text editor of your choice.
2. Within the `entityengine.xml` file, configure each database as a separate `datasource` element.
3. If desired, define a unique `delegator` element and `group-map`.
4. Save and close the `entityengine.xml` file.
5. Restart OFBiz.

How it works...

The Entity Engine rebuilds its runtime configuration of configured data sources each time it restarts. To tell OFBiz which data sources to connect with, add a `datasource` element declaration to the `entityengine.xml` configuration file for each database needing an Entity Engine-managed connection. There is no limit to the number of `datasource` elements you may configure within the `entityengine.xml` file.

To associate one or more entities with an Entity Engine-managed connection, use the `delegator` element. This element allows you specify precisely which entities are to be managed per defined connection. There is no limit to the number of `delegator` elements you may add to the `entityengine.xml` file.

Entities defined within a `delegator` element are grouped according to "entity groups", where an "entity group" is a collection of entities defined in an entity group definition file. There is no limit to the number of entities or entity groups supported by the OFBiz Entity Engine.

Creating entity groups

To effectively manage an unlimited number of entities, databases, and database connections, the Entity Engine groups together entities that map to tables on the same physical database. For example, out-of-the-box, all the OFBiz ERP entities that are physically implemented as tables on the Derby database are grouped together in the `org.ofbiz` entity group.

Getting ready

There is no need to create new entity groups if your entities will be part of the OFBiz schema. You can use the default OFBiz instance group-name of `org.ofbiz`.

How to do it...

To add more entities that are not part of the Derby entity group, or if you wish to separate out your entities into different entity groups, create new entity groups as shown here:

1. Within the `entityengine.xml` file (`~framework/entity/config/entityengine.xml`), define a `delegator` for the group with a pointer to the `datasource` database configuration element. Each `delegator` is defined with a `delegator` element as shown here:

```
<delegator name="default" entity-model-reader="main"
            entity-group-reader="main" entity-eca-reader="main"
            distributed-cache-clear-enabled="false">
  <group-map group-name="org.ofbiz"
            datasource-name="localpostnew"/>
  <group-map group-name="org.ofbiz.olap"
            datasource-name="localderbyolap"/>
</delegator>
```

2. Within the `ofbiz-component.xml` file, create one or more `entity-resource` declarations, each pointing to the location of an entity group definition file as shown here:

```
<entity-resource type="group" reader-name="main" loader="main"
                 location="entitydef/entitygroup_olap.xml"/>
```

3. The entity group definition file must have a valid version number and XSD schema declaration, as follows:

```
<?xml version="1.0" encoding="UTF-8"?>
<entitygroup xmlns:xsi="http://www.w3.org/2001/XMLSchema-instance"
             xsi:noNamespaceSchemaLocation=
                   "http://ofbiz.apache.org/dtds/entitygroup.xsd">
```

4. Add one or more `entity-group` XML declaration statements. Each `entity-group` declaration adds a single entity to the specified group as shown here:

```
<entity-group group="org.ofbiz.olap" entity="CurrencyDimension"/>
```

5. Restart OFBiz.

How it works...

OFBiz uses entity groups to collect together all the entities to be accessed using the same Entity Engine-managed connection. The Entity Engine labels and otherwise identifies unique database connections using `delegators`. Entity groups are primarily a convenience for easily mapping database connections, delegators, and specific entities.

Disabling automatic database checks

There are times when you don't want OFBiz to check the database and/or make entity changes on system startup. For example, you may be using the Entity Engine and OFBiz to retrieve data from a read-only database.

Getting ready

Using an editor or IDE of your choosing, open the Entity Engine configuration file:

```
~framework/entity/config/entityengine.xml
```

How to do it...

To change the default Entity Engine startup behavior, follow these simple steps:

1. For each database (`datasource`) that you wish to turn checking off, find the following configuration attributes and set them to `false`:

   ```
   check-on-start="false"
   add-missing-on-start="false"
   ```

2. Save and close the file.
3. Restart OFBiz.

How it works...

Each time OFBiz starts up, it checks the `entityengine.xml` configuration file to determine which databases to connect to and how to handle missing tables, columns, and/or primary and foreign keys. Setting these values to `false` tells OFBiz to not perform startup checks or initialization-time repairs on the databases so configured.

Mapping database data types

One of the primary benefits of using the Entity Engine over direct SQL calls to access data is that OFBiz abstracts the details of how data is physically stored, away from the user. When making a request for data through the Entity Engine, the user does not need to know where the data is physically located or how it is formatted. The Entity Engine handles all the details of data mapping for the user in real time.

Since physical data storage formatting varies widely from database vendor to vendor, the Entity Engine must map these variations to consistent data type values for use within the OFBiz framework.

Getting ready

The following steps have to be performed before adding or modifying data type mapping:

1. Entity engine field types are configured in separate field type definition files, one for each database in use. To determine which field type definition file to use, consult the `entityengine.xml` file. Each field type file is defined with a `field-type-name` element XML declaration.

2. Find the database configuration declaration for the field(s) you wish to change by locating the `datasource` element with the appropriate `name` attribute value. For example, if you wish to change the database field type definitions for the database called `localderby`, find the `name` attribute that has the value of `localderby`.

3. Once the desired data source is identified and the `datasource` element is located, observe the `field-type-name` attribute's value. For example, in the default out-of-the-box `entityengine.xml` file, the `field-type-name` value for `localderby` is `derby` as shown here:

```
<datasource name="localderby"
        <!--Note: file contents removed for clarity -->
            field-type-name="derby"
```

4. Locate the appropriate `field-type` element declaration given the `field-type-name` value from step 3. For example, in the following `field-type` element, we see that the field type definition file for the `derby` data source is `fieldtypederby.xml` (Note: the location of `fieldtypederby.xml` defaults to `~framework/entity/fieldtype`):

```
<field-type name="derby" loader="fieldfile"
            location="fieldtypederby.xml"/>
```

How to do it...

Adding or modifying a data type mapping may be performed by following these steps:

1. Open the existing field type definition file for the database as configured in the `entityengine.xml` file. Use the process described earlier to find the appropriate file corresponding to the database data type needing modification.

2. To change an existing field type definition, edit the appropriate entry in the field type definition file. For example, to change the definition of the OFBiz data type `currency-amount`, edit the `field-type-def` element as shown here:

```
<field-type-def type="currency-amount" sql-type="NUMERIC(18,2)"
                java type="java.math.BigDecimal">
  <validate method="isSignedDouble"/>
</field-type-def>
```

3. To add a new field type definition, add an element of type `field-type-def` to the document. Don't forget to close the element with a `</field-type-def>` tag.

4. Save and close the file.

5. If necessary, run `ant clean-install` to remove any existing data.

6. If necessary, run `ant run-install` to reinstall any seed data.

7. Restart OFBiz.

How it works...

The Entity Engine automatically maps low-level database data types to data types that are consistent across all Entity Engine-managed databases using the mapping definitions found in field type definition files. In this way, OFBiz offloads the tedious and often error-prone task of converting physical database data storage formats for application use from the developer.

In the following example, an OFBiz data type is shown and then the equivalent storage data types per database are given. Using the Entity Engine as the layer between database access and application logic, the OFBiz developer need only reference the data as an OFBiz data type. There is no need to worry about the vagaries of the individual storage mediums in use. If the underlying database changes, applications will continue to work transparently as applications read and write OFBiz data type(s) to the Entity Engine and not the target database.

OFBiz data type: date-time			
	sql-type	sql-type-alias	java-type
Oracle	TIMESTAMP	TIMESTAMP(6)	java.sql.Timestamp
PostgreSQL	TIMESTAMPTZ		java.sql.Timestamp

Creating a new entity definition file

Entities are defined in entity definition XML document files. By convention, entity definition files are located in a containing Component's `entitydef` directory. This may be changed by editing the Component's `ofbiz-component.xml` file.

How to do it...

To define a new entity definition file, follow these few steps:

1. Check the `ofbiz-component.xml` file to make sure there is an `entity-resource` element that locates an entity definition file. For example:

```
<entity-resource type="model" reader-name="main" loader="main"
                 location="entitydef/entitymodel.xml"/>
```

2. Using your favorite operating system or IDE tool, add entity definition files in the directory locations specified in the `ofbiz-component.xml` file shown earlier. Make sure each file has the appropriate XML version and XSD declarations in the beginning of the file:

```
<?xml version="1.0" encoding="UTF-8"?>
<entitymodel xmlns:xsi="http://www.w3.org/2001/XMLSchema-instance"
          xsi:noNamespaceSchemaLocation=
                   "http://ofbiz.apache.org/dtds/entitymodel.xsd">
```

3. Make sure the new entity definition file has a closing XML element tag (`</entitymodel>`).

4. Insert as many entity definitions within this file as needed.

5. Save and close the file.

6. Restart OFBiz to make any changes to the `ofbiz-component.xml` file effective.

How it works...

OFBiz is made aware of entity definition files by placing one or more declarations about the files within a Component's `ofbiz-component.xml` file. There is one such declaration for each entity definition file located within the containing Component.

Creating a new entity model

The Entity Engine supports an unlimited number of entity definitions spread across an unlimited number of data sources. To create a new entity, sometimes called the entity model, is simply to add the entity's definition to an entity definition file.

Getting ready

Make sure you have an entity definition file defined in an existing `ofbiz-component.xml` file.

How to do it...

To create a new entity, follow these steps:

1. Open an existing entity definition file or create a new one.

2. Add one or more `entity` elements as shown here. Please note: XML declarations shown below are for demonstration purposes only. Statements have been removed to make reading easier:

```
<entity entity-name="EntityName"
        package-name="org.ofbiz.somePackageName"
```

```
          title="My New Entity">
   <!-- Entity definition XML declaration(s) go here.
        Removed for demonstration purposes -->
</entity>
```

3. Each `entity` element will have one or more of the following declarations added:

   ❑ `field` element declarations within the `entity` element:

   ```
   <field name="someFieldName" type="any defined type">
   </field>
   ```

   ❑ `prim-key` elements to define the primary key for this entity:

   ```
   <prim-key field="primaryKeyField"/>
   ```

   ❑ `relation` elements.

4. Close the `entity` element with a closing tag (`</entity>`).

5. Save and close the file.

6. Restart OFBiz to make the entity definitions effective.

How it works...

When OFBiz first starts up, it checks the data model as defined by configured entities in valid entity definition files. Any new entries in entity definition files are checked for configuration integrity and added to the OFBiz data model automatically.

There's more...

The following table summarizes many common entity configuration settings:

entity element tag (Required)		
Attribute name	**Required?**	**Usage**
`entity-name`	Yes	The name used to uniquely identify this entity.
`table-name`	No	The equivalent database table name. If this value is the same as that of the value specified by the entity-name, then this attribute may be left out of the definition.
`package-name`	Yes	Used to organize entities. The suggested best practice is to use the `org.ofbiz.somepackage` syntax, although there are no checks on these values.

To configure one or more primary keys for an entity, add an XML declaration similar to the following:

prim-key element tag (Not required)		
It is not required to have a primary key declaration. However, it is highly recommend for both referential integrity and performance improvements. An entity may have an unlimited number of primary key fields defined. Some databases have restrictions on the length of the primary key.		
Attribute name	**Required?**	**Usage**
field	Yes	This is the name of the field.

If performance is an issue, you may optionally configure one or more index elements for an entity. Indexes are configured as shown here:

index element tag (Not required)		
Attribute name	**Required?**	**Usage**
name	Yes	Name to use when using this index. Note: there is a limit of 18 characters or less for this value.
unique	No	Valid values: true, false. Default: false
index-field element tag		
name	Yes	The name of the entity field to use as the index.

To configure the following entity behavior for an individual entity, use the settings as shown here:

Configure an XML declaration similar to the following:	Behavior
no-auto-stamp="true"	By default, OFBiz will create the following entity fields: lastUpdatedStamp, lastUpdatedTxStamp, createdStamp, createdTxStamp for all entities. Additionally, these fields are automatically updated as appropriate. In cases where you are reading and writing to a non-OFBiz database entity, you may want to turn off this behavior.
never-cache="true"	Set this entity to never be cached.
sequence-bank-size= "Integer Value"	Set the range of sequence identifiers used when getting a new sequence identifier using Entity Engine interfaces. The default is "10".

Field `elements` map the target database columns to the equivalent OFBiz field definition. To add one or more column definitions as field entries, use the `field` element with the following attribute settings:

field element tag (Required)		
Field elements configure one or more columns for the entity.		
Attribute name	**Required?**	**Usage**
`name`	Yes	This is the name of the field.
`col-name`	No	If the database table column name is different from the equivalent entity field name, set the value here.
`type`	Yes	This value may be any supported field type value as defined in the appropriate `fieldtype` definition file for this database.
`encrypt`	No	To instruct OFBiz to use its own encryption algorithm to encrypt and decrypt this field's value before storage and upon retrieval, set as `true`.
		Note: setting field encryption in this manner is not the same as using the target database encryption support.
		Default: `false`
`enable-audit-log`	No	If set to `true`, the Entity Engine will record any changes to this field in an `EntityAuditLog` entity.
		Default: `false`
`non-null`	No	Sets not-null constraints on the database (instead of the field type).
		Default: `false`

Just as physical database tables may be associated with one another through defined "relationships", OFBiz entities may be related. Use the `relation` element attribute settings to define one or more relational associations between the defined entity and any other OFBiz entities as described here:

relation element tag (Not required)		
This element configures one or more relationships for the associated entity. An entity may be related to an unlimited number of other entities using these XML relationship declarations:		
Attribute name	**Required?**	**Usage**
`type`	Yes	Valid values: `one`, `many`, `one-nofk`
		Note: OFBiz automatically creates a foreign key for one-to-one entity relationships. If you don't want a foreign key created, use the `one-nofk` value.
`fk-name`	Yes	An "alias" or name to use for this field, when used as a foreign key.
		Note: this must be 18 characters or less.
`rel-entity-name`	Yes	The name of the entity that is the target in this relationship. All relationships are defined from the defined entity to a target entity as specified using the `rel-entity-name` attribute.
key-map element tag		
This element is required if the related entity primary key fields do not have the same name as the entity being defined.		
There may be an unlimited number of `key-map` elements per entity.		
`field-name`	Yes	The field name from the defined entity that represents the primary key used in this relationship.
`rel-field-name`	Yes	The name of the primary key in the related entity used to configure this relationship.

Modifying an existing entity model

To change the entity model where the physical characteristics of the underlying database changes, you must rebuild the target database table as well as modify the corresponding entity model to coincide with these changes.

 Note: simply changing an entity's configuration will not reconfigure the physical database tables and column definitions on the target database.

To change an entity model where the existing column structure is not affected, for example, to add a new relationship definition for an entity, may not require first changing the target database

Getting ready

First of all, ensure the following:

1. If necessary, back up any data in the target database table(s) as modeled by the entity. You may use a third-party database specific backup tool or the OFBiz WebTool's **Entity XML Export** tool located at:

   ```
   https://localhost:8443/webtools/control/xmldsdump
   ```

2. If required, drop the table from the database. You may use the database vendor's tool, third-party database specific tool, or the OFBiz WebTool's **Entity SQL Processor**. To use the **Entity SQL Processor**, log in to WebTools and navigate to:

   ```
   https://localhost:8443/webtools/control/EntitySQLProcessor
   ```

   In the **SQL Command** text box, enter in a command similar to the following SQL DROP statement and click the **submit** button. Note: do not add a trailing semi-colon. This will drop the indicated table:

   ```
   DROP TABLE "tablename"
   ```

How to do it...

To modify an existing entity, follow these steps:

1. For changes that reflect modifications to the physical characteristics of the data on the target database, remove the target table from the database as indicated earlier.

2. Using any text editor, open the entity definition file containing the entity model to change.

3. Modify the entity model definition by editing the existing entity definition.

4. Save and close the entity definition file.

5. Restart OFBiz to make the modified entity model effective. For tables that have been removed from the target database, OFBiz will attempt to recreate the table using the entity's new definition.

6. If necessary, reload any data that may have been saved.

How it works...

OFBiz entities are models of physical storage repositories such as databases. When the underlying medium changes, for example, columns within an RDBMS table are reconfigured, OFBiz must be told how to adjust its view of the data. OFBiz cannot rearrange existing data. It can only modify its model of that data.

By default, OFBiz can, however, if configured to do so, instruct a data source to create new tables, fix certain key assignments, and create or remove table relationships based on configured entity models when it starts up.

Building a view-entity

OFBiz view-entities are a convenient way of constructing SQL JOIN statements. They do not force the creation of database tables or map to database tables as do entity definitions, but rather they allow OFBiz to create runtime views of related tables so that users may easily access joined tables without creating complicated SQL JOIN statements.

Getting ready

View-entities are defined in entity definition files along with entity definitions. Make sure you have an entity definition file (to use for any view-entities) configured in an existing `ofbiz-component.xml`.

How to do it...

The process for creating one or more view-entities is similar to that of creating an entity definition, and can be done by following these steps:

1. Open an existing entity definition file or create a new one.

2. Add one or more `view-entity` elements as shown here. Please note: XML declarations shown below are for demonstration purposes only. Statements have been removed to make reading easier:

   ```
   <view-entity entity-name="EntityName"
                package-name="org.ofbiz.somePackageName"
                never-cache="true" title="My New View Entity">
      <!-- Entity definition XML declaration(s) go here.
           Removed for demonstration purposes -->
   </view-entity>
   ```

3. Close the `view-entity` element with a closing tag (`</view-entity>`).

4. Save and close the file.

5. Restart OFBiz to make the view-entity definition effective.

6. Use the WebTools **Entity Reference - Interactive Version** to see if the new view-entity was successfully created (`https://localhost:8443/webtools/control/entityref`).

7. Programmatically, view-entities are accessed in the same manner as entities.

How it works...

OFBiz view-entities are a convenient way to create SQL `JOIN` statements (joining together table column data from two or more tables) using XML declarations instead of SQL statements. The Entity Engine automatically creates the SQL `JOIN` statement any time the view-entity is accessed.

View-entities may be created or removed from the OFBiz Entity Engine data model at any time using the mentioned recipe. View-entities are read-only, and attempts to store data using a view-entity will fail.

There's more...

An OFBiz view-entity has one or more participating "member" entities. As a convenient way to refer to a member entity, you must create an entity level alias for that member using the `member-entity` element as shown here:

member-entity element tag		
Create a shortcut alias for each view-entity participating member.		
Attribute name	**Required?**	**Usage**
entity-alias	Yes	Two-letter to four-letter alias or abbreviation used for the remainder of this definition to represent the full entity name as given in the `entity-name` attribute.
entity-name	Yes	The name of an existing entity.
		Note: this attribute is case-sensitive. The value in this field must match an existing entity name.

Each member entity may have one or more field aliases defined for any existing entity field. All fields are referenced using field aliases within the context of the view-entity. To create field-level aliases, use the `alias` element tag as shown here:

---

alias element tag

For example, an `alias` element definition of:

```
<alias entity-alias="OH" name="orderId" >
```

Refers to the field `orderId` in the entity aliased within the `member-entity` as `OH`. If `OH` is aliased as `OrderHeader`, then this alias refers to the `orderId` field in the `OrderHeader` table.

Attribute name	Required?	Usage
entity-alias	Yes	Use the entity's alias as configured in the `member-entity` element instead of the real entity name.
name	Yes	The field from the aliased entity to use as part of this definition.

complex-alias element tag

Within the `alias` element, you may have one or more `complex-alias` elements defined. `complex-alias` elements are a mechanism for configuring filters on one or more return fields.

operator	Yes	Any supported mathematical operator for the field's data type.

One or more fields to be joined using the operator-supplied operator. Fields are defined using the `complex-alias-field` element tag.

If all fields for an entity should be returned when calling this view-entity, you may use the shortcut `alias-all` element as defined here:

---

alias-all element tag

Return all the fields for the specified entity alias.

Attribute name	Usage
entity-alias	Use the entity's alias as configured in the `member-entity` element instead of the real entity name.

To create a SQL OUTER JOIN (that is, a JOIN on two tables where records from the joined tables may not have matching pairs), use the view-link element to define the relationship between one entity and another target entity, and set the rel-optional value to true:

view-link element tag (Optional)		
Attribute name	**Required?**	**Usage**
entity-alias	Yes	The alias for the entity participating in this relation.
rel-entity-alias	Yes	The alias of the related entity.
rel-optional	No	Valid values: true, false
		Default: false
key-map element tag		
The key-map entity defines the table relationship.		
field-name		The name of the field as defined by the entity pointed to by the entity-alias attribute value.

See also

View-entities may be quite complex. For an in depth treatment of this subject, please see **The Open For Business Project: Entity Engine Guide** at:

http://ofbiz.apache.org/docs/entity.html

6

OFBiz Security

In this chapter, you will find useful information on:

- ▶ Securing communications ports
- ▶ Disabling demonstration user accounts
- ▶ Protecting OFBiz web pages
- ▶ Creating user accounts
- ▶ Protecting applications using security groups
- ▶ Protecting views ("Tarpitting")
- ▶ Retrieving forgotten passwords
- ▶ Changing a password
- ▶ Adding or changing SSL certificates
- ▶ OFBiz web application single sign-on (the external login key)

 Note: if you are wondering why the screenshots in this chapter do not exactly match the out-of-the-box OFBiz web page views, then be advised that the visual theme has been changed from the default to one that makes it easier to view navigation links on backend OFBiz web applications. Managing OFBiz visual themes is discussed in *Chapter 10*.

Introduction

In this chapter, we discuss strategies for securing your OFBiz installation and web applications ("webapps"). Such strategies take many forms allowing you, the OFBiz owner, maximum flexibility in designing and deploying the security policies that make the most sense for your business needs.

To begin with, OFBiz is distributed with a minimum of security features turned on. This is intentional to facilitate ease of initial software evaluation, customization, and testing. When your deployment requirements are known, security controls may be applied as required. While there are not many out-of-the-box security configuration settings that should be attended to before going into production, it is highly recommended that, at a minimum, you consider changing the default **HyperText Transfer Protocol (HTTP)** and **HyperText Transfer Protocol Secure (HTTPS)** communications ports and disabling demonstration login accounts.

Beyond these basic administrative security tasks, we shall also introduce in this chapter topics ranging from web page authentication settings to the use of an "external login key" to enable OFBiz web Application single sign-on.

 Caution: the suggestions in this chapter do not obviate the need for a comprehensive enterprise security policy nor the implementation of a network and/or server-based firewall.

Securing communications ports

OFBiz relies heavily on the underlying TCP/IP networking stack, as well as the embedded Catalina/Tomcat servlet container in which it runs for Internet communication support. For example, the Catalina servlet container provides all the basic HTTP and HTTPS connection handling on the default IP ports of 8080 and 8443 respectively. Ports 8080 and 8443 by convention do not require any special usage privileges on the hosting system. This means that any non-privileged user may startup an OFBiz instance from the install directory.

A downside of running web servers on ports 8080 and 8443 is that client browsers expect to find URLs on ports 80 and 443. Port 80 is used for non-secure connections while port 443 is used for secure, HTTPS-based communications. To run a web server on IP ports 80 and 443 often requires special privileges, sometimes called "root" or "superuser", on the host server. When OFBiz is configured to run on these ports, it is considered by some to be more secure.

A second set of ports, 9990 and 9991, that should be secured before deploying OFBiz in a production environment, are ports used to access the BeanShell interpreter through the TELNET protocol. You may either disable these ports or protect them using an external firewall.

How to do it...

Communication ports 80 and 443 may be set up by the following steps:

1. To change the HTTP/HTTPS ports, open the following file:

    ```
    ~framework/base/config/ofbiz-containers.xml
    ```

2. To change the default HTTP port from 8080 to 80, first locate the `http-connector` property. Within the `http-connector` specification, find the `port` property. Edit this property value as shown:

```
<property name="http-connector" value="connector">
  <!--Note property declarations removed. See file for details.-->
  <property name="port" value="80"/>
  <!--Note property declarations removed. See file for details.-->
</property>
```

3. To change the default HTTPS port from 8443 to 443, first locate the `https-connector` property. Within the `https-connector` specification, find the `port` property. Edit this property value as shown:

```
<property name="https-connector" value="connector">
  <!--Note property declarations removed. See file for details.-->
  <property name="port" value="443"/>
  <!--Note property declarations removed. See file for details.-->
</property>
```

4. To change or disable the default BeanShell ports, locate the `beanshell-container` property. To disable these ports, wrap the entire container definition in XML comments (`<!-- -->`). To change the ports, edit the property values as shown:

```
<container name="beanshell-container"
           class="org.ofbiz.base.container.BeanShellContainer">
  <property name="telnet-port" value="9911"/>
  <property name="app-name" value="OFBiz"/>
</container>
```

5. Save and close the file.
6. Restart OFBiz to make IP port configuration changes effective.

How it works...

The OFBiz distribution comes integrated with the Catalina servlet container. This container provides the basic communication support necessary for OFBiz to act as a web server on the Internet. As with most of OFBiz, the Catalina servlet container is completely configurable. What you get out-of-the-box are generic settings based on the experience of the project team.

All available Tomcat/Catalina servlet container configuration parameters are exposed in the `~framework/base/config/ofbiz-containers.xml` file within the named container element. When OFBiz starts up, it passes the configuration settings in this file to the Tomcat/Catalina container(s) for processing. This means that you may tune your servlet container instance by changing settings in this file.

Note: when HTTP and HTTPS ports are changed to values under 1000, most operating systems will require superuser or root privileges before OFBiz may be restarted. Therefore, if you change these ports as described here you may first need to be the root or system user before starting OFBiz.

There's more...

If you change servlet container HTTP/HTTPS settings, you probably will want to change the following settings within the ~framework/webapp/config/url.properties file. These settings are used internally by OFBiz to support automatic URL conversions. These settings are not passed to the servlet container:

```
port.https.enabled=Y
port.https=443
port.http=80
```

There are several other TCP/IP ports that OFBiz uses and that you should be aware of when configuring firewalls or other software running on the same server as an OFBiz instance.

 Note: it is possible to run many instances of OFBiz on the same server if care is taken to set TCP/IP so there are no conflicts.

These ports include, but are not limited to:

▶ **Database Ports**: Any port(s) used by the entity engine as configured in ~framework/ entity/config/entityengine.xml will need safe passage through any firewall if the target database system(s) are remotely located.

▶ **RMI/JNDI ports**: Details of using OFBiz as either a provider of Remote Method Invocation (RMI)/Java Naming and Directory Interface (JNDI)-based services are beyond the scope of this book. However, RMI may be used in a number of places throughout the code base, and RMI IP port settings are a consideration when readying OFBiz for production environments. The primary RMI configuration file used when setting up an OFBiz RMI server is the ~framework/base/config/ofbiz-containers.xml file.

RMI may also be configured for use with the Service engine as either a service client or by settings in this file: ~framework/service/config/serviceengine.xml (defaults to 1099).

 For more information concerning RMI configuration, please see the Apache OFBiz **FAQ-Tips-Tricks-Cookbook-HowTo** located on the OFBiz Wiki: http://cwiki.apache.org/confluence/x/9ABk

See also

There are many other Catalina/Tomcat settings in the `ofbiz-containers.xml` file that may affect OFBiz security and performance. To see a complete list of Tomcat/Catalina-specific settings, please refer to the appropriate Tomcat documentation available at:

`http://tomcat.apache.org`

For more information on TCP/IP port usage, please see **Apache OFBiz Technical Production Setup Guide**:

`https://cwiki.apache.org/confluence/display/OFBTECH/`
`Apache+OFBiz+Technical+Production+Setup+Guide`

Disabling demonstration user accounts

Out-of-the-box, OFBiz comes with demonstrations for many of the ERP applications that make up the project. These demos are purposely distributed with privileged user login accounts enabled to showcase role base permission checking. Before moving an OFBiz instance into production, at a minimum these demonstration privileged accounts should be disabled: "flexadmin", "bizadmin", "demoadmin", "ltadmin", and "supplier".

How to do it...

To disable demonstration user accounts, follow these steps:

1. Log in into the **Party Manager** application using the default username "admin" and password "ofbiz".

2. Bring up the profile of the account you wish to disable by first locating the account using the **Find Parties** on **Party Manager** web page as shown here:

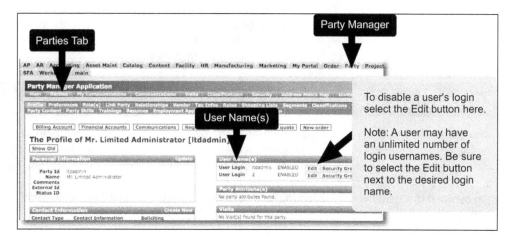

3. Under the **User Name(s)** section of the account on the **Profile** web page, click the **Edit** button to bring up the profile's HTML form to **Update UserLogin Security Settings** as shown here:

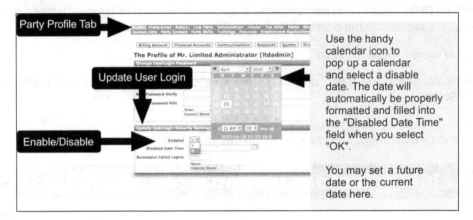

4. Change the **Enabled** drop-down select box to **N**.

5. Add the **Disabled Date Time** using the calendar icon. If no disable time is selected, the current time will automatically be inserted in this field. Entering a value in this field allows you to select future dates for disabling.

6. Hit the **Save** button to make the change immediately effective.

7. Perform this set of tasks for every account that requires disabling.

How it works...

The **Party Manager** application provides a convenient UI to manage user accounts such as those provided with the demonstration software. Disabling an account is an effective way of turning off OFBiz access for any user.

Disabling an account has the added advantage of allowing you to re-enable that user login at any future date without needing to recreate it. Further, by disabling an account instead of removing it, you maintain a record of that user's login and system activities.

Protecting OFBiz web pages

Any web page may be set to require user authentication by way of the OFBiz login process by setting the corresponding `request-map` entry in the `controller.xml` file. A user need only log in one time per session as OFBiz will check each request for a protected web page against a requesting visitor's login status. If the requestor is already logged in, they will not be asked to login again. If the visitor is not logged in, they will be presented with an HTML login form.

Getting ready

Identify the web application and the web page, OFBiz Service, or OFBiz Event that requires user authentication.

How to do it...

You can protect your web pages by following these steps:

1. Open the appropriate `controller.xml` file containing the request-map entry for the web page to protect.

2. Edit the `request-map` entry for the URI to be protected by setting the `security` element's `auth` attribute to `true`. For example, the following request-map has both the authorization and encryption (`https`) attributes for the `authview` request-map set to true:

```
<request-map uri="authview">
  <security https="true" auth="true" />
  <response name="success" type="view" value="main" />
</request-map>
```

3. That is all you need to do to force a user to log in before accessing your web page. Note: there is no need to restart OFBiz. All `controller.xml` file changes are immediate.

How it works...

Each web application has its own `controller.xml` file used to map incoming HTTP/HTTPS requests with the appropriate OFBiz web application Event, Service, or web page view. When a request for a URL that has been configured to require authentication is made, OFBiz first checks the user's session, and if the user is already logged in, will let the user proceed to the URL. If the user is not yet logged in, OFBiz will present the configured login web page and form.

When presented with the login form, the user must enter a valid user login name and password. Values entered on this form are compared against known user account values as stored within the database.

Once the user has successfully logged in, the user's identification credentials are made part of the user's session by including them within a `userLogin` session attribute, available programmatically by accessing the `HttpServletRequest` object.

There's more...

To override `controller.xml` authentication settings for an entire OFBiz instance, use your favorite text editor to modify the `~framework/webapp/config/url.properties` file and change the following global URL conversion setting as shown here:

```
port.https.enabled=N
```

Restart OFBiz to make this change effective.

Setting this property as shown overrides all `controller.xml` settings for the entire instance. All URL requests will be serviced using the HTTP port. Any explicit requests for secure port access, for example, `https://www.myserver.com` will automatically be routed by OFBiz to the non-secure URL equivalent.

While not necessarily a security setting, session timeouts are configured within the web application deployment descriptor file per OFBiz webapp. The `~webapp/webappName/WEB-INF/web.xml` file is used directly by Tomcat to configure parameters specific to an individual web application. To set Tomcat session timeouts, add an entry similar to the following:

```
<session-config>
  <session-timeout>60</session-timeout> <!-- in minutes -->
</session-config>
```

Creating user accounts

OFBiz user accounts are a handy mechanism to manage information about users. OFBiz supports a rich set of user account management tools allowing for the collection and maintenance of account information in the form of user "profiles".

> OFBiz "users" are one of several different types of objects collectively known as "Parties". Users' characteristics are defined within the data model using the "Party" and various other associated entities. For the remainder of this chapter, we shall consider OFBiz "users" as those willing participants in OFBiz business processing that have OFBiz accounts, and that have a row/record in the OFBiz "Party" entity/table.

Only a user with administrative privileges may create accounts on behalf of another user. Similarly, only privileged user(s) may view or change another user's profile information.

> Note: out-of-the-box, users may create accounts for themselves without any special privilege. For example, the OFBiz e-commerce demonstration web store allows site visitors to create accounts as desired.

How to do it...

To create user accounts, follow these steps:

1. Navigate to the **Party Manager** application and log in as the administrative user. (Out-of-the-box, log in as "admin" with a password of "ofbiz").

2. Select the **Parties** tab.

3. Select the **Create New** tab. This will bring up the **Create New Party Detail** HTML menu selection form as shown in the following figure. Select from one of the provided **Create** links as shown here:

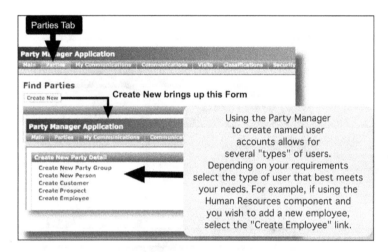

4. Selecting the appropriate **Create New Party Detail** link from step 3 will bring up a tailored **Edit Personal Information** HTML form as shown in the following figure. Initial user profiles may be built automatically depending on the type of user being created. The **Edit Personal Information** form will enforce valid form field data entry based on user type.

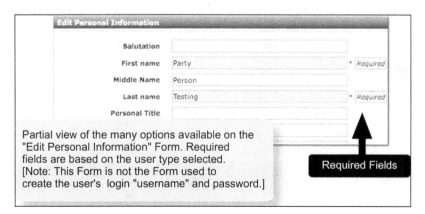

5. Submit the **Edit Personal Information** HTML form to create the new user account by clicking the **Save** button. This will bring up the **Profile** page for the newly created user account.

6. To assign the new user a unique login username and password, select the **Create New** button located to the right of the **User Name(s)** section of this page. For example, we have created a new user named "Party Testing" and set up a default user login username of "testLoginId" as shown:

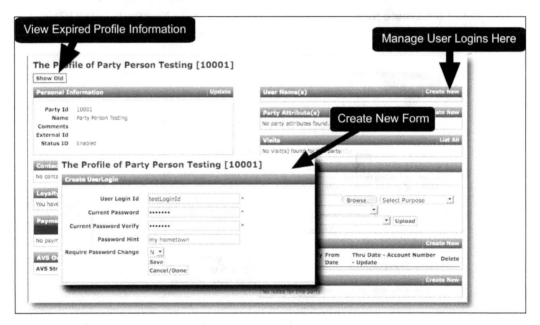

How it works...

OFBiz tracks users by giving each user an account and a profile. The user's profile includes one or more unique user login identifiers called login "usernames". Access to secured parts of OFBiz are protected by requiring a user to log in using the assigned username and password. At login time, OFBiz associates the logged in user with any access permissions and application-based task roles they may have as part of their profile.

Using the OFBiz **Party Manager** allows privileged administrative users all the tools necessary to create new user accounts and assign account profile information.

There's more...

Global user profile security defaults are set in the following properties file:

`~framework/security/config/security.properties`

Global options include:

- The minimum password length. Out-of-the-box, this value is five consecutive characters. Blank (" ") characters are not permitted in passwords.

- The number of failed attempts after which the user's account will be disabled. This number defaults to three.

- The length of time to disable a user's account should they fail to log in after the consecutive login attempt value. After this elapsed time, the user's account will automatically be re-enabled and they may attempt to log in again.

- The encryption algorithm to use to encrypt passwords. The default is the one-way, internal SHA encryption algorithm.

Protecting applications using security groups

"Security groups" allow for fine-grain permission checking, on a user-by-user basis, across an entire OFBiz web application ("webapp"). If you have webapps needing protection based on a user's permissions—that is, a user's authorization to perform various business processing tasks—and not just login authentication, then using security groups may be the answer.

How to do it...

To protect an OFBiz webapp using security groups, proceed as described here:

1. In the `ofbiz-component.xml` file for the component containing the webapp to be secured, add one or more security groups using the `base-permission` attribute. To add multiple security groups, separate each group name with a comma (","). In the following example, we configure the `OFBTOOLS` security group association for the `myapp` webapp:

```
<webapp name="myapp" server="default-server"
        location="webapp/myapp" mount-point="/"
        base-permission="OFBTOOLS" app-bar-display="false"/>
```

2. In the `controller.xml` file within the `myapp` webapp (or whichever webapp you are securing using security groups), set the corresponding `request-map` entry `security` element's `auth` attribute to `true` as shown here. This will force user login when requests for the web page are made.

```
<request-map uri= "mywebpage">
  <security https="false" auth="true" />
  <response name="success" type="view" value="somewebpage" />
</request-map>
```

3. Restart OFBiz and test coverage by trying to access a protected web page. Observe that you may be able to log in, but that you will be denied access to the webapp if the user login used is not a member of the appropriate security group(s).

4. Associate one or more users with the configured security group. A security group must also be associated with each user that you wish to authorize access to your protected web application. To associate one or more security groups with a user, you may use the security group's **Add UserLogin to Security Group** form by selecting the **User Logins** tab as shown here:

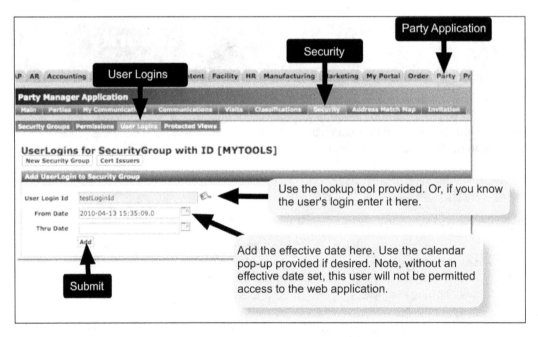

How it works...

Security groups may be used to apply fine-grain authorization or permission enforcement checks to individual web pages and portions of a web page within a protected web application.

Using the following diagram, security group processing may be described as follows:

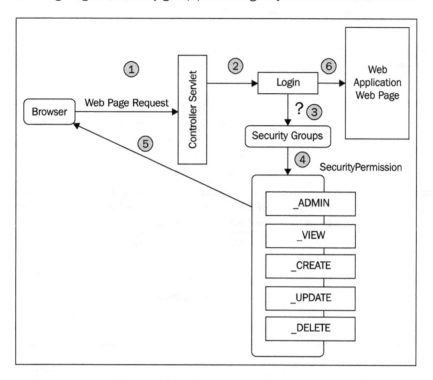

When a visitor makes a request for an OFBiz web page, the **Controller Servlet** (1) checks to see if the request-map `security` element's `auth` attribute is set to `true` for the web page. If it is, the visitor is presented a **Login** form(2). After successful login, OFBiz checks to see if the webapp is configured to require further access mediation based on **Security Groups** (3). If there are no security groups configured for a webapp, the visitor—now an OFBiz user—is allowed access to the web page.

If the webapp has one or more security group(s) configured, OFBiz checks to see if the user is a member of all configured groups. If not, the user is allowed to log in but is denied access to the web page and any protected web page(s) within the protected webapp.

Note: if the user successfully logs in, but is not a member of all the configured security group(s), they are still logged in to the OFBiz instance. This means they may access any other OFBiz webapp(s)/web page(s) requiring authentication as long as they are a member of all configured security group(s) for that web page(s)/webapp(s). They may always access any web page(s)/webapp(s) that require authentication but are not protected by security groups.

If the user is a member of all the configured security group(s), the user is assigned the appropriate **Security Permissions** (4) and allowed to continue (5) to the protected web page as shown in the previous diagram:

Once a user gains access to a webapp protected by security groups, they are permitted or denied use of OFBiz resources accessed through the web page, based on **Security Permissions**. Out-of-the-box, there are five security permissions that may be applied to mediate access to OFBiz resources. They are shown here:

Security permission	Usage (rights are cumulative. For example, a user must have both DELETE and UPDATE permissions to perform update and delete operations using provided forms).
_VIEW	View only access rights. Minimum permission necessary to access a protected webapp.
_CREATE	Allows the user to create new entities.
_DELETE	Allows the user to delete entities.
_UPDATE	Allows the user to update entities.
_ADMIN	Includes all other permissions.

 Note: you may also create your own security permission(s) and use these within your web application to control access to any or all processing logic.

There's more...

Security groups and security permissions are an extremely flexible tool that may be used as needed to protect any OFBiz web application. In the following example, we apply two new security groups to the myapp web application:

```
<webapp name="myapp" server="default-server" location="webapp/myapp"
        mount-point="/" base-permission="MYTOOLS,MYPLACE"
        app-bar-display="false"/>
```

The MYTOOLS and MYPLACE security groups are not part of the OFBiz distribution, and must be created. To create a new security group, use the **Party Manager** application as shown here:

1. Log in to the **Party Manager** application.
2. Select the **Security** tab.
3. Select the **New Security Group** tab.
4. Enter the name of the new security group and any description, and submit the HTML form. That is all you need do to create a new security group.

Security groups are like containers that hold one or more security permission(s). To associate one or more security permissions to a security group, for example, the MYTOOLS security group created earlier, use the **Party Manager** application as shown here:

1. Edit the MYTOOLS security group by selecting it from the list of security groups displayed on the **Party Manager** application's **SecurityGroups List** as shown here:

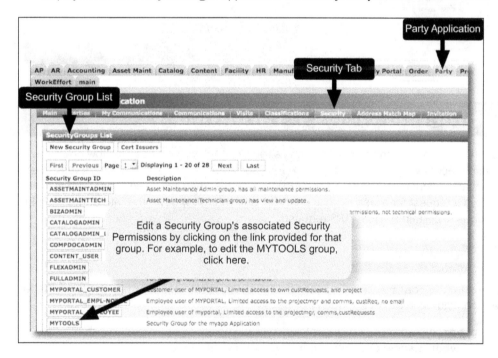

2. Selection of the security group on the **SecurityGroups List** web page will bring up the **Edit Security Group** form for this security group. Select the **Permissions** tab to bring up the **Edit Security Group Permissions** form.

3. From the **Add Permissions (from list) to SecurityGroup** form select an existing security permission from the drop-down select box provided and hit the **Add** button. Continue adding as many security permissions as desired.

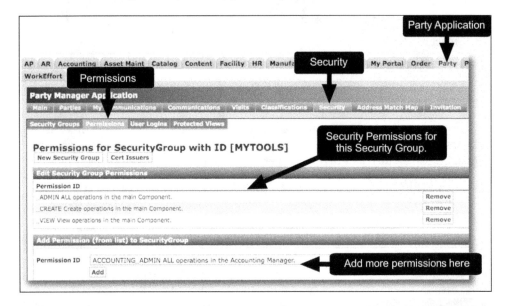

Protecting views ("Tarpitting")

"Tarpitting" gets its name from e-mail anti-spamming techniques used to slow down the rate at which repetitive access requests for e-mail services are honored by mail servers. The tarpitting concept may be applied to OFBiz web pages when you need to limit the number of times a request for a web page is honored, and thus slow down the rate at which OFBiz responds to certain HTTP/HTTPS requests.

Getting ready

Make sure the `controller.xml` file containing your protected view has the following Java class configured in the `preprocessor` section:

```
<preprocessor>
  <event name="checkProtectedView" type="java"
         path="org.ofbiz.webapp.control.ProtectViewWorker"
         invoke="checkProtectedView"/>
</preprocessor>
```

How to do it...

To control the rate at which certain OFBiz web pages are honored, use the security group's protected view option as shown here:

1. Log in to the **Party Manager** application.

2. Select the **Security** tab to bring up the **SecurityGroups List**.

3. Select the desired security group for the protected web page from the list provided to bring up the **Edit Security Group with ID** web page.

4. Select the **Protected Views** tab.

5. For the requested **View Name**, enter in the view name as configured within the `controller.xml` view-map entry. For example, if you have a view-map similar to the following:

```
<view-map name="MyProtectedScreen" type="screen"
          page="some page location" />
```

6. The name to enter is `MyProtectedScreen`.

7. Enter in other field values as desired. (Note: the "tarpitting" value is the value entered for the field labeled `Duration`. This is the length of time during which the web page view will not be available).

8. Submit the Form by hitting the **Add** button. Web page view monitoring and protection is immediate and does not require an OFBiz restart.

How it works...

The OFBiz controller servlet is the initial point of contact for all HTTP/HTTPS requests. This servlet, modeled after the **Model-View-Control** (**MVC**) design pattern, is responsible for handling all aspects of HTTP/HTTPS request processing, including selecting web page views for the requestor and delegating business processing to other OFBiz servlets, Services, and Events.

Adding the `ProtectViewWorker.java` program to a controller's configuration (via the `controller.xml` file) tells the controller to pay special attention to certain view requests and, based on the configuration parameters set within the **Party Manager** application, handle those requests appropriately.

There's more...

By default, a blank web page is presented when a protected view is blocked. You may change this behavior by editing the `~framework/security/config/security.properties` file and modify the following line: `default.error.response.view=view:viewBlocked` to match a request-map entry as shown here:

```
<request-map uri="viewBlocked">
  <response name="success" type="view" value="viewBlocked" />
</request-map>
<view-map name="viewBlocked" type="screen"
      page="component://common/widget/CommonScreens.xml#viewBlocked"/>
```

Retrieving forgotten passwords

If you do not know the plaintext password for a user, the password may not be retrieved. However, the existing password may be removed and a new one issued for the user either by implementing an HTML form similar to those found on the e-commerce demonstration and shown here:

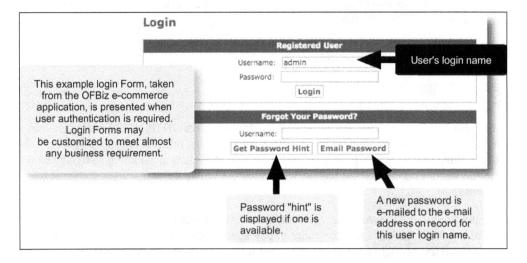

Or by using the **Party Manager** application as the administrative user ("admin") and creating a new password for a user. To implement a form-based automatic password creation service similar to that shown above, follow the given recipe.

 Note: for security reasons, OFBiz password encryption is a one-way process. There is no way to programmatically recover the plaintext value of a password once it has been encrypted by OFBiz.

Getting ready

In the `controller.xml` file for the webapp from which your user's web page view will be providing the forgotten password e-mail service, make sure you have a `request-map` entry that maps the user's request for a new password to the OFBiz `forgotPassword` event as shown here:

```xml
<request-map uri="forgotpassword">
  <security https="true" auth="false"/>
  <event type="java" path="org.ofbiz.securityext.login.LoginEvents"
         invoke="forgotPassword"/>
  <response name="success" type="view" value="login"/>
  <response name="error" type="view" value="login"/>
</request-map>
```

How to do it...

To add a feature to allow the user to request that a new password be e-mailed, follow the process outlined here:

1. Open the FreeMarker file (or OFBiz widget) containing the HTML form that will allow the user to e-mail a new password.

2. If using a FreeMarker template file to create the HTML form and web page view, add lines similar to the following:

```html
<#-- Note: the user must supply a valid userLoginId in the
     "Username" field for this to work -->
<#-- If they don't, an error message will be returned -->
<form method="post" action="<@ofbizUrl>forgotpassword</@ofbizUrl>"
      name="forgotpassword" style="margin: 0;">
  ${uiLabelMap.CommonUsername}: 
  <input type="text" size="20" class="inputBox" name="USERNAME"
         value="<#if requestParameters.USERNAME?has_content>
                   ${requestParameters.USERNAME}
                <#elseif autoUserLogin?has_content>
                      ${autoUserLogin.userLoginId}
                </#if>"/>
  <input type="submit" name="EMAIL_PASSWORD" class="smallSubmit"
         value="${uiLabelMap.CommonEmailPassword}"/>
</form>
```

3. Save and close the file. Changes are immediate and do not necessitate OFBiz restart.

How it works...

A request to the `forgotpassword` URI as mapped in the `controller.xml` file calls an OFBiz Event that:

1. Takes the provided form request parameter of `USERNAME`.
2. Looks up the associated `userLoginId` and primary e-mail address for the provided `USERNAME`.
3. Creates a new password for that `userLoginId`.
4. E-mails that password to the primary e-mail address on file within the user's profile.

If the user does not have a primary e-mail address on file or an unknown `USERNAME` is passed, control is passed back to the user and an error message is displayed.

Changing your password

Any user may change their own password at any time. For e-commerce application users, passwords may be changed using the **Profile** tab located along the top navigation bar:

```
https://localhost:8443/ecommerce/control/viewprofile
```

Users of OFBiz backend applications, for example, the **Order Entry** or **Accounting** applications, may use the **MyPortal** application to change passwords.

How to do it...

The following demonstrates use of the MyPortal application to change a password:

1. Log in to the **MyPortal** application:

   ```
   https://localhost:8443/myportal/control/main
   ```
2. Select the **My Profile** tab to bring up the **My Profile** web page.
3. Under the **Create New** section of the **My Profile** web page, click the **Edit** button next to the **User Login** label to bring up the **Change User Login Password** form.
4. Enter the current password.
5. Enter a new password. Passwords must be at least five characters in length and not contain any blanks.
6. Verify the typing of the new password by entering it again.
7. Save the form by clicking the **Save** button.

How it works...

The **MyPortal** application provides a handy UI for non-e-commerce OFBiz users to manage profile information such as password changes. **MyPortal** is password-protected and therefore, when a user requests access to it, they must first log in and be authenticated before initiating any profile changes. In this way, OFBiz is able to verify the user's identity, including the existing password for the account in which the user logged in, prior to the user submitting a change request.

Adding or changing SSL certificates

Secure Sockets Layer (**SSL**) is the protocol used by OFBiz to provide secure communications between browser clients and OFBiz webapps. Through SSL, secure communication sessions are enabled by using public and private keys to encrypt and decrypt messages on a user-by-user basis.

Internet web servers implementing SSL keep public keys in "certificates". When a browser or other web-based client lands on a secure web page, it will first query the server's SSL certificate to determine the server's identity, and then, based on that information, decide to request the server's public key so that it may continue to communicate using encrypted transmissions.

 Note: technically, the out-of-the-box servlet container (the "Catalina" servlet container and the "Tomcat" engine) provides the certificate exchange and encryption/decryption support. The OFBiz code seamlessly integrates this support so that applications need not worry about the details of secure Internet communications.

Because the certificate containing the public key is used to identify the OFBiz server as a trusted source, most deployed OFBiz instances replace the out-of-the-box default public key certificate (provided primarily as a convenience) with one that has been signed and therefore authenticated by a third-party called a **Certificate Authority** (**CA**).

While it is not necessary to have a certificate signed to operate a secure OFBiz instance, nor is it necessary to change the out-of-the-box certificate, it is highly recommended to do so. The process for exchanging the default out-of-the-box SSL certificate for another certificate, either signed by a CA or a self-signed one, is described in this recipe:

Getting ready

All roads to certificate replacement start with creating new keys and certificates. A suggested tool to use for key and certificate creation is the **KeyTool**. This collection of utilities is usually provided as part of the operating system and/or Java SDK you may be using. If not, you may find out more information here:

```
http://java.sun.com/j2se/1.5.0/docs/tooldocs/solaris/keytool.html
```

How to do it...

To create signed certificates, proceed as follows:

1. Since the SSL public key is derived from the private one, you must create the private key first and then use that key to create the public key. If you are using KeyTool, you can create the public key, private key, and the special file needed to store your keys and certificates, called the `keystore`, with the following command:

   ```
   keytool -genkey -keyalg RSA -alias server -keystore mykeystore.jks
   ```

   You will be presented with a number of questions. Answer as appropriate for your server installation. The answers will be used to generate the certificate and key(s).

2. Create a **Certificate Signing Request** (**CSR**). A CSR is a document created by KeyTool that asks that the enclosed certificate be signed by a third-party. CSR can be created by giving this command:

   ```
   keytool -certreq -alias server -keyalg RSA -file certreq.csr
           -keystore mykeystore.jks
   ```

3. Send your CSR to a CA to be signed. CAs known to work with OFBiz include Verisign, Thawte, Comodo, GeoTrust, CACert.org, and FreeSSL. (See the OFBiz Wiki for details).

4. If instead you wish to self-sign your own certificate, run a command similar to the following. Answer the questions as appropriate for your server. This will create a self-signed certificate and automatically store it in the designated `keystore`.

   ```
   keytool -selfcert -alias server  -keyalg RSA -keystore
   mykeystore.jks
   ```

5. If you sent your certificate off to be signed, download your signed certificate from the CA.

6. Import your signed certificate containing your public key into the `keystore` using a KeyTool command similar to the following. If you self-signed your certificate, you will not need to perform this step as this was already done in step 4.

   ```
   keytool -import -alias server -trustcacerts -file mysignedcert.cer
           -keystore mykeystore.jks
   ```

That is all you need to do to get a self-signed certificate into the keystore for OFBiz to use.

If you have created a new `keystore` file as in the examples above, you need to tell OFBiz how to access this new repository.

> Note: creating a new `keystore` as shown here is recommended for new installations to establish a server trust chain.

To inform OFBiz where a `keystore` is located and the password to use when accessing this file, edit the `ofbiz-containers.xml` file as shown here. (Note: the `keystorePass` property value is the password you created for the keystore in step 1):

`~framework/base/config/ofbiz-containers.xml`

```
<property name="keystoreFile"
        value="framework/base/config/mykeystore.jks"/>
<property name="keystorePass" value="newpassword"/>
<!-- Note the keystore type needs to match the type used when
    creating the keystore -->
<property name="keystoreType" value="PKCS12" />
```

How it works...

Using the `ofbiz-containers.xml` file as a reference, OFBiz automatically initializes the Catalina/Tomcat servlet container when it starts up, with the essential elements necessary to handle secure, encrypted SSL browser communications. Beyond initial servlet container setup, OFBiz leaves the details of web server and browser key exchange and SSL encryption to the servlet container.

There's more...

You may also use the **OpenSSL** toolkit to create SSL keys and certificates. To do so, follow these steps:

1. Create the private key:

   ```
   openssl req -new -key privkey.pem 4096
   ```

2. Using the private key, create a CSR to be sent to a CA to be signed:

   ```
   openssl req -new -key privkey.pem -out cert.csr
   ```

3. Send the CSR to a trusted CA. Signed certificates from the following CAs are known to work with OFBiz.

4. Create the keystore and import your private key:

```
keytool -genkey - keyalg RSA -alias server
        -keystore mykeystore.jks
keytool -import -alias server -keystore mykeystore.jks
        -privkey.pem
```

5. CSRs are returned as valid certificates. Import your signed certificate into the keystore using a command similar to the following. (Note: different CA have slightly different installation instructions. Follow those provided as appropriate):

```
keytool -import  -alias server -keystore mykeystore.jks
        -privkey.pem
```

See also

Please refer to the OFBiz **FAQ-Tips-Tricks-Cookbook-HowTo** on the OFBiz Wiki:

```
http://cwiki.apache.org/confluence/x/9ABk
```

OFBiz single sign-on and the external login key

If an OFBiz user (whose session has not expired) stays within the processing domain of a single OFBiz webapp, they will not need to log in more than once. But, because of the nature of TCP/IP sessions and servlet container behavior, users moving between OFBiz webapps may be prompted to log in once for each OFBiz webapp they wish to access. Since any single OFBiz instance may support an unlimited number of webapps, certain users such as administrators may need to log in many times in the course of performing a single administrative task.

To help mitigate this situation, OFBiz provides a handy mechanism called the "External Login Key". This feature enables logged in users to move between OFBiz web applications requiring authentication without having to log in more than one time.

Note: because the external login key implementation depends on the user's session, there may be times when the external login key appears not to work. This may happen when a user has multiple browser windows open (each representing a unique TCP/IP session) at the same time, and is moving among browser window sessions and webapps running within the same OFBiz instance.

Getting ready

Implementing the external login key mechanism requires two distinct activities. Both activities must be implemented for this to work:

1. Turn on external login key checking for each participating webapp within the appropriate `controller.xml` file.

2. Create a dynamic "external login key" request parameter and append it to the navigation link for each link that forwards a user to a participating OFBiz webapp web page.

How to do it...

To enable single sign-on, perform the following steps:

1. To turn on external login key checking for an OFBiz webapp, make sure the following Java class is configured within the `preprocessor` portion of the `controller.xml` file for that webapp. Conversely, to remove external login key checks, remove or comment out this line from the `controller.xml` file:

```
<preprocessor>
   <!-- Events to run on every request before security
        (chains exempt) -->
   <event name="checkExternalLoginKey" type="java"
          path="org.ofbiz.webapp.control.LoginWorker"
          invoke="checkExternalLoginKey"/>
</preprocessor>
```

2. Adding an external login key to an HTML location reference (HREF) within a FreeMarker template is easy. Use the `externalLoginKey` session attribute as shown here:

```
<a href=
"<@ofbizUrl>
/myofbizwebapp/control?externalLoginKey=${externalLoginKey!""}
</@ofbizUrl>">
  Click Here
</a>
```

How it works...

Regardless of which OFBiz webapp a user logs in to, an external login key is generated for that user for each successful login. This key is placed in the user's session and available programmatically for OFBiz applications to use when dynamically creating navigation location links to other OFBiz applications. Dynamic OFBiz webapp navigation links are created by adding the key as a request parameter to the link.

In this way, web page requests for OFBiz webapps with the user's unique external login key may be created each time a user lands on an OFBiz web page. The user may then select one of these links to another OFBiz webapp and automatically have their current external login key passed to the target OFBiz webapp and web page.

There's more...

If you are using OFBiz Menu widgets to build lists of HTML location references and you want to provide external login keys for these references, OFBiz provides a convenient syntax for adding external login keys as shown here:

```
<menu-item name="findQuote" title="${uiLabelMap.OrderOrderQuotes}" >
  <link target="/ordermgr/control/FindQuote" url-mode="inter-app">
    <parameter param-name="partyId"/>
    <parameter param-name="externalLoginKey"/>
  </link>
</menu-item>
```

7
WebTools

In this chapter, we shall discuss several WebTools, including tools and utilities for:

- Cache maintenance
- Changing debug settings
- Exporting database data to XML documents
- Loading databases from XML documents
- Managing internationalization labels
- Using the SQL processor
- Exploring the entity reference tool
- Viewing OFBiz usage statistics
- Uncovering artifact information
- Working with temporal expressions

Introduction

Out-of-the-box, OFBiz comes with many tools designed to help manage your OFBiz instance. One set of tools specifically for use with the "framework" portion of the code base, that is, those parts of OFBiz that make up the underlying core or support platform and which are found starting in the `framework` directory, are called the "WebTools".

The WebTools toolkit is front-ended with a separate OFBiz Component, webapp (located as a sub-directory under the `framework` directory), and UI, called the "WebTools" Application. This webapp consolidates the many day-to-day OFBiz administrative system health checks, system and application tuning utility access points, and configuration interfaces under a single UI umbrella.

All WebTools are password-protected and require administrative privileges and user membership in the "OFBTOOLS" security group to access and use. Out-of-the-box, the default administrative user login is "admin" and the password is "ofbiz". If these user credentials have not been changed, they may be used to access all WebTools features and facilities discussed in this chapter.

The main WebTools UI web page is located at:

```
https://localhost:8443/webtools/control/main
```

From the menu selections on this web page, you may navigate directly to the desired tool. Or, if you prefer, navigate directly to the target tool using its URL.

Cache maintenance

OFBiz, like most enterprise class software, uses caching techniques to improve system performance by placing often used data in memory (and sometimes on disk) "caches". Since the OFBiz framework is an all-inclusive deployment platform, there are many opportunities to employ caching methodologies. From database access to web page screen construction and teardown, OFBiz implements many independently configurable caching stores. Each cache may be tuned independently of all others using the WebTools "cache maintenance" tool.

From the **Cache Maintenance** web page, you may view all currently active caches and statistics on a per cache basis. In addition, you may, with one mouse click, clear and reload all active caches as well as expire all stale cache data, and run the Java garbage collector.

For individual caches, you may set limits on the number of cache entries, called "elements", or allow an unlimited number. For caches with a set limit on the number of entries, OFBiz automatically handles element expiration and removal using a least recently used algorithm. OFBiz tracks cache hits (the number of times a request for a cached element was satisfied by finding the element in cache) and misses and reports these statistics on the WebTools **Cache Maintenance** web page.

Getting ready

To get started with the WebTools **Cache Maintenance** tool, either navigate to the WebTools main web page and select **Cache Maintenance**, or go directly to the tool's URL located at `https://localhost:8443/webtools/control/FindUtilCache`. If you have not already logged in, you will be prompted to log in. Enter the administrator's username and password. If these have not changed since initial system download, the administrative user's name is "admin" and the password is "ofbiz".

How to do it...

Once logged in, follow these steps:

1. From the **Cache Maintenance** page shown, observe the following OFBiz cache statistics: total memory allocated to all caches, free memory, used memory, and maximum available memory. The maximum and minimum values displayed should be within the ranges set for the Java JVM when the system was started.

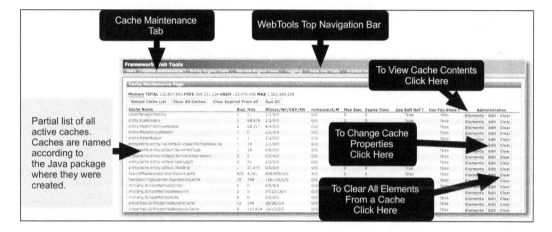

2. To clear all caches and reload the cache list, click the **Clear All Caches** button followed by the **Reload Cache List** button as shown in the figure.

3. To view individual cache entries, called "elements", in real-time as the system is running, select the **Elements** tab adjacent to the target cache. Elements include the cache "key" (either a piece of data such as a `GenericValue`, a file, or pointer to a file) and the size of the element in bytes.

4. To edit individual cache settings, click the **Edit** button adjacent to the cache of interest. Per cache configuration settings include the maximum size (0 indicates none), Expire time (0 indicates do not expire).

How it works...

OFBiz implements caching to help maximize system performance through minimizing I/O operations. For example, to reduce the number of database and/or disk accesses required to support business applications, certain operations such as Entity Engine database request and/or web page views benefit greatly from caching.

Each OFBiz Component and Application may implement one or more caches by calling the generic OFBiz caching utility (the `UtilCache` Java class). You may even implement your own cache for a custom Application using the `UtilCache` utility, and then manage that cache using the WebTools **Cache Maintenance** web page.

Out-of-the-box, many of the framework Components such as the Entity Engine, Service Engine, and widget tools implement caching that you may easily monitor and tune using the WebTools UI described here.

There's more...

Out-of-the-box, OFBiz has been set with all the default cache settings needed to run the demonstration Applications provided. These setting are tuned for the development installation and may not be adequate for a production environment where transaction volumes are significantly higher than testing scenarios.

> Note: initial startup cache settings are configured in the `~framework/base/config/cache.properties` file. If you change any cache property using WebTools and then restart your instance of OFBiz, settings in `cache.properties` will overwrite any WebTools settings. Please see the `cache.properties` file concerning the latest information regarding initial system setup suggestions, especially as they apply to production-ready deployments.

The OFBiz caching utility places no limits on the number and/or size of caches that may be active at any time. The complexity of the OFBiz caching scheme derives from the number of caches and how the settings of any one cache may impact other caches and memory availability, and not the actual caching implementation.

At some point, given a finite amount of physical computer memory, there may be memory utilization contention based on element caching. Each OFBiz instance will behave differently under different runtime transaction loads, and it is incumbent upon the OFBiz administrator to use the provided WebTools cache maintenance utilities to find the optimum settings for any single OFBiz deployment.

See also

Note: please see the OFBiz Javadocs `UtilCache` for more technical information concerning implementation and usage of the OFBiz caching scheme:

`http://ci.apache.org/projects/ofbiz/site/javadocs`

Changing debug settings

OFBiz system event logging and debug tools are an integral part of the OFBiz experience. Whether you are monitoring a deployed system or developing a new OFBiz Component or webapp, OFBiz wide runtime event logging and debugging support is your best troubleshooting tool. Out-of-the-box, event logging is based on the Apache log4J logging tool (`http://logging.apache.org/log4j`) and may be enabled or disabled using the WebTools interface without restarting OFBiz. If enabled, log4j logging levels (the triggers that tell log4j when to write an Event message to the log file) may also be adjusted during normal system operations.

Getting ready

To get started and manage OFBiz logging features, either navigate to the WebTools main web page and select the **Logging** navigation tab, or go directly to the tool's URL located at: `https://localhost:8443/webtools/control/LogConfiguration`. If you have not already logged in, you will be prompted to log in. Enter the administrator's username and password. If these have not changed since initial system download, the administrative user's name is "admin" and the password is "ofbiz".

How to do it...

Debug settings can be changed by following these steps:

1. To adjust logging levels, select the **Log Configuration** navigation tab from the main **Logging** web page.
2. Add or remove check box selections as desired. Each check box represents a logging level. Note: logging levels are independent of one another. For example, if you want "warning" and "error" messages posted to the logfile, select **Warning** and **Error**. No other messages, including "fatal" messages, will be posted.

3. Click **Update** as shown in the following figure. That's all you need to do. No need to restart OFBiz or change any code.

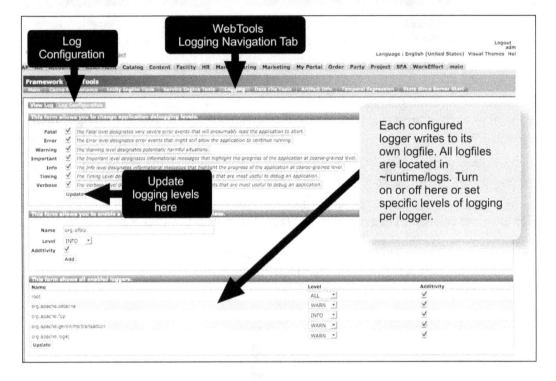

4. To completely disable all event logging, scroll down the **Log Configuration** web page to the section labeled: **This form shows all enabled loggers**. Next to each defined logger, select the **OFF** drop-down menu option. Click the **Update** button and all logging will be turned off. You do not need to restart OFBiz to make this effective.

How it works...

Out-of-the-box, OFBiz system-level logging is based in an implementation of Apache log4j. (http://logging.apache.org/log4j/index.html). Log4j provides a facility to implement one or more "loggers". These loggers write consistently formatted text entries to one or more logfiles based on settings configured here and in a Log4j initial configuration setting file found at ~framework/base/config/debug.properties.

 Note: Apache log4j may be replaced or supplemented when running in other servlet containers and/or web application servers. Alternative logging tools are configured in ~/framework/base/config/debug.properties. Configuring such environments is beyond the scope of this book.

One of the basic tenants of Apache log4j is that event logging statements may be placed within the code and selectively triggered by the type of Event that occurs. Logging Event types trigger logging "levels". For example, when an Event type of "Fatal" occurs, the logger, if configured to do so, will post messages to one or more logfiles as "Fatal" level messages.

This means that in your code, you may place logging statements to only write messages when a "Fatal" Event occurs. Of course, the developer will need to determine what constitutes a "Fatal" Event and write statements accordingly. But log4j doesn't really care except to log a message to the designated logfile when the "Fatal" Event code path is executed.

There are seven independently configured levels of logging defined in OFBiz: "Fatal", "Error", "Warning", "Important", "Info", "Timing", and "Verbose". The OFBiz project has integrated Apache log4j in such a way as to make using logging levels easy. All the software developer need do is import the `org.ofbiz.base.util.Debug` Java class and call the appropriate `Debug` object method. Formatting of the message, including adding the source code line number and a timestamp when the method was invoked, are automatically handled by the `Debug` Java class, as is message routing to the correct logfile.

For example, if you would like to post a message to the logfile from within a Java program only when the **Warning** level is turned on, write a statement similar to the following:

```
Debug.logWarning(
"This message should only be written when logging Warning messages",
 module);
```

From the WebTools **Logging Configuration** web page, you may selectively turn on posting of individual message levels as necessary. There is no need to recode your program or restart OFBiz.

There's more...

All OFBiz logfiles are found in the `~/runtime/logs` directory. At any time, you may remove any of the files in `~/runtime/logs` directory without damaging system operations. Once a logfile is removed, OFBiz will cease posting messages to it. The next time OFBiz is started, it will recreate the file automatically. If you would like to clean any of the files while OFBiz is running and then have logging commence to a clean file without restarting OFBiz, try first removing the file and then recreating an empty file. On a Unix system, you may use the Unix `touch` command to create an empty file. For example:

```
cd ~runtime/logs
rm ofbiz.log
touch ofbiz.log
```

Over the years, as the complexity of OFBiz has grown, the project, in an effort to make troubleshooting and error reporting easier, has created separate logfiles for certain framework processing such as a special logfile for the Catalina servlet container and Formatted Objects Processing (Apache FOP).

The WebTools **Log Configuration** settings allow for controls that not only enable and disable the primary OFBiz logfile but also for managing other configured loggers.

From the main **Logging** web page, you may select the **View Log** navigation tab. This will bring up an HTML formatted version of the main OFBiz log (ofbiz.log) as shown. This tool may prove extremely useful if you are working on a remote OFBiz system and do not have command line or filesystem access to the OFBiz logfile directory. Note: you will need to refresh the web page to see real-time updates to this file:

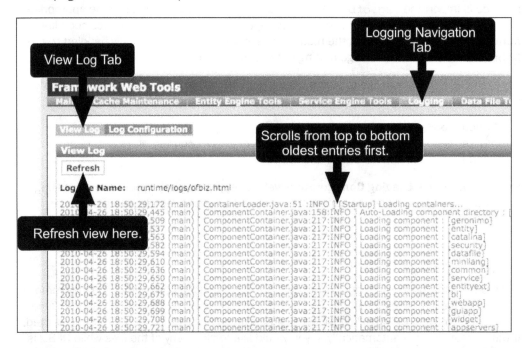

Exporting database data to XML documents

The OFBiz WebTools interface provides utilities to easily export data from any OFBiz data source or part of an OFBiz data source, including all configured databases. All data source exports copy from the target source and save data as one or more plain text XML document file(s). These files may be then directly imported to other OFBiz managed data sources using the OFBiz XML data import tools.

Note: at any time, you may export data from your database(s) using any third-party tools available. This section provides information on how to use OFBiz to manage the exporting of data from any configured data source.

Getting ready

When using the **XML Data Export** tools to copy data from an OFBiz managed data source, OFBiz must have write access to the destination directory where you plan on saving the exported data. Alternatively, you may elect to export data to the browser's web page view. In this case, you will not need file system write permissions to perform this task.

To get started and use the **XML Data Export** tool, either navigate to the WebTools main web page and select **XML Data Export** from the main web page menu, or go directly to the tool's URL located at `https://localhost:8443/webtools/control/xmldsdump`. If you have not already logged in, you will be prompted to log in. Enter the administrator's username and password. If these have not changed since initial system download, the administrative user's name is "admin" and the password is "ofbiz".

How to do it...

To export a database to an XML document, perform the following steps:

1. If you are exporting to the local file system, enter this directory location for the field labeled **Output Directory**. This is an absolute directory location and not relative to the OFBiz install directory.

2. To have all data exported to a single file, enter the name of that file in the **Single Filename** field provided. If you do not enter a value here, each entity will be exported to its own file.

3. To limit the number of records/rows to be exported, enter the desired values in the **Max Records Per File** field.

4. To specify date filters, enter dates or use the calendar icons provided.

5. Select one or more entity(s) to export from by checking the HTML checkbox next to each entity name provided. Or, alternately, to export all the entities defined, click the **Check All** button.

6. Click the **Export** button. Success and/or error messages are reported directly to this web page.

How it works...

Wherever it can, OFBiz uses well-formed XML documents as a basis for the task at hand. Exporting data from an OFBiz Entity Engine-managed data source is no exception. The **XML Data Export** tool reads data from one or more target data source-managed entities, formats that data as a plain text string, and then writes out the data according to the entity's defined model using XML syntax. The end result is a text file that contains one or more XML declarations, each representing a row (or record) from the data source.

By using the entity's own model to describe exported data (the entity's entity definition as found in an entity definition file), OFBiz preserves enough information about the data so that it may, in turn, be reloaded into another Entity Engine-managed data source.

Loading database(s) from XML documents

The OFBiz WebTools interface provides a number of utilities to help load data, from one or more files and/or directories, into any Entity Engine data source (including databases). In this section, we shall examine loading data from XML document files using the WebTools **Entity XML Tools**.

Getting ready

Make sure the data to be loaded is formatted correctly as the OFBiz **XML Data Import** tool requires files to be in XML document format beginning with an `entity-engine-xml` element tag and ending with the appropriate closing tag as shown:

```
<entity-engine-xml>
  <!-- This is a comment and is valid within a data file -->
  <EntityName fieldName="someValue"
            anotherFieldName="someOtherValue" />
  <!-- You may have as many entity/field declarations as desired
       within a single file -->
</entity-engine-xml>
```

Each XML element within the XML data file represents a record (or row) to be inserted into the indicated entity. Within an element's declaration, each attribute represents a column (or field) within the entity. Attribute names must be valid entity field names. There are many examples of this formatting throughout the code base as this is the format used to construct seed and other data loaded automatically by the ANT data loading directives.

To get started and use the **XML Data Import** tool, either navigate to the WebTools main web page and select **XML Data Import** from the main web page menu, or go directly to the tool's URL located at `https://localhost:8443/webtools/control/EntityImport`. If you have not already logged in, you will be prompted to log in. Enter the administrator's username and password. If these have not changed since initial system download, the administrative user's name is "admin" and the password is "ofbiz".

How to do it...

A database can be loaded from an XML document by following these steps:

1. To import an XML document file directly to the target data source, enter either the absolute location on the local hard drive (and not a directory location relative from the OFBiz installation directory) of the file or the URL of this file. URLs may be for files local to the OFBiz instance in use or remotely located. Click the **Import File** button to submit this form. Success and error messages are posted on this web page.

2. Alternatively, you may insert one or more XML declarations, or cut and paste one or more XML declarations into the provided HTML form's TEXTAREA. Click the **Import Text** button as shown:

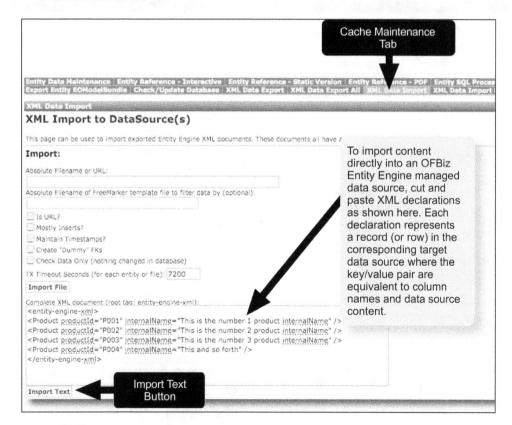

3. File imports, if successful, are added to the data source immediately. No need to restart OFBiz.

How it works...

The **XML Data Import** tool takes one or more well-formed XML document file(s) and copies data from each file as instructed by the XML declarations within the file. Each XML file must contain one or more element(s) that declares the entity to be loaded, as well as element attributes that define the entity fields and the data values to load.

There's more...

When loading files using the **XML Data Import** tool, care must be taken to load files in the proper order so that foreign-key integrity is preserved. When loading multiple files, loading is sequential and a failure in any file will terminate the loading process and roll back all previously loaded data.

Managing internationalization labels

OFBiz "labels" are the mechanism used to handle the locale-sensitive translation of many HTML form elements. While the underlying internationalization and localization support within OFBiz is implemented using Java `ResourceBundles`, and is for the most part transparent to the application developer, the manual management of the translated objects that make up these resources is the subject of this section.

At last count, there are over 10,000 unique labels defined. Each of these labels has the potential of being translated into any supported language. To see at a glance all labels, and quickly edit a translation for a label, you may use the OFBiz **Label Manager** tool.

 Note: for optimum performance when using the OFBiz **Label Manager**, make sure you set your JVM memory settings to the highest possible values supported by your hosting machine.

Getting ready

To get started with the WebTools **Label Manager** tool, either navigate to the WebTools main web page or go directly to the tool's URL located at:

```
https://localhost:8443/webtools/control/SearchLabels
```

If you have not already logged in, you will be prompted to log in. Enter the administrator's username and password. If these have not changed since initial system download, the administrative user's name is "admin" and the password is "ofbiz".

How to do it...

To edit labels, follow these steps:

1. Once on the **Label Manager** page, bring up the **Filter Labels Info By** HTML form.
2. Use the search filtering tool to specify a unique label file and/or key, or, to display all labels, click the **Find** button.
3. To edit a label, select the label from the results screen and edit as appropriate.
4. Save the edit.

How it works

OFBiz "labels" are part of the internationalization and localization support built-in to the OFBiz code base. "Labels" are the "key" portion of the key/value pair that make up the information needed to identify the translation of a particular text string. This key is used to look up translation maps in "label files". Any FreeMarker document and/or OFBiz widget may employ one or more "labels" to provide user session-based translations (called "localization").

> Note: although the underlying support exists to translate OFBiz "labels" to any known language, only a few languages have complete translation maps in place.

Under the covers, OFBiz implements internationalization and localization using the Java `ResourceBundle` class. "Labels" are stored in files, usually located in a Component's `config` directory where the label's use originated. For example, within the `Order` Component's `config` directory, there are several "label" files: `OrderEntryLabels.xml`, `OrderErrorUiLabels.xml`, and others. These files include one or more property "keys" that represent the "label" as it would appear in an HTML document.

As part of the construction of a web page using the Screen widget, any files containing locale labels are configured within the `actions` portion of the screen's definition. You may see how this works by examining the contents of the `actions` element within a screen's definition. If a declaration for a "property-map resource" is present, then one or more label files are available within the context for this web page.

For example, if, within a FreeMarker template, you have an HTML text string with FreeMarker markup as shown here:

```
${uiLabelMap.OrderWhereShallWeShipIt}
```

The `uiLabelMap` is the name of the map that has been placed in the context, containing the translation of the `OrderWhereShallWeShipIt` "label". To make all this work in real time, each user's session has an attribute indicating the locale to use for that session. OFBiz automatically takes the locale attribute, looks up the "label" in the specified map, in this case the `uiLabelMap`, and returns the translated value.

There's more...

You may edit "label" files by hand at any time if you know the location of the file in which the label is stored. Using the OFBiz **Label Manager** makes locating and editing OFBiz translation files (resource bundles) easy and painless.

If you wish to make available only certain language/locale translations for a particular instance of OFBiz, you may edit the following property file and control precisely which locales are available for user selection at runtime:

~framework/common/config/general.properties

Modify the locales.available property as shown here:

```
# To only display the following locale specific labels:
locales.available=fr,nl,zh,en,it,es,ja,de
```

Using the SQL processor

There are instances, especially when testing, where accessing an Entity Engine data source directly without using the Entity Engine delegator methods prove useful. For example, if you need to test a query before embedding it within the logic of your Application, or if you need to drop a table from a database, you can use the **SQL Processor** tool to communicate SQL statements directly to the target database.

Getting ready

To get started with the WebTools **SQL Processor** tool, either navigate to the WebTools main web page and select the **Entity SQL Processor**, or go directly to the tool's URL located at:

https://localhost:8443/webtools/control/EntitySQLProcessor

If you have not already logged in, you will be prompted to log in. Enter the administrator's username and password. If these have not changed since initial system download, the administrative user's name is "admin" and the password is "ofbiz".

How to do it...

The **SQL Processor** tool can be used to communicate SQL statements directly to the target database by following these steps:

1. Navigate to the **SQL Processor** web page as shown earlier. This will bring up an HTML form that allows you to select the desired data source from the **Group** drop-down box and enter in a single SQL statement, as shown in the figure:

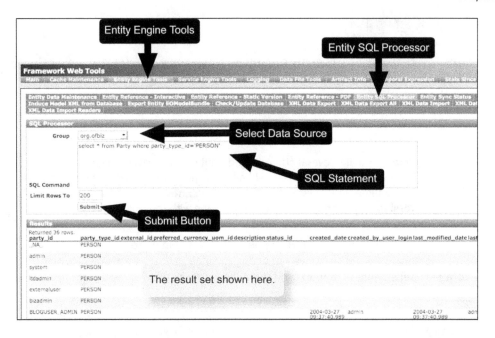

2. To limit the number of records/rows returned, enter a value in the **Limit Rows To** field.

3. Click the **Submit** button.

How it works...

The OFBiz **SQL Processor** form takes the selected **Group** and finds the configured data source for that group. It then takes the SQL statement as entered in the HTML TEXTAREA named **SQL Command** as shown in the screenshot and calls the Java org.ofbiz.entity.jdbc. SQLProcessor to process the statement. Result sets and error messages are returned to the web page.

Exploring the entity reference tool

With over 1,000 unique entities that come with OFBiz out-of-the-box, the **Entity Reference - Interactive Version** is an indispensable tool for understanding and managing the runtime aspects of all the different OFBiz data sources that may be connected through the Entity Engine. Using this tool, you may:

▶ List all connected database tables, columns, and record content

▶ Observe all entity relationships and move between related entity views, with easy, one-click navigation links

▶ Add and remove data from database tables (if no foreign key relationships are violated) using the HTML forms provided

Getting ready

To get started with the WebTools **Entity Reference - Interactive Version** tool, either navigate to the WebTools main web page and select the **Entity Reference - Interactive** link, or go directly to the tool's URL:

```
https://localhost:8443/webtools/control/entityref
```

> Note: there are several other related Entity Engine tools available on the main WebTools menu. And while all these navigation links eventually lead to the same end, make sure you select the **Entity Reference - Interactive Version** for best results and to follow along with the rest of this section.

If you have not already logged in, you will be prompted to log in. Enter the administrator's username and password. If these have not changed since initial system download, the administrative user's name is "admin" and the password is "ofbiz".

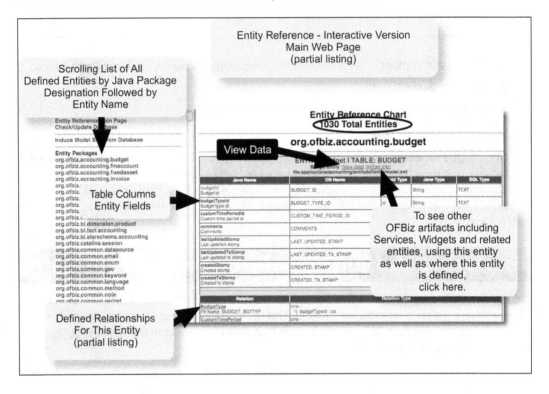

How to do it...

You can easily explore around the entity reference tool by following these steps:

1. Once you have found your way to the **Entity Reference Chart** web page, which is the main web page for the **Entity Reference - Interactive Version** tool, you may observe at a glance the total number of entities defined.

2. Scrolling down the page, you will see a table-like view of each entity, grouped by package name (if the entity has been defined as being part of a package name), followed by a list of any relationships the entity is a participant in.

3. To find the record (or row values) for an individual entity, select the **[View data]** link to bring up the corresponding **Find Value** web page. For example, to find all **Budget** entity records, select the **[View data]** link under the **org.ofbiz.accounting.budget** entity view. This will bring up the **Find Values** web page for the selected **Budget** entity as shown below. (Note: in this case, we are informed that no records were found).

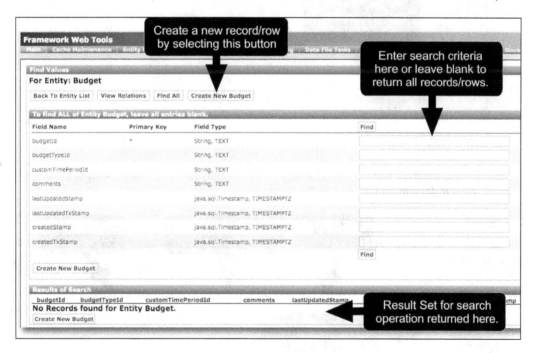

4. We can add a `Budget` record by clicking the **Create New Budget** button to bring up the **Edit Value** web page shown:

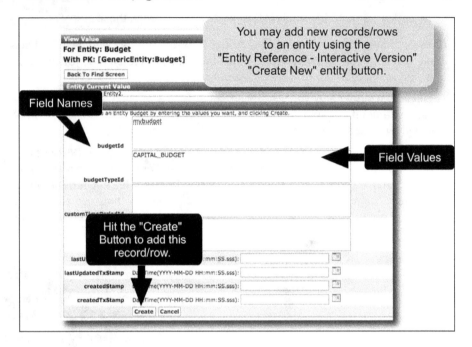

Note that for the `Budget` entity, the field `budgetTypeId` is a foreign key and, therefore, if entered as part of this new record, it must already exist.

5. Finally, we may view all the relations that any entity is a participant in by clicking the **View Relations** button on the **Find Values** web page.

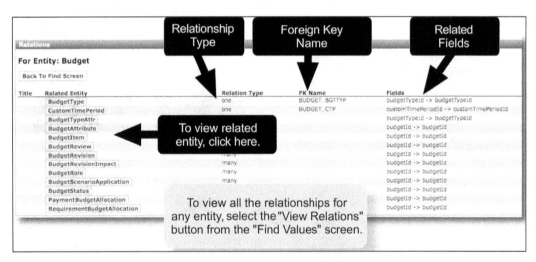

How it works...

The **Entity Engine - Interactive Version** tool provides a handy organized view into all the data sources the current instance of the OFBiz Entity Engine are configured to manage. For anyone needing to work with any OFBiz Entity Engine data source, this tool provides a convenient jumping-off point to navigate among entities, data sources, database tables, and rows that make up an OFBiz installation.

Viewing OFBiz usage statistics

The OFBiz **Stats Since Server Start** is the place to go to see web page statistics at a glance and in detail. The statistics are broken down by HTTP/HTTPS requests, and direct requests via `controller.xml` request-maps for OFBiz Events, Services, and `view-map` entries.

Getting ready

To get started with the WebTools tool, either navigate to the WebTools main web page and select the **Stats Since Server Start** top navigation link, or go directly to the tool's URL located at:

```
https://localhost:8443/webtool/control/StatsSinceStart
```

If you have not already logged in, you will be prompted to log in. Enter the administrator's username and password. If these have not changed since initial system download, the administrative user's name is "admin" and the password is "ofbiz".

How to do it...

Once logged in, you can view usage stats by the following steps:

1. The **Stats Since Server Start** tool is a display of the web traffic experienced over a set period of time. By default, and if you have not cleared any of the server web page hit counters, this display covers the time since OFBiz was restarted. To clear all counters without restarting OFBiz, select the **Clear Since Start Stats** link as shown in the figure:

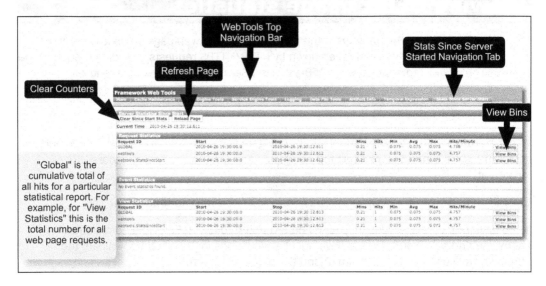

2. Web page hit statistics are grouped into "bins" where a bin contains statistics for one or more 15-minute interval. To see a breakdown by web page and bin, click the **View Bins** button adjacent to **Request ID** desired.

3. The statistics as displayed on this web page may be refreshed by clicking the **Reload Page** button.

How it works...

Every HTTP/HTTPS request for every web page served by OFBiz (a "hit") is automatically recorded by the control servlet for the webapp servicing the request in the `ServerHit` database table. OFBiz tracks information about where a visitor came from and how long it takes OFBiz to service each request.

Uncovering artifact information

A little used but highly valuable tool that could save you hours of time researching how the various pieces of OFBiz fit together, the **Artifact Info** utility is a necessity for easily assembling OFBiz piece-part information (where OFBiz pieces are called "artifacts") into a coherent story. Artifacts may include anything and everything that goes into making up your OFBiz instance. This WebTool utility works with the following OFBiz artifacts: entities, widgets (screen, form, menu, tree), Events, Services, and `controller.xml` files.

 Note: to use this tool, set your min and max memory within your OFBiz startup file (or on the command line) generously as assembling artifact information consumes large amounts of memory!

Getting ready

To get started with the WebTools **Artifact Info** tool, either navigate to the WebTools main web page and select the **Artifact Info** navigation link, or go directly to the tool's URL located at:

`https://localhost:8443/webtools/control/ArtifactInfo`

If you have not already logged in, you will be prompted to log in. Enter the administrator's username and password. If these have not changed since initial system download, the administrative user's name is "admin" and the password is "ofbiz".

How to do it...

There are a number of ways to use the **Artifact Info** tool, and the reader is encouraged to experiment and find methods best suited to their needs. Some of these are listed:

1. To find artifacts associated with a particular Component or webapp, enter information as shown here:

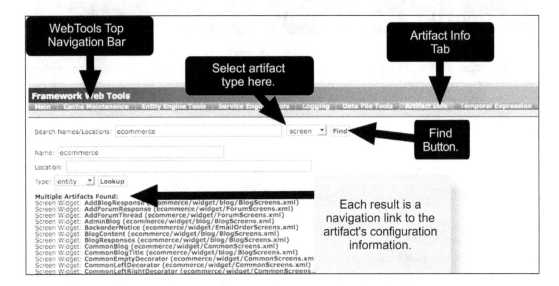

2. To follow a link, for example, to delve deeper into the artifacts found for the e-commerce screen to see details about the `AddBlogResponse` Screen widget, click on the link provided. This will bring up a web page similar to the following:

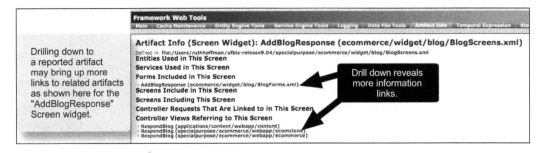

3. To view artifact information for a specific entity, for example, the `ElectronicText` entity as shown here, return to the main **Artifact Info** web page and select **entity** from the pull-down menu provided. Enter **ElectronicText** in the **Search Names/Locations** field.

4. Click the **Find** button to bring up a web page similar to the following:

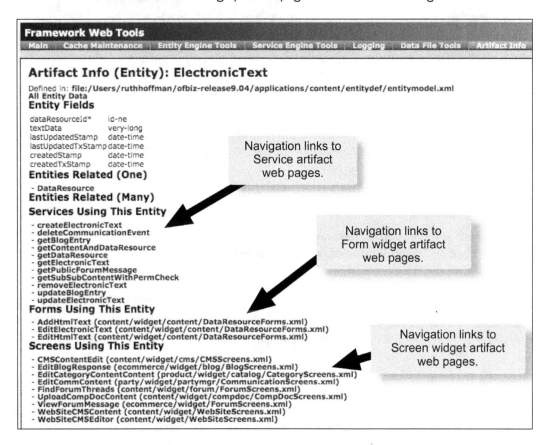

How it works...

Since OFBiz knows the configuration of every artifact in advance of any usage, it can programmatically assemble all the relationships involved in any single artifact, including information about how other artifacts are used to build one by parsing all its configuration tables and building a dynamic, runtime view of the relationships that exist among all the artifacts.

Working with temporal expressions

OFBiz "temporal expressions" are a formal system or grammar used to describe the timing associated with the occurrence of recurring system events. Each expression represents a declaration about when and how often an Event may occur. Expressions may be used as single declarations, for example, run a Service every day at 9:00 pm or as a union, intersection, or difference of one or more ranges of time.

Using the OFBiz temporal expressions tool, you may edit an existing expression—OFBiz comes with several predefined—and/or create your own expressions and use them in conjunction with other OFBiz business processing logic.

Getting ready

To get started with the **Temporal Expressions** WebTools tool, either navigate to the WebTools main web page and select the **Temporal Expressions** link, or go directly to the tool's URL located at:

```
https://localhost:8443/webtools/control/findTemporalExpression
```

If you have not already logged in, you will be prompted to log in. Enter the administrator's username and password. If these have not changed since initial system download, the administrative user's name is "admin" and the password is "ofbiz".

How to do it...

You can edit or create temporal expressions by following these steps:

1. To list all currently defined temporal expressions, leave the **Find Temporal Expression** HTML form empty and click the **Find** button. This will bring up a list of the available expressions.

2. To modify any existing expression, select the navigation link provided adjacent to the expression. This will bring up the **Temporal Expression Maintenance** HTML form. Make changes to this expression as desired. Click the **Save** button to make the changes effective.

3. To add a new temporal expression, click the **Create** button from the **Find Temporal Expression** page. This will bring up the **Temporal Expression Maintenance** page where you may add a new expression of the types supported. Once a new expression has been defined, click the **Save** button.

4. There is no need to restart OFBiz to make the changes effective.

How it works...

Temporal expressions are used throughout the OFBiz code base as a consistent method of describing schedules and Event timing. Expressions are persistent in the OFBiz database (the `TemporalExpresson`, `TemporalExpressionAssoc`, and `TemporalExpressionChild` entities) and managed as resources available for use by any OFBiz Application, Component, or end user. The WebTools **Temporal Expressions** tool provides an HTML form-based interface for managing these OFBiz resources.

There's more...

For the curious, there is a really nice write-up on OFBiz temporal expressions on the OFBiz Wiki:

```
https://cwiki.apache.org/confluence/display/OFBENDUSER/
Temporal+Expressions
```

8

Web Services

In this chapter, we shall look at various techniques to build OFBiz web service providers and consumers. In particular, you will find information on:

- Requesting web services using URL parameters
- Requesting web services using an `HttpClient`
- Creating `HttpClient` and passing XML documents
- Creating XML-RPC web service clients
- Becoming an XML-RPC web service provider
- Generating a WSDL document
- Building SOAP messaging clients
- Creating SOAP compliant web services

Introduction

Ask five people what "web services" are and you will likely get at least six different opinions. Because the term evokes such ambiguity, we need to set ground rules for this chapter and define what we mean by "web services". Therefore, for the purposes of this book, "web services" are the interactive exchange of messages from one system to another using the Internet as the network transport and HTTP/HTTPS as the messaging protocol. Message exchange transpires without human intervention and may be one-way—that is, called without an immediate response expected—or two-way.

Web services operate as producer/consumer systems where the producer—called the "service provider"—offers one or more "services" to the "consumer"—sometimes referred to as the "client". In the web services world, Internet-based service providers advertise and deliver service from locations throughout the Web. The Internet, and the Web in particular, serve as the highway over which potential web service clients travel to find service providers, make contact, and deliver products.

Service-oriented by design, OFBiz is a natural for building and deploying both web service clients and web service providers. Any OFBiz web application (webapp) may both consume web services and act as a web service provider within the same application or in an unlimited number of OFBiz webapps.

Within the web service producer/consumer model, service providers are responsible for accepting and validating requests for service and delivering the product. Consumers must find service providers, request service, and accept delivery of the product. There are a number of ad-hoc and formal standards that have evolved over the last few years to help facilitate the business of enabling web services, including, but not limited to, URL parameter passing, XML-RPC, and Simple Object Access Protocol (SOAP) based messaging. OFBiz provides built-in support with tools and integration points to make implementing both service provider and consumer web services a snap.

Requesting web services using URL parameters

There are many web service providers that require nothing more than URL parameter passing to request a service. These service providers take HTTP/HTTPS request parameters as appended to a prospective consumer's URL, and process requests according to the passed parameter values. Services are delivered back to the requestor through the client's HTTP/HTTPS response message or as a separate HTTP/HTTPS request message exchange.

An example of such a real world web service is the PayPal **Payments Standard** payment processing service. This web service expects requests to come in on an advertised URL with request particulars appended to the URL as request parameters. Prospective consuming systems send HTTP/HTTPS request messages to the PayPal URL asking for service. Once a request for service has been accepted by PayPal, the Payments Standard web service responds and delivers service using the HTTP/HTTPS response message.

A separate web service, also involving PayPal, called the **Instant Payment Notification** (**IPN**) web service is an example of a web service in which parameters are passed on the URL from the service provider to a consumer such as OFBiz. In this case, OFBiz listens on a configured URL for an HTTP/HTTPS request message from PayPal. When one is received, OFBiz responds appropriately, taking delivery of PayPal service.

Note: to implement a PayPal IPN client within an OFBiz web application, you must provide PayPal a destination URL that maps to a valid OFBiz request-map, and then process any incoming URL parameters according to the PayPal IPN directions.

Getting ready

To act as a web service client and pass parameters on the URL within an OFBiz Java Event or Service, make sure you include the following Java packages in your program:

```
import java.io.IOException;
import java.net.URL;
import java.net.URLConnection;
import javax.Servlet.http.HttpServletRequest;
import javax.servlet.http.HttpServletResponse;
```

How to do it...

To request a service using URL parameters, follow these steps:

1. Within an existing OFBiz Java program (either an Event, Service, or any other) method, create a Java `HashMap` containing the name/value pairs that you wish to pass on the URL. For example:

   ```
   Map parameters = UtilMisc.toMap("param1", "A", "param2", "B");
   ```

2. Use the OFBiz-provided `UtilHttp.urlEncodeArgs` method to properly encode the parameters directly from the `HashMap` into a Java `String`. For example:

   ```
   String encodedParameters = UtilHttp.urlEncodeArgs(parameters,
                                                       false);
   ```

3. Build a URL and add the encoded parameter string to the URL:

   ```
   String redirectUrl = "http://www.somehost.com";
   String redirectString = redirectUrl + "?" + encodedParameters;
   ```

4. Send the request by way of the `HttpServletResponse` object's redirect method.

   ```
   try {
       response.sendRedirect(redirectString);
   }
   catch (IOException e) {
       // process errors here
       return "error";
   }
   ```

How it works...

In a very simple web service client scenario, OFBiz acts on behalf of a user or another OFBiz process and makes a web service consumer request of a remote service provider. The request is sent using a HTTP/HTTPS request message with one or more service parameters appended to the URL. The URL is the location on the web of the service provider.

Because the scenario described above is a one-way message exchange—that is, the request message is delivered to the destination URL, but OFBiz does not wait around for a response message—there must be assumptions made about how the web service provider will deliver service. Many times, service is delivered through a totally separate message exchange, initiated by first making the one-way request as described earlier.

To illustrate how this may play out, we consider the PayPal Payments Standard web service. This web service may be invoked from OFBiz in at least two different ways. For example, one approach is to include an HTML form on an OFBiz web page with a **Submit** button. The **Submit** button when clicked redirects the browser (with the request message) to the PayPal web service site passing the form contents as is.

An alternative implementation is to have an HTML form on an OFBiz web page with a **Submit** button that, when clicked, forwards the browser's request of an OFBiz Service (or Event). In this case, the OFBiz Event or Service will take the form attribute values (from the request message) and create a URL for the PayPal web service location. The original form attribute values and any other information as provided by the context or through database reads is appended to the URL. OFBiz then redirects the user's original request message using the sendRedirect method on the HttpServletResponse object to effectively send the user, by way of a browser and an appropriately crafted URL, to the PayPal web service.

Building URL request parameters out of plain Java strings can be tricky given the nature of the characters used to construct request parameters and delimit multiple parameter strings. For example, how do you pass a space character as part of a parameter when spaces are used as delimiters?

Enter URL encoding. URL encoding takes certain characters, deemed "special" characters, and "escapes" them so that they may be used as part of a request parameter string. OFBiz provides an easy-to-use encoder (and decoder) method(s): the UrlEncodeArgs method on the UtilHttp utility that takes as an argument a Java Map and returns an encoded string that may then be appended to a URL as shown earlier.

 Note: an exhaustive treatment of URL encoding is beyond the scope of this book. For more information on HTML and ASCII character codes and encoding symbols, please see http://www.ascii.cl/htmlcodes.htm

There's more...

The `UrlEncodeArgs` method has two modes of operation: selecting the `false` method-parameter value will encode using only an ampersand (`&`) symbol while the `true` parameter value tells OFBiz to use `&amp` as the encoding string. Based on the web service provider's instructions, you will need to determine which mode is appropriate for your application.

Many web services do not require encoded values. You will need to verify for each service whether or not it is necessary to encode and decode URL parameters. For example, the PayPal IPN web service sends request parameters without any encoding. When returning IPN messages, the client web service is, however, instructed to encode parameters.

PayPal IPN is strictly a server-to-server (there is no human intervention) messaging system where message traffic is transported across the web from one server URL to another. PayPal is the web service provider while, in this scenario, OFBiz acts as the web service client. It works something like shown in the following diagram:

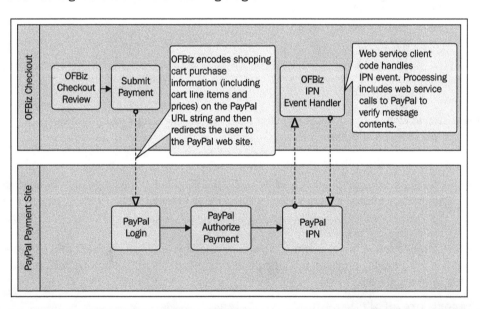

Requesting web services using an HttpClient

Many web services are implemented using HTTP/HTTPS request methods and parameters passed as part of the request's message body. These requests for service mimic a user sitting at a browser submitting HTML forms and waiting for server response. Service providers read HTTP/HTTPS request header information and name/value request message parameter pairs, and deliver service through the HTTP/HTTPS response message.

Writing clients for these types of web services usually require a synchronous call to the service provider. From within your OFBiz client code, you initiate a call to a service provider and then wait until a response (or timeout) is received. Unlike the PayPal Payments Standard service described earlier, the OFBiz client program does not redirect HTTP/HTTPS request messages to another URL.

There are a number of examples within the out-of-the-box OFBiz project of service providers that use the HTTP/HTTPS request message body to exchange information with OFBiz clients. They include, but are not limited to:

- Authorize.net Payment Services
- ClearCommerce Payment Services
- Go Software RiTA
- ValueLink Prepaid/Gift Card Payment Services
- DHL, FedEx, United Parcel Services (UPS), and United States Post Office Shipping Services
- CDYNE Web Based Services
- PayPal Payments Pro

Getting ready

The first step in writing any web service client is to gather the following information about how the target web service operates:

- The URL on the web for the service provider
- Any connection parameters and/or HTTP/HTTPS request message header settings that must be passed as required by the service provider
- The HTTP/HTTPS connection verb (get, post, or other)

Within a Java program, to send and receive web service messages as a client and use the built-in HTTP client utility provided by OFBiz, make sure you have the following Java packages imported in your program:

```
import org.ofbiz.base.util.HttpClient;
import org.ofbiz.base.util.HttpClientException;
```

How to do it...

You can request a web service by following these steps:

1. Create a connection string that includes the URL of the target web service and the type of request:

   ```
   String connectString =
           "http://www.some_web_service_url.com/serviceName";
   ```

2. Within your Java program, create an instance of the `HttpClient` object with the URL/connection string passed to the constructor as shown here:

```
HttpClient http = new HttpClient(connectString);
```

3. Create the content of your request as dictated by the target web service provider. For example, some web services expect XML documents; others, simple string parameters. A web service that expects a string of name/value pairs could be coded as follows:

```
http.setParameter("Param1", "X");
http.setParameter("Param2", "Y");
```

4. Send your request using the appropriate method on the `HttpClient` object. For "get" requests, use the `get` method. For "post" requests, use the `post` method as shown here:

```
try {
    response = http.post();
}
catch (HttpClientException e) {
    // Process error conditions here
}
```

5. Handle any service response inline. Unlike the asynchronous nature of the PayPal IPN web service described earlier, `HttpClient` based web services process return calls inline with the initial web service call. Under the covers, the `HttpClient` utility handles all the network connection set up and lower-level message transmissions.

6. There is no need to release or close the connection as OFBiz manages the handoff of connections.

How it works...

When using the `HttpClient` to access web services remote to OFBiz, you send the consumer-side call synchronously; that is, you wait for the return from the remote web service call within your program. The OFBiz integration of the `HttpClient` utility manages the details necessary to open the network connection, maintain direct request and response message exchanges, and close the connection upon completion of processing.

There's more...

The OFBiz implementation of the `HttpClient` object provides several convenience constructors, which may be useful depending on your processing needs. These include:

```
// To create a new client object and connect using a URL object
// instead of a String
URL url = "https://www.some_host.com/";
HttpClient http = new HttpClient(url);

// To create a new client object using a Java Map containing
// request parameters
HttpClient http = new HttpClient(url, UtilMisc.toMap("param1", "X",
                                                     "param2", "Y");

//To create a new client object with a parameter map and
// header settings
HttpClient http = new HttpClient(connectString,
                                 UtilMisc.toMap("param1", "X"),
        UtilMisc.toMap("User-Agent, "Mozilla/4.0"));
```

See also

OFBiz provides an integration of the Apache `HttpClient` software package: the **Jakarta Commons HTTP Client** that is accessed by creating a new `HttpClient` object. Any method you can call on, the original Apache `HttpClient` object is available in the OFBiz implementation. This includes full support for HTTPS (SSL) clients. For more information, please see the Jakarta Commons HTTP Client web page:

`http://hc.apache.org/httpclient-3.x/`

Creating HttpClients and passing XML documents

There are many examples within the OFBiz out-of-the-box code base of web service clients that call real world web services and pass XML documents as part of the payload. These web services clients use the `HttpClient` as described in the previous recipe in addition to XML document preparation utilities to build the necessary message content used to communicate with external web services.

In this section, we discuss how to write your own web service client(s) and exchange XML documents with one or more external-to-OFBiz web services providers.

Getting ready

The first step in writing any web services client is to gather the following facts about how the target web service operates:

- The URL on the web for the service provider
- Any connection parameters and/or HTTP/HTTPS request message header settings that must be passed as required by the service provider
- The HTTP/HTTPS connection verb (get, post, or other)

To write a web service client that passes one or more XML documents, import at least the following into your Java program:

```
// Use these to build an XML document
import org.ofbiz.base.util.UtilXml;
import org.w3c.dom.Document;
import org.w3c.dom.Element;
import org.xml.sax.SAXException;

// Use these to send/receive web services client services:
import org.ofbiz.base.util.HttpClient;
import org.ofbiz.base.util.HttpClientException;
```

How to do it...

To create an HttpClient and pass XML documents, follow these steps:

1. Create a connection string that includes the URL of the target web service and the type of request:

```
String connectString =
        "http://www.some_web_service_url.com/serviceName";
```

2. Within your Java program, create an instance of the HttpClient object with the URL/connection string passed to the constructor as shown here:

```
HttpClient http = new HttpClient(connectString);
```

3. Create the XML document as prescribed by the target web service. For example, the following code snippet was taken from the UpsServices.java program where an XML document is sent to the target web service:

```
Document rateRequestDoc =
    UtilXml.makeEmptyXmlDocument("RatingServiceSelectionRequest");
Element rateRequestElement = rateRequestDoc.getDocumentElement();
rateRequestElement.setAttribute("xml:lang", "en-US");
```

```
// XML request header
Element requestElement =
        UtilXml.addChildElement(rateRequestElement, "Request",
                                rateRequestDoc);
// Code removed…

// Example, setting up required and optional XML document
// elements: the pickup type
Element pickupElement =
        UtilXml.addChildElement(rateRequestElement, "PickupType",
                                rateRequestDoc);
// Code removed…

// Example setting more elements, this time: package info
String maxWeightStr =
        UtilProperties.getPropertyValue(serviceConfigProps,
                        "shipment.ups.max.estimate.weight", "99");
BigDecimal maxWeight = new BigDecimal("99");
// Code removed…

// Use OFBiz UtilXml utility to create the XML document
try {
    rateRequestString = UtilXml.writeXmlDocument(rateRequestDoc);
}
catch (IOException e) {
    String ioeErrMsg =
        "Error writing RatingServiceSelectionRequest XML Document"
        + " to a String: " + e.toString();
    Debug.logError(e, ioeErrMsg, module);
    return ServiceUtil.returnFailure(ioeErrMsg);
}
// More code removed…

// Call to the method that eventually calls the UPS web service
try {
    rateResponseString =
                sendUpsRequest("Rate", xmlString.toString());
}
catch (UpsConnectException e) {
    // Process errors here
}
```

4. Invoke the `HttpClient` object to call the target web service and pass the XML document within the request message. For example, using the `UpsServices.java` program from step 3, the call to the `HttpClient` object looks something like the following:

```
public static String sendUpsRequest(String upsService,
                String xmlString) throws UpsConnectException {
    // Code removed...
    HttpClient http = new HttpClient(conStr);
    // You may set a timeout in milliseconds
    http.setTimeout(timeout * 1000);
    http.setAllowUntrusted(true);
    String response = null;
    try {
        response = http.post(xmlString);
    }
    catch (HttpClientException e) {
        // Process errors here
    }
    // Handle the return response as necessary here
}
```

5. Process the response from the web service call inline.

6. There is no need to release or close the connection as OFBiz manages the handoff of network connections transparent to the developer.

How it works...

The `HttpClient` utility may be used to send and receive XML documents as directed by web service providers. When using the `HttpClient`, web service client requests are made inline with code logic. Once established, communications between the `HttpClient` and the target web service are streamed directly across the HTTP/HTTPS connection, bypassing OFBiz.

Creating XML-RPC web service clients

XML-RPC-based web services expect service requests in the "XML-RPC" specification format. If you need to access a web service as a client using XML-RPC, then this section is for you. OFBiz provides a utility based in the Apache XML-RPC project that exposes everything necessary to easily write Java-based XML-RPC clients.

Getting ready

Gather the following information about how the target web service operates:

- ▶ Determine the URL of the web service provider
- ▶ Determine the procedure, function, and/or method to be called
- ▶ Determine any connection parameters

Don't forget to import the following:

```
import org.apache.xmlrpc.client.XmlRpcClient;
import org.apache.xmlrpc.client.XmlRpcClientConfigImpl;
import org.apache.xmlrpc.XmlRpcException;
import java.net.URL
```

How to do it...

To create XML-RPC web service clients, follow these steps:

1. Create an instance of the `XmlRpcClient` object as shown here:

   ```
   XmlRpcClient client =  new XmlRpcClient();
   ```

2. Create an instance of the `XmlRpcClient` configuration object:

   ```
   XmlRpcClientConfigImpl config = new XmlRpcClientConfigImpl();
   ```

3. Set the `XmlRpcClient` configuration with the target URL and other parameters as dictated by the web service provider. Wrap the call to the URL in a `try/catch` block as shown:

   ```
   try {
      config.setServerURL(new URL(
                "http://localhost:8080/webtools/control/xmlrpc"));
   }
   catch (MalformedURLException me) {
       // Add error processing here
   }
   ```

4. Set configuration parameters as shown here. For example, if the target web service requires basic HTML form authentication, set the `config` object as shown:

   ```
   config.setBasicUserName("admin");
   config.setBasicPassword("ofbiz");
   ```

5. Associate the `config` object with the `XmlRpcClient` object:

   ```
   client.setConfig(config);
   ```

6. Marshal any parameters that are to be sent to the web service:

```
Object[] params = new Object[]{10, "message from xml-rpc client"};
```

7. Call the web service by invoking the `execute` method on the client object. Don't forget to specify the remote procedure, function, or Java method to call. Wrap the call in a `try/catch` block:

```
try {
    Integer result = (Integer) client.execute("testSvc", params);
}
catch(XmlRpcException xe) {
    // Add error processing here
}
```

8. Process results.

How it works...

The XML-RPC standard is a remote procedure calling mechanism that may use HTTP/HTTPS as the network transport. (Note: XML-RPC may also run over RMI). XML-RPC web service consumers specify a procedure (or Java method) name and requesting parameters in an XML request document, and the web service provider returns, as payload within the HTTP/HTTPS response message, an XML document with either a service response or error message.

XML-RPC procedure parameters may be (in the vocabulary of the XML-RPC specification) scalars, numbers, strings, dates as well as complex records (or "struct(s)"), and arrays structures. Practically speaking, the Apache XML-RPC implementation supports all primitive Java types including long, byte, short, double as well as calendar objects, timezone setting, and milliseconds.

The response format has a content-type of `text/xml`. The body of the response contains a single XML structure containing a `methodResponse` element, a single `params` element that contains a `param` element.

See also

For more details, visit the **XML-RPC Specification** page at:

```
http://www.xmlrpc.com/spec
```

Becoming an XML-RPC web service provider

XML-RPC provides a straightforward XML-based mechanism for providing web-based services such as publishing information. Any OFBiz Service may act as an XML-RPC web service provider simply by setting the Service's `export` configuration setting to `true` and using the OFBiz XML-RPC event handler (`org.ofbiz.webapp.event.XmlRpcEventHandler`) wrapper to receive XML-RPC requests and route them to the proper OFBiz Service for handling.

Getting ready

OFBiz provides an XML-RPC event handler, extending the basic `XmlRpcHttpServer` that comes with the integrated Apache XML-RPC libraries. To use it, you must include an entry in a `controller.xml` file of the web application where the XML-RPC call will be published. This entry should look something like the following. (If the following line does not already exist either within the `common-controller.xml` file or your local web application's `controller.xml` file, add it to either file):

```
<handler name="xmlrpc" type="request"
        class="org.ofbiz.webapp.event.XmlRpcEventHandler"/>
```

You must also include a `request-map` similar to the following that instructs the OFBiz controller for the web application handling the XML-RPC request to use the generic OFBiz XML-RPC handler:

```
<!-- No need to track server hits or visits for an XML-RPC URI -->
<!-- Also note: the XML-RPC request will contain the name of the
     OFBiz Service to call -->
<request-map uri="xmlrpc" track-serverhit="false"
             track-visit="false">
  <event type="xmlrpc"/>
  <response name="error" type="none"/>
  <response name="success" type="none"/>
</request-map>
```

Finally, the target Service called through the XML-RPC execute method must exist and must have, in its Service definition, the `export` flag set to `true`. For example, if the following client call (in Java) is invoked by a remote consumer:

```
<service name="myTestService" engine="java" export="true"
         validate="false" require-new-transaction="true"
         location="org.ofbiz.common.CommonServices"
         invoke="testService">
  <description>Test service</description>
  <attribute name="defaultValue" type="Double" mode="IN"
             default-value="999.9999"/>
  <attribute name="message" type="String" mode="IN" optional="true"/>
  <attribute name="resp" type="String" mode="OUT"/>
</service>
```

How to do it...

To enable XML-RPC service provider, follow these steps:

1. Create a Service as a method in any existing OFBiz Service's class (or create a new class) that takes the standard OFBiz Service's context map parameters and processes them. For example, the following OFBiz Service is called `myTestService`. This Service could be deployed using the Service definition shown:

```
public static Map<String, Object> myTestService(
            DispatchContext dctx, Map<String, ?> context) {
    Map<String, Object> response = ServiceUtil.returnSuccess();
    if (context.size() > 0) {
        for (Map.Entry<String, ?> entry: context.entrySet()) {
            Object cKey = entry.getKey();
            Object value = entry.getValue();
            // Process Service parameters
        }
    }
    return response;
}
```

2. Rebuild the Component containing the new Service.

3. Restart OFBiz.

4. Test with an XML-RPC client.

How it works...

The OFBiz XML-RPC event handler acts as a wrapper for any OFBiz Service that may want to provide web services based on the XML-RPC specification. It is called from the controller servlet when HTTP/HTTPS request messages are received for the configured URL.

The XML-RPC event handler, based on the Java Apache XML-RPC libraries, manages all the web service interface details such as extracting the XML elements from the request message and passing those to the target Service as name/value pairs (in the standard OFBiz Service context map.) It also handles authentication and the formatting of the HTTP/HTTPS response message, based on the results returned from the Service call, to the web service consumer.

As a result, the developer of any XML-RPC web service need only concentrate on the business logic of the Service and not on the details of implementing the XML-RPC specification.

Please see the **Apache XML-RPC Server** website:

```
http://ws.apache.org/xmlrpc/server.html
```

OFBiz SOAP messaging clients

Simple Object Access Protocol (**SOAP**) is a protocol for exchanging structured information in a decentralized, distributed environment. It is XML-based and consists of three parts:

- An envelope that defines a framework for describing what is in a message and how to process the message
- A set of encoding rules for expressing instances of application-defined data types
- A convention for representing remote procedure calls and responses

To illustrate just how easy it is to use OFBiz to create an unlimited number of SOAP-based web service clients, we shall discuss writing an SOAP-based client to request service from a real world web service: the U.S. National Weather Service's National Digital Forecast Database (NDFD). This web service provides a number of useful weather-related products. To keep our example simple, we shall request service from the NWS operation that provides the latitude and longitude for a given (valid) ZIP code. (Note: this web service only supports ZIP codes for the Continental United States, Alaska, Hawaii, and Puerto Rico).

 For more information about the NWS web service, please see:
```
http://www.nws.noaa.gov/forecasts/xml/
```

To view the WSDL for all the operations supported by this web service, point your web browser to:

```
http://www.weather.gov/forecasts/xml/SOAP_server/ndfdXMLserver.php#
```

To see the WSDL for just the zip code operation, select the **LatLonListZipCode** link.

Getting ready

Verify that the web service is up and running by viewing the WSDL in your browser:

```
http://www.weather.gov/forecasts/xml/DWMLgen/wsdl/ndfdXML.wsdl
```

While technically not part of the creation of an SOAP web service client, to illustrate many of the points of this chapter we shall describe a simple HTML form that allows us to enter in ZIP codes from a browser instead of hardcoding values in our SOAP client-code. This form shall be part of the myWebapp main web page built elsewhere in this book. In this way, we may also return results in real time to the same web page as contains the form.

In addition to the HTML form, we shall build an OFBiz Service that takes the web page form, creates the appropriate SOAP message envelope, and calls the NWS web service.

For all this to work, we will also need to create a request-map in the myComponent Component's myWebapp webapp controller.xml file that maps the form's URI request location to our OFBiz Service. To get started, the steps are as follows:

1. Create an HTML form to allow for dynamic and repeated entry of a ZIP code value. Shown here is a simple form created on the myWebapp (within myComponent). When the **run test** button is clicked, this form will call an OFBiz Service. This can be seen in the following figure:

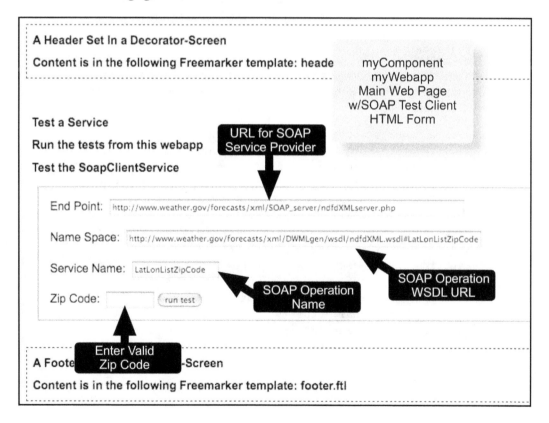

2. The (abbreviated) HTML form looks something like this:

```
<form name="soapClient"
        action="<@ofbizUrl>soapClientService</@ofbizUrl>"
        method=post>
  <#-- HTML removed to improve readability -->
  <label for="01">Zip Code:</label>
  <input type="text" id="01"  name="param1" value="" size="7"/>
  <input id="smt"  style="display: inline" type="submit"
          class="smallSubmit" value="run test"/>
</form>
```

3. Add a request mapping in the `controller.xml` file for the `myWebapp` webapp:

```
<!-- ======= Testing Soap Client ===== -->
<request-map uri="soapClientService">
  <security https="false" auth="false"/>
  <event type="service" invoke="soapClientService"/>
  <response name="success" type="view" value="main"/>
  <response name="error" type="view" value="main"/>
</request-map>
```

4. Add a Service model definition in an existing Service definition file for the OFBiz Service that will accept web page form parameters and send them to the NWS service:

```
<service name="soapClientService" engine="java"
        location="org.ofbiz.myComponent.myNewclasses.MyWebServices"
        invoke="soapClientService">
  <description>Example SOAP client web service</description>
  <attribute name="endPoint" type="String" mode="IN"
              optional="true"/>
  <attribute name="namespace" type="String" mode="IN"
              optional="true"/>
  <attribute name="serviceName" type="String" mode="IN"
              optional="true"/>
  <attribute name="param1" type="String" mode="IN"
              optional="true"/>
  <attribute name="result" type="String" mode="OUT"
              optional="true"/>
</service>
```

How to do it...

In this section, we look at the specifics of creating an SOAP client to call the U.S. National Weather Service web service and get the latitude and longitude given a ZIP code as passed from an HTML form:

1. Import the following JAR files:

```
// All the magic is in the following Axis client classes
// They do all the hard work of creating SOAP wrappers
// and dealing with the XML
import org.apache.axis.client.Call;
import org.apache.axis.client.Service;

// We also need these JAR files
import javax.xml.namespace.QName;
import java.net.MalformedURLException;
import java.net.URL;
import java.util.ArrayList;
import java.util.List;
import java.util.Map;
```

2. Code the client request based on the WSDL. Note that we have already studied the WSDL and know what the remote service is looking for. The following method, called the soapClientService OFBiz Service, is all that is needed to call the NWS web service and return an XML document containing our Service response:

```
public static Map<String, Object> soapClientService(
                    DispatchContext dctx, Map context) {
    Map results = FastMap.newInstance();
    results.put("result", "success");
    // Get everything we need out of the context (the HTML Form)
    String endPoint = (String) context.get("endPoint");
    URL endpoint = null;
    // Define the web services end point as a URL
    try {
        endpoint = new URL(endPoint);
    }
    catch (MalformedURLException e) {
        Debug.log("Location not a valid URL" +e);
    }
    Service service = null;
    Call call = null;
    try {
        // Instantiate a new Axis Service object
        service = new Service();
```

```
        // And create a call object from the Service
        call = (Call) service.createCall();
        call.setTargetEndpointAddress(endpoint);
        String nameSpace = null;
        // Just in case, validate the FORM variables
        if(UtilValidate.isNotEmpty(
                    (String) context.get("namespace"))) {
            nameSpace = (String) context.get("namespace");
        }
        String serviceName = null;
        if(UtilValidate.isNotEmpty(
                    (String) context.get("serviceName"))) {
            serviceName = (String) context.get("serviceName");
        }
        // This is how we tell NWS which procedure to invoke
        call.setOperationName(new QName(nameSpace,serviceName));
        // Since this is an artificial program and we know
        // that there is only a single input parameter for this
        // service that is the zip code, we are just going
        // to force it. Making this Service more generic is left
        // as an exercise for the reader.
        String zipcode = (String) context.get("param1");
        // This is where we make the call and let OFBiz and Axis
        // do all the heavy lifting
        Object ret = (String) call.invoke(new Object[] {zipcode});
        // And, hopefully, we return in line with a useful result
        results.put("result", ret.toString());
    }
    catch (Exception e) {
        Debug.log("Exception when running our SOAP client test: "
                    +e);
        results.put("result", "error: ");
    }
    // Note: we are returning the results as is and not extracting
    // each parameter as sent by the NWS web service.
    return results;
}
```

3. Build the myComponent Component.

4. Restart OFBiz and navigate to myComponent webapp using:

```
http://localhost:8080/mywebapp/control/main
```

How it works...

Like other web service clients, OFBiz SOAP-based clients first request access to a remote web service and then, when access is granted, consume the Service directly from the service provider inline with the programming logic in which they are embedded. Using the OFBiz SOAP integration greatly simplifies the business of writing SOAP web service client code.

In this example, results are returned directly to the calling web page as shown here:

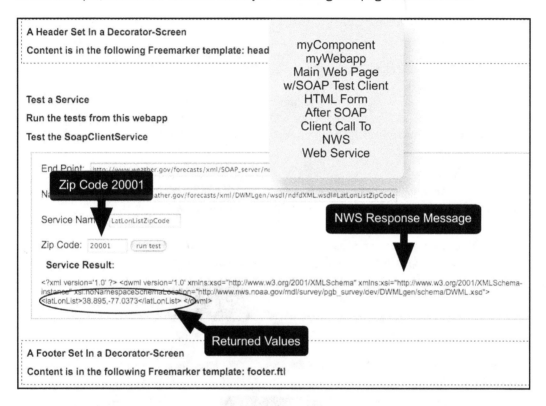

There's more...

You may use the WebTools **Run Service** service utility to invoke the NWS service by making a few simple changes to the Service definition for the `testRemoteSoap` Service that is part of OFBiz out-of-the-box. The `testRemoteSoap` Service definition is found in:

```
~framework/common/servicedef/services_test.xml
```

The following is the code:

```
<!-- the location = endpoint -->
<!-- invoke parameter is the name of the service to invoke
     for example LatLonListZipCode -->
<service name="testRemoteSoap" engine="soap" export="true"
         location=
 "http://www.weather.gov/forecasts/xml/SOAP_server/ndfdXMLserver.php"
         invoke="LatLonListZipCode">
  <description>A service to invoke the NWS web service</description>
  <namespace>
    http://www.weather.gov/forecasts/xml/DWMLgen/wsdl/
    ndfdXML.wsdl#LatLonListZipCode
  </namespace>
  <attribute name="ZipCode" type="String" mode="IN"/>
  <attribute name="invoke" type="String" mode="IN" />
  <attribute name="result" type="String" mode="OUT"/>
</service>
```

 Note: the out-of-the-box OFBiz Service definition for the `testRemoteSoap` calls a web service that is no longer operational. It will not work as is.

After changing the `testRemoteSoap` Service definition, you may invoke the Service without creating a web page or HTML form using the WebTools **Run Service** utility as shown here:

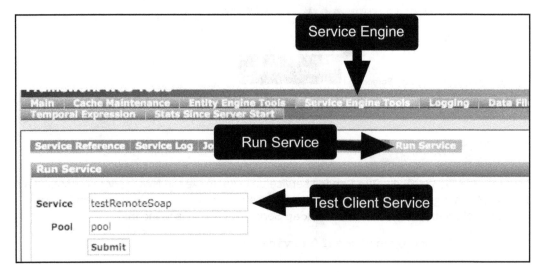

Submitting the **Run Service** form will bring up a form that will allow entry of the required ZIP code input for the NWS web service as shown here:

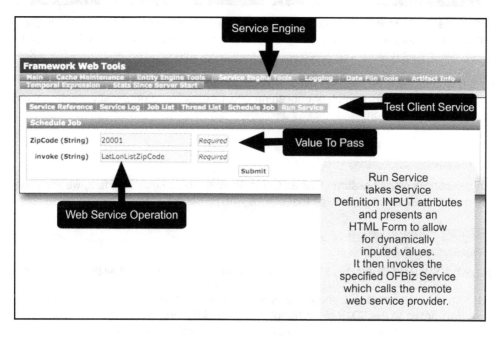

Hitting the **Submit** button will run the `testRemoteSoap` OFBiz Service that, in turn, calls the NWS web service `LatLonListZipCode` procedure with the ZIP code as entered on the **Run Service** form as part of the service request. Web service return values or an error code are displayed on the **Schedule Job** web page as shown here:

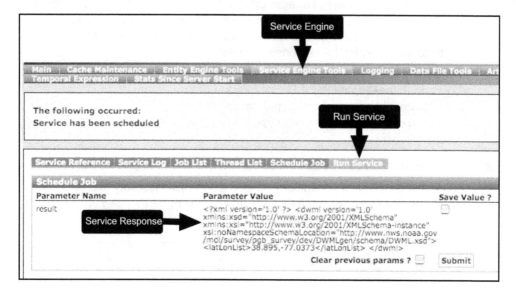

Generating a WSDL document

Web Service Descriptor Language (**WSDL**) is an XML-based grammar used to define the interface provided by a web service. Web service providers publish—on the Web—one or more WSDL(s) describing how an interested service consumer may connect and consume a Service.

The work of creating SOAP web service's WSDLs by hand can be tedious and error-prone. Fortunately, OFBiz makes the job of publishing WSDLs easy by automatically creating them from a Service's definition.

Getting ready

For this section, we shall assume that an OFBiz Service already exists. In fact, we shall use as an illustration the `testSvc` Service that comes with OFBiz out-of-the-box.

How to do it...

To publish a SOAP WSDL for this Service, or any other OFBiz Service, follow these simple steps:

1. To indicate that a URL should be handled as a SOAP web service request and be forwarded to the SOAP event handler, add the following line to the `controller.xml` file for the OFBiz webapp where the web service will be exposed:

   ```
   <handler name="soap" type="request"
            class="org.ofbiz.webapp.event.SOAPEventHandler"/>
   ```

2. Add one or more `controller.xml` `request-map` definitions for the location of the SOAP-based web service(s). For example, the following is taken from the WebTools Component `controller.xml` file. Note response types are set to `none`. This indicates that the Service will handle the caller's response message by streaming directly to the HTTP/HTTPS response variable:

   ```
   <request-map uri="SOAPService">
     <event type="soap"/>
     <response name="error" type="none"/>
     <response name="success" type="none"/>
   </request-map>
   ```

3. Make sure the Service's definition has the `export` attribute set to `true`.

4. Ensure that the Service's definition has all the settings necessary to create a valid WSDL. For example, at a minimum, define the engine as `soap` and provide `location` and `invoke` attribute values as shown here:

   ```
   <service name="testSoap" engine= "soap" export = "true"
            location=
   ```

```
               "http://localhost:8080/webtools/control/SOAPService?WSDL"
               invoke="testSvc">
   <description>A SOAP Service with WSDL found here </description>
   <attribute name="message" type="String" mode="IN"
               optional="true" />
   <attribute name="response" type="String" mode="OUT" />
</service>
```

5. Create a WSDL as follows: (You can see this in your browser by going to the
    location attribute value specified in the Service definition):

```
<wsdl:definitions targetNamespace=
                        "http://ofbiz.apache.org/service/">
   <wsdl:message name="testSoapResponse">
     <wsdl:part name="resp" type="xsd:string"/>
   </wsdl:message>
   <wsdl:message name="testSoapRequest">
     <wsdl:part name="message" type="xsd:string"/>
   </wsdl:message>
   <wsdl:portType name="testSoapPortType">
     <wsdl:operation name="testSoap">
       <wsdl:input message="tns:testSoapRequest"/>
       <wsdl:output message="tns:testSoapResponse"/>
     </wsdl:operation>
   </wsdl:portType>
   <wsdl:binding name="testSoapSoapBinding"
                 type="tns:testSoapPortType">
     <soap:binding style="document"
           transport="http://schemas.xmlsoap.org/soap/http"/>
     <wsdl:operation name="testSoap">
       <soap:operation soapAction=
               "http://localhost:8080/webtools/control/SOAPService"
           style="rpc"/>
       <wsdl:input>
         <soap:body encodingStyle=
                    "http://schemas.xmlsoap.org/soap/encoding/"
                 namespace="http://ofbiz.apache.org/service/"
                 use="literal"/>
       </wsdl:input>
       <wsdl:output>
         <soap:body encodingStyle=
                    "http://schemas.xmlsoap.org/soap/encoding/"
                 namespace="http://ofbiz.apache.org/service/"
                 use="literal"/>
       </wsdl:output>
```

```
        </wsdl:operation>
      </wsdl:binding>
      <wsdl:service name="testSoap">
        <wsdl:port binding="tns:testSoapSoapBinding"
                name="testSoapPort">
          <soap:address location=
                "http://localhost:8080/webtools/control/SOAPService"/>
        </wsdl:port>
      </wsdl:service>
    </wsdl:definitions>
```

6. If this is a new Service or if you have changed some Service definition settings, restart OFBiz to make the changes effective. That is all you need to do.

How it works...

The OFBiz `ModelService` object provides a handy set of methods that can take an instance of a Service's definition and dynamically construct a WSDL based on configured attributes. For example, the following table maps WSDL XML specification requirements to OFBiz Service definition elements and attributes:

Element	Usage	OFBiz service definition attribute
definitions	The root element. Declares the name of the web service.	name attribute.
types	Declares the data types supported and transmitted by the web service.	Taken from the INPUT/OUTPUT attributes defined for the Service.
message	Describes one or more "messages". Messages have a name and may have "parts" that may refer to parameters and/or return values. Each message declares a one-way request or one-way response operation.	message attribute if provided.
portType	portType is used to combine messages into a complete one-way or round-trip service delivery operation.	invoke attribute. Where the invoke represents the web service operations. Note: for a web service that supports many operations, you will need to provide one or more service definitions.
binding	The network transport is declared through the binding. SOAP-specific details are declared here.	Default to SOAP because the engine setting is SOAP.
service	The URL (Web address) for this web service.	location attribute.

To create a WSDL from a Service's definition, OFBiz simply gets the service's model from the service dispatch context and passes configuration settings to a WSDL generation tool (provided by the Apache Axis library).

When a request for an OFBiz resource comes across the wire and the destination is a URL of an OFBiz Service that has been mapped to the OFBiz SOAP event handler, OFBiz first checks to see if the request has a WSDL request parameter affixed to it. If it does, then OFBiz will automatically call the service `DispatchContext` object's `getWSDL` method to get the WSDL, based on the Service's definition, and return the WSDL as part of the HTTP/HTTPS response message.

 Note: this only works if you first define an OFBiz service and then force requests for that Service to be processed by the SOAP Event handler.

Creating SOAP-compliant web services

If publishing SOAP web service WSDLs seemed rather easy, then publishing SOAP-based web services is not much harder. OFBiz makes the task of taking any service and making it SOAP compatible a snap. This leaves the Service designer and developer to figure out how to process the business logic that makes up your service's product.

In this section, we shall create a new OFBiz SOAP-based web service. We shall proceed by first creating an OFBiz Service, and then configuring this service to use the existing OFBiz SOAP event handler, so that we may transparently handle SOAP messages. That is all we need to do to become an SOAP-based web service provider.

Our OFBiz Service is very simple: when a consumer asks for service at our published web service URL, we respond by:

1. Querying the configured data source (database) for a list of product names.
2. Returning to the client, an XML document with the product list, in the properly wrapped SOAP envelope.

To keep this simple, we shall rely on previously discussed work and will create our web service within the `myWebapp` OFBiz web application ("webapp") and `myComponent` OFBiz Component built as part of a previous chapter. Therefore, our `controller.xml` file will be located in:

`~/hot-deploy/myComponent/webapp/myWebapp/WEB-INF/controller.xml`

Getting ready

For this recipe, we first need to ensure the following:

1. To indicate that a URL should be handled as an SOAP web service request and be forwarded to the SOAP event handler, add the following line to the `controller.xml` file for the OFBiz webapp where the web service will be exposed:

    ```
    <handler name="soap" type="request"
            class="org.ofbiz.webapp.event.SOAPEventHandler"/>
    ```

2. Add one or more `controller.xml` `request-map` definitions for the location of the web service(s). For example, the following is taken from the WebTools Component `controller.xml` file. (Note response types are set to `none`. This indicates that the service will handle response back to the caller by streaming directly to the HTTP response variable):

    ```
    <request-map uri="getProductName">
      <event type="soap"/>
      <response name="error" type="none"/>
      <response name="success" type="none"/>
    </request-map>
    ```

3. Add a Service definition for the SOAP Service in a Services definition file of choice. Remember to set the `export` attribute to `true` as well as the `location`, `engine`, and `invoke` attributes accordingly:

    ```
    <service name="soapWebService" engine="soap" export="true"
        location=
         "http://localhost:8080/myWebapp/control/soapGetProductNames"
        invoke="soapWebService">
      <attribute name="message" type="String" mode="IN"
                optional="true"/>
      <attribute name="resp" type="String" mode="OUT"/>
    </service>
    ```

How to do it...

To create a SOAP-compliant service, follow these steps:

1. Create the target OFBiz Service. If using Java, create a method in an existing Services class file (preferably a services file) or create a new Java class file. For example:

    ```
    // Very Simple SOAP Web Service
    // Takes on INPUT parameters and returns a List of product names.
    // What makes this a web service? The Service Definition
    ```

```
// and a controller.xml request-map setting using the
// "soap" engine type
public static Map<String, Object> soapWebService(
                      DispatchContext dctx, Map context) {
    Map result = ServiceUtil.returnSuccess();
    GenericDelegator delegator = dctx.getDelegator();
    List<String> names= FastList.newInstance();
    try {
        List gvList =delegator.findList("Product",
                          null,null,null,null,false);
        names = EntityUtil.getFieldListFromEntityList(gvList,

                      "productNames", false);

        result.put("productNames", names);
    }
    catch(GenericEntityException ge) {
        return ServiceUtil.returnError("error message");
    }
    return result;
}
```

2. Build the Java class file containing the OFBiz Service method.

3. Restart OFBiz.

4. Observe the WSDL by directing your browser to:

   `http://localhost:8080/myWebapp/control/getProductNames/`
   `soapWebService?wsdl`

   or to see all the services available from this OFBiz instance:

   `http://localhost:8080/myWebapp/control/getProductNames?WSDL`

5. Test with a remote SOAP-based consumer.

How it works...

The following diagram shows at a high level the interaction between the OFBiz SOAP Event handler and an OFBiz Service that implements the processing logic for an SOAP-based web service:

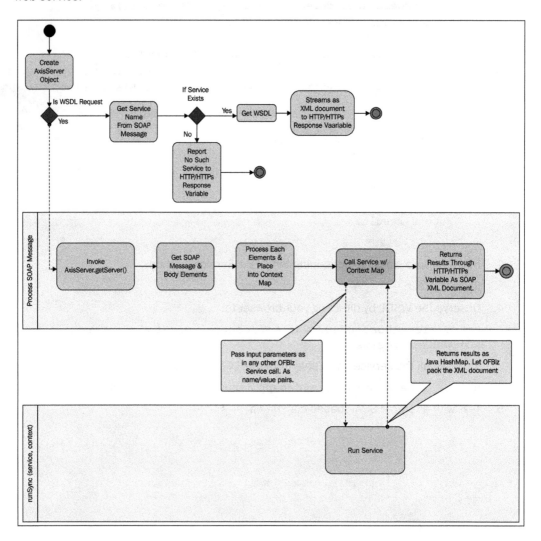

The OFBiz SOAP Event handler does all the hard work of taking the incoming HTTP/HTTPS request and peeling off the SOAP envelope to reveal all the included SOAP messages. Once extracted, the SOAP messages are further processed and used to find the appropriate OFBiz Service to invoke and to pass service INPUT parameters as a service would normally expect to see them: as a name/value pair map structure.

The SOAP Event handler invokes the target service and then takes any results from the service invocation and creates the proper XML document response message as well as the HTTP/HTTPS response message SOAP wrapper.

Finally, the Event handler sends the HTTP/HTTPS response message back to the web services client.

In many cases, the OFBiz SOAP Event handler provides all the SOAP and XML document preparation necessary to publish an OFBiz Service as a web service as is.

9
OFBiz Tips and Tricks

In this chapter, find helpful hints regarding the following:

- ▶ Fixing Java memory allocation errors
- ▶ Reloading OFBiz seed and demo data
- ▶ Creating new seed data files
- ▶ Changing the administrative user's password
- ▶ Creating a new administrative user login
- ▶ Getting the OFBiz version number
- ▶ Building an OFBiz instance
- ▶ Building a single OFBiz Component
- ▶ Creating a new OFBiz Component or Application
- ▶ Creating a FreeMarker transformation
- ▶ Preparing data using Groovy
- ▶ Pop-up a new browser window (FreeMarker)
- ▶ Installing an OFBiz Visual Theme
- ▶ Creating an OFBiz Visual Theme

Introduction

While the recipes in this book are presented in no particular order, an attempt has been made to group related topics together under the same chapter heading. This chapter is organized a bit differently. It is a collection of mostly unrelated recipes that are important and should be discussed, but that don't fall within the purvey of any of the existing chapters.

Fixing Java memory allocation errors

If you get a Java memory error similar to that shown in the following figure on either an OFBiz error page or in the OFBiz logfile, you may or may not be able to continue running OFBiz. JVM memory allocation is configured in the startup file(s) or, if you are starting OFBiz from the command line, as a parameter passed to the Java executable.

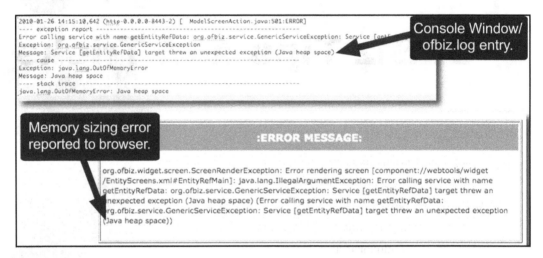

Getting ready

First of all, ensure the following:

1. If OFBiz is already running, shut it down by either running the shutdown script provided or killing the associated Java process.

2. Navigate to the OFBiz install directory.

How to do it...

Java memory allocations like the one shown in the earlier figure can be fixed by following these steps:

1. If you are using startup files such as `startofbiz.sh` for Unix systems or `startofbiz.bat` on a Windows computer, open the appropriate startup file. If you are starting OFBiz from the command line, you simply enter in the new parameters as part of the initial Java command.

2. For example, to change the JVM heap setting within the `startofbiz.bat` file, locate the line that reads:

   ```
   "%JAVA_HOME%\bin\java" -Xms128M -Xmx512M -jar ofbiz.jar >
   runtime\logs\console.log
   ```

3. Change the -Xms128M and -Xmx512M values to something more appropriate to your system's capabilities. For example, to set these values to 512 MB and 1024 MB respectively, make the following changes:

```
"%JAVA_HOME%\bin\java" -Xms512M -Xmx1024M -jar ofbiz.jar >
runtime\logs\console.log
```

4. Save your changes.

5. Restart OFBiz.

How it works...

As with all Java programs, OFBiz runs entirely within a Java Virtual Machine (JVM). The JVM is responsible for providing OFBiz with a number of runtime environmental Services, including memory management. The JVM makes initial memory allocations from the parameters passed at invocation.

There's more...

Details concerning Java's memory management support is beyond the scope of this book. All you need to know to configure OFBiz, however, is that the parameters used to tell the JVM how much memory to allocate for the entire OFBiz runtime instance are:

```
-msXXm  -mxXXm
```

Where ms is the initial "heap-size" in megabytes (or millions of bytes). In this situation, the "heap-size" refers to the memory allocated and available for OFBiz to use as it sees fit.

mx is the maximum heap-size. The mx value should not be larger than your computer's physical memory size.

For example, -ms512m -mx2000m sets an initial heap size of 512 MB and a maximum size of 2 GB.

Reloading OFBiz seed and demo data

You may rebuild OFBiz and reload all configured databases with distribution data from the original seed and demo data files included in the download at any time. If you have not changed the original data loading configuration, the procedure discussed here will return your OFBiz database to its initial state.

The state of the official OFBiz download site is in a constant state of flux. As of this writing, Release 9.04 downloads acquired from the stable release download link require a build as described here before they will work correctly. This could change at anytime. Be aware of this requirement and act accordingly

Note: "seed" data is considered essential to successful OFBiz operations. "Demo" data is provided by the various applications to demonstrate the workings of application features and functions.

Getting ready

Before following this recipe, ensure these steps are performed:

1. Navigate to the OFBiz install directory.
2. If OFBiz is running, shut it down.
3. Open a command line or console window.

How to do it...

To return the OFBiz database to its initial state by reloading all "seed" and "demo" data, run the provided ANT tool as follows:

1. From the command line, execute the following command:

   ```
   ant run-install
   ```

2. Restart OFBiz.

How it works...

Running the provided ANT script with a target of `run-install` starts up OFBiz and instructs it to reload the database with all available data. OFBiz will search the current instance's installation environment looking for configured data files to load, and then load those files' data into the database. Upon completion of this process, OFBiz shuts down and returns control to the command-line prompt.

There's more...

Running ANT `run-install` without first removing existing data will write data as record updates to the database. Many times you will want to first purge the database of existing data, and then run the ANT script with the `run-install` target to return the database to its initial, out-of-the-box state. To first remove all the data from the configured database(s), run the following from the OFBiz install directory:

```
ant clean-data
```

If you want to remove all log files, compiled class files, as well as data from the database, you can run the following ANT command from the install directory:

```
ant clean-all
```

Creating new seed data files

Seed data files are used to load the OFBiz database—sometimes referred to as "seeding" the database—with data whenever the ANT database data loading targets are called. You may create new seed data files as needed. Each Component may have one or more seed data files, and OFBiz supports an unlimited number of seed data files across the installation.

Getting ready

Navigate to the top-level directory for the component that will contain the new seed data file.

How to do it...

Follow this recipe to create new seed data files:

1. Open the ofbiz-component.xml file in an editor of your choice.

2. Add an entity-resource XML declaration with the seed data file's location as shown here. The location attribute contains the location of the file relative to the containing Component. The reader-name attribute tells OFBiz when to load the file based on ANT targets.

   ```xml
   <entity-resource type="data" reader-name="seed"
                    loader="main" location="data/mainSeedData.xml"/>
   <!-- For data to be loaded on the "demo" pass, use the
        reader-name of demo -->
   <entity-resource type="data" reader-name="demo"
                    loader="main" location="data/mainDemoData.xml"/>
   ```

3. Create a new seed data file by copying any existing seed data file and removing everything from the file except the initial version declaration and the start and end entity-engine-xml declarations. For example, when opened in a plain text editor, your file should look something like the following:

   ```xml
   <?xml version="1.0" encoding="UTF-8"?>
   <entity-engine-xml>
   </entity-engine-xml>
   ```

4. Add one or more entries to this file representing the data to be loaded. The basic format for an entry is:

   ```xml
   <EntityName1 fieldName1 = "value"...fieldNameN="value" />
   ```

5. Save the file.

6. Navigate to the OFBiz Install directory.

7. Run the ANT database load script.

```
ant run-install
```

8. Restart OFBiz.

How it works...

OFBiz provides a flexible database data loading environment by allowing the user to configure which data files should be loaded when the ANT tool is used. Within the `ofbiz-component.xml` file, the presence of the `entity-resource` element tells OFBiz that there is a data file to load, where that file is located, and under what circumstances to load data from that file into the database. This last piece of information is configured using the `reader-name` attribute. The `reader-name` attribute is set to a "reader" (for example, a `reader-name` of `seed`) based on which ANT target should be used to load the file. The following table translates reader-name values to ANT targets.

 Note: some `reader-name` values and equivalent ANT targets are cumulative in that they not only load files for the specified reader, but may also load other files. For example, the `run-install` target loads all data files, including `seed` and `demo`.

If you want to load only specific types of data into the database using ANT commands, the following table maps the `reader-name` (type of data to load) with the equivalent ANT command to use:

reader-name value	ANT command (target)	Usage
NA	ant clean-data	To clean all data from the database in preparation for clean build.
demo	ant run-install	Loads all types of data files.
seed	ant run-install-seed	Load seed data. For example, geographic information.
seed-initial	ant run-install-initial	Loads seed-initial type only.
ext	ant run-install-extseed	Loads seed data types: seed, seed-initial, and ext.
ext-test	ant run-install-exttest	Loads seed data types: seed, seed-initial, ext, ext-test in that order.

There's more...

By choosing to run various ANT data loading scripts depending on your needs, you may selectively load data from files into the database while leaving other database entities untouched. This is a helpful facility should you need to repeatedly load seed or demo data while testing.

Within data files to be loaded using the ANT tool, all entity field values are represented as strings. OFBiz manages the translation of the string value to the target database data type. If you want a verbatim or literal value to be loaded in the database or value that contains characters XML parsers view as "special" or "trigger" values, then wrap your value with CDATA sections as shown here:

```
<fieldName><![CDATA[verbatim string goes here!]]></fieldName>
```

Changing the administrative user's password

If you are the OFBiz administrator and you forget this user's password, you could be out of luck since the administrator (the "admin" user login) has all the privileges necessary to perform any OFBiz task, including logging in and assigning the admin user a new password.

If you find yourself in this situation, there is no easy way to retrieve this password such that you may use it to log in. The only solution to this problem is to reset the password by directly manipulating the correct entity in the database, or let OFBiz do that for you using the following recipe.

Getting ready

Before following this recipe, ensure these steps are performed:

1. Navigate to the OFBiz install directory.
2. Open a command line or console window.
3. If you are running OFBiz, it is best to stop it at this time.

How to do it...

To reset the admin password, follow these steps:

1. From the OFBiz install directory, run the following command:
   ```
   ant load-admin-user-login -DuserLoginId=admin
   ```
2. Restart OFBiz.

3. Log in to OFBiz as the admin user where the login user name is "admin" and the password is "ofbiz".

4. When prompted to change the admin user's password, enter the new password or "ofbiz" to maintain the existing value.

How it works...

This `ant` command rebuilds OFBiz and reloads the database with a single entity containing the admin user's login password of "ofbiz". It also sets a flag indicating that the next time this user logs in, they must change this password. Based on this flag setting, when next the admin user logs in, they will be prompted to change the password. At that time, the password may be reset to a new value or the "ofbiz" value can be re-entered.

There's more...

You can always change the admin password using the OFBiz **Party Manager** application, assuming you can log in as "admin". In fact, that is the preferred method. This recipe is intended to be used in those situations where the admin user cannot log in to access the **Party Manager**. As such, ensure that access to this ANT script is well protected from malicious use.

Creating a new administrative user

To change the default administrative user's login from "admin" to another value, follow this recipe.

Getting ready

Ensure these steps are performed:

1. Navigate to the OFBiz install directory.

2. If OFBiz is already running, shut it down.

3. Open a command line window.

How to do it...

To create a new administrative user, perform these steps:

1. Type in the following `ant` command where `NewUserLoginName` is the value for the user login identifier:

```
ant load-admin-user-login -DuserLoginId=NewUserLoginName
```

The NewUserLoginName as shown must be less than or equal to 255 ASCII characters in length, and not contain any back or space characters.

2. Restart OFBiz.

3. Log in to OFBiz as the administrative user using the new login name as entered in step 1 and using a password of "ofbiz".

4. When prompted to change the administrative user's password, enter the new password or "ofbiz" to maintain the existing value.

How it works...

Similar to the process for changing the admin user's password as described in the previous recipe, this ant command rebuilds OFBiz and loads the database with a single entity containing the admin user's new login name as passed from the ant invocation and a password of "ofbiz". It also sets a flag indicating that the next time this user logs in using this new login name, they must change the password. When next the administrative user logs in, they will be prompted to change the password. At that time, the password may be reset to a new value or the "ofbiz" value can be re-entered.

There's more...

The administrative user's login and password may be changed in this way any number of times.

Getting the OFBiz version number

You may use the ANT build script found in the install directory to easily find the OFBiz version number.

 Note: this recipe only works if you are running a copy of OFBiz downloaded from the Subversion repository and you have a Subversion client on your CLASSPATH. Pre-built packages of 9.04 versions downloaded from the official Apache OFBiz website download page do not support this feature at the time of this writing.

Getting ready

There are no special prerequisite requirements to perform this task.

How to do it...

You can find the OFBiz version by following these steps.

1. From the install directory, open a command line or console window (note: you do not need to stop OFBiz to perform this task).

2. Type in the following command:

   ```
   ant svninfo
   ```

3. You will observe results as shown:

   ```
   Buildfile: build.xml
   svninfo:
         [echo] Creating svninfo
         [echo] Rev:903429
       [delete] Deleting: /opt/release9.04/runtime/svninfo_tmp.xml
         [echo] Done!
   BUILD SUCCESSFUL
   Total time: 3 seconds
   ```

4. The [echo] Rev:903429 line gives us the version number as 903429.

How it works...

OFBiz uses the ANT Java build tool to both build OFBiz code creating Java executables and manage the OFBiz build process. The version number returned from the ANT command line invocation is the "last changed revision", meaning this is the last version that saw an actual commit to the code base.

 Note: the "last changed revision" may not be the same as the version number associated with your download. To find the version number of your download, you will need to either run the Subversion command to get the version number or, if you don't have Subversion installed locally, retrieve the version number from your download directly from the text file that contains this information.

There's more...

If you are running Subversion locally, you may use Subversion to determine the OFBiz version number as shown here:

1. From the install directory, open a command line.

2. Type in the following command:

   ```
   svn info
   ```

3. Observe the results as posted to the command line:

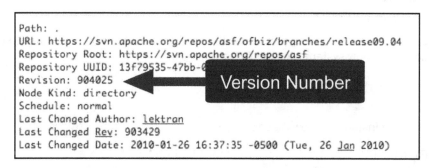

```
Path: .
URL: https://svn.apache.org/repos/asf/ofbiz/branches/release09.04
Repository Root: https://svn.apache.org/repos/asf
Repository UUID: 13f79535-47bb-0
Revision: 904025
Node Kind: directory
Schedule: normal
Last Changed Author: lektran
Last Changed Rev: 903429
Last Changed Date: 2010-01-26 16:37:35 -0500 (Tue, 26 Jan 2010)
```

Version Number

In addition to using ANT or Subversion to determine the installed version, you may also go directly to the location on disk where the version information is kept. You may need to resort to this if you do not have Subversion installed or if your ANT file is corrupt. The process is shown here:

1. Navigate to the OFBiz install directory.

2. Find the `.svn` sub-directory as shown in the figure.

3. From inside the `.svn` directory, locate the `entries` file.

4. Open this file in any text editor and observe the version number information as shown here:

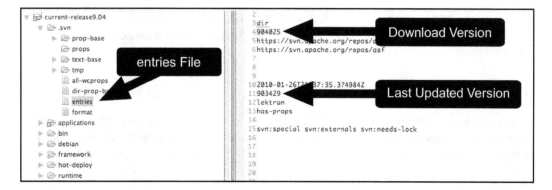

Building an OFBiz instance

OFBiz may be rebuilt from source code at any time. Included with the download are all the scripts necessary to recreate OFBiz from source by the following recipe.

Getting ready

The following prerequisites have to be ensured:

1. Navigate to the OFBiz install directory.
2. Open a command-line window.
3. Stop OFBiz if it is running (either use the provided script per the operating system in use or, for Unix systems, kill the OFBiz process).

How to do it...

To build an OFBiz instance, follow these steps:

1. From the OFBiz install directory, run the following command:

   ```
   ant
   ```

2. When the command-line prompt is returned, restart OFBiz. Rebuilds are effective after restart.

How it works...

OFBiz consists of many artifacts, including plenty of Java code. To recompile and reassemble the OFBiz Java code into an executable package, the Apache ANT Java build tool is used. Without making further changes from the initial download, invoking `ant` from the OFBiz install directory without any targets (parameters) instructs `ant` to run the `build` target as configured in the provided `build.xml` file.

If run from the OFBiz install directory, ANT will transverse each sub-directory and invoke any `build.xml` files present. In this way, OFBiz may be rebuilt from a single location and invocation.

There's more...

If you have downloaded a checkout from Subversion, you will need to build OFBiz before you can successfully start the OFBiz instance. Use the following command to both build OFBiz and create/load the database:

```
ant run-install
```

The entire OFBiz project code base may be "built" at any time. Alternatively, each Component may be built independently from the rest of the project if necessary.

Reasons for rebuilding the entire project may include, but are not limited to:

- Download from Subversion source code repository requires build before startup
- Run JUnit tests
- Reload/rebuild the database
- Changes to a Java program
- Addition of new Java programs (called a Java "class" file)

Reasons to rebuild a single Component may include:

- Patching a Java source file
- Adding/modifying a Java file

See also

For more information on the Apache ANT Java build tool, please see the official Apache ANT website:

```
http://ant.apache.org
```

Building a single OFBiz Component

Each OFBiz Component may be built independently from any other Component. If you only want to add, modify, or delete Java code within a single Component, there is no need to build the entire distribution. You may simply rebuild the Component in which the code is located. You don't even need to stop the currently running instance until after the build is complete and you are ready to test your new build.

Getting ready

Ensure the following prerequisites:

1. Navigate to the Component you wish to rebuild.
2. Open a command-line window.

How to do it...

Build an OFBiz Component by following these steps:

1. From the command line, invoke the following ANT command (on a Unix system):

   ```
   ant
   ```

2. Return to the OFBiz install directory and restart OFBiz.

How it works...

Each OFBiz Component has a `build.xml` customized to rebuild that Component in its root directory location. By navigating to the top-level directory for any Component and invoking the `ant` command at that location, you automatically tell `ant` to use the `build.xml` file located there as its configuration setting.

 If you want to do this in Windows, you will need to specify the path to the `ant` batch file.

Creating a new OFBiz Component or Application

Recent developments within the OFBiz community have resulted in the download distribution containing an ANT script to quickly and easily build new OFBiz Components and Applications.

Getting ready

Ensure the following prerequisites:

1. Decide on a name for the new Component. For example, if you want to call your new Component "myComponent" then the name will be `myComponent`.

2. Determine if the Component will have an OFBiz Application (sometimes referred to as a "webapp") associated with it. Do you want to be able to log in to this Component? If so, then you will need to have at least one OFBiz Application associated with this Component.

3. If the Component is to have an OFBiz Application (a "webapp"), determine a name for this Application. For example, if you wish to call the webapp "myWebApp" then the Application's name is `myWebApp`.

4. Navigate to the OFBiz install directory.

5. If OFBiz is already running, shut it down.

How to do it...

To create a new OFBiz Component, follow these steps:

1. From the command line, type in the following `ant` command:

   ```
   ant create-component
   ```

2. Answer the command-line prompts as described here:

Command line prompt	What to enter
Component name:	The name of the Component. This becomes the directory name and will be used to reference the Component for future access. Do not use spaces between Component name parts. For example, "My New Component" is not a valid Component name. Try "MyNewComponent" instead.
Component resource name:	Resource names are used internally to OFBiz. You can enter in any value here; however, the value `main` is the typical response.
Webapp name:	The name of your OFBiz application. This is used as the directory name for the component sub-directory that is the new OFBiz Application. Do not use spaces for this value. For example, "My New Webapp" is not a valid name. Try "MyNewWebapp" instead.

3. Restart OFBiz.

4. Navigate your browser to:

   ```
   http://localhost:8080/${component_name}/control/main
   ```

   where `${component_name}` is the name of your new Component. For example, if your Component name is `myComponent`, navigate to:

   ```
   http://localhost:8080/myComponent
   ```

How it works...

ANT takes the values as entered on the command line and creates a Component directory structure in the hot-deploy parent directory. This skeletal directory is given an `ofbiz-component.xml` file and all the necessary sub-directories needed for an OFBiz web application ("webapp"). If a "webapp" name and base permissions are provided, the script will install a default HTML login form inside the webapp directory along with a basic controller.xml file configured to enforce user login.

There's more...

Components may be created in any of four locations within OFBiz. Best practices and practical considerations suggest creating new Components in the `hot-deploy` directory because:

▶ Adding a Component in this location does not require any further OFBiz configuration changes

▶ These Components are the last to be loaded, so if there are any Component dependencies, for example, you need data loaded from a framework Component, that has already been loaded

Components may be created without web application interfaces. For example, if you have a new Component that only provides services for other Components or that adds entities to the database, you may not need to build a web interface. If this is the case, there is no need to create the web application portion of the Component.

Creating a FreeMarker transform

If none of the existing FreeMarker transforms meet your requirements, you may always create your own. FreeMarker transforms are Java classes configured to perform an inline conversion when used within a FreeMarker template.

How to do it...

To create your own FreeMarker transform, follow these steps:

1. Create the Java class that implements the `TemplateTransformModel` Java class.

2. Rebuild the Component containing the transform.

3. Add the transform's Java class package name to the following Java property file so that it will be loaded on the CLASSPATH and available for use:

   `~framework/webapp/config/freemarkerTransforms.properties`

4. Restart OFBiz.

5. Use the transform in a FreeMarker template by wrapping content in the transform tags.

How it works...

Writing a Java FreeMarker transformation is a simple way of extending FreeMarker data formatting capabilities for use across the entire OFBiz instance.

There's more...

There are many examples of custom FreeMarker transformations within the OFBiz distribution. For example, the `content` Component has implemented a number of these to assist in the sometimes tricky transformation of raw data into human readable formats:

```
~content/src/org/ofbiz/content/webapp/ftl
```

Preparing data using Groovy

You can use Groovy scripting language to prepare data for any presentation layer screen rendering tool, including the FreeMarker templating engine and OFBiz widgets.

Getting ready

Groovy has been integrated into the OFBiz framework, so using it is as simple as creating a text file with Groovy code and then pointing one or more Screen widget `actions` declarations to the location of the Groovy file.

 Note: a side effect of integration is that execution context information, including the HTTP/HTTPS request message and request parameters, are always available in the Groovy runtime context.

By convention, Groovy files are located in the `webapp/WEB-INF/actions` directory of a containing Component. For example, we could have a Groovy file named `myGroovyFile.groovy` located in the `~myComponent/webapp/WEB-INF/actions` directory.

How to do it...

To prepare "Groovy" data, follow these steps:

1. Create a new text file or open an existing file.
2. Import any required Java classes.
3. Add any Groovy statements, including calls to the entity engine to extract data.
4. Add Groovy statements to move any prepared data to the context.
5. Close the file and save. Groovy files have the `.groovy` suffix.

 Note: changes to Groovy script files do not require OFBiz restarts to be effective.

How it works...

Separating web page layout and style from data is the stuff Model-View-Controller (MVC) web application design patterns are made of. The OFBiz framework enables MVC separation through a number of architectural features, including the separation of web page screen (or "view") definitions from the data that is presented by the views. Web page views and screen layouts may be built using a variety of tools, including the OFBiz Screen widget, FreeMarker templates, and/or other OFBiz widgets.

All these tools support context aware, runtime merging of screen view definitions with data gathered and manipulated using the Groovy scripting language.

There's more...

Groovy is a dynamic scripting language with syntax similar to Java and with many additional features "inspired" by languages such as Python, Ruby, and Smalltalk (`http://groovy.codehouse.org`). Some commonly used Groovy patterns found within the OFBiz code base are listed in the following table:

Usage	Groovy code
Import statements	`import.java.util*;` `import org.ofbiz.base.util.UtilMisc;`
To load request parameters from a Form or URL HTTP/HTTPS request	`myRequestParam=parameters.someParam;`

Set request parameters into the context directly from a URL request	`// Note: all request parameters are`
	`// assumed to be Strings`
	`// Unless otherwise converted`
	`context.paramA+ "_X" = parameters.AparamA`
	`context.paramB+ "_Y" = parameters.AparamB`

Create a new Java List structure Check for an empty list	`newList = [];` `if(newList) { // do something }`
Create an empty Java Map structure (key, value pairs)	`someMap = [:];` `someMap.keyName=value;`

"Safe Navigation Operator" (Used to avoid `NullPointerException`)	`Z = ObjectY.find("Q");`
	`R = Z?.AA?.BB`
	`// R is null if Z or ZZ.AA are null`

"Elvis Operator"	`context.someStringValue = someStringValue`
	`?: "Default Value";`
	`    context.someNumber =`
	`someNumber + x ?: 0;`

"For" loops	`ListOfGenericValues.each {`
	`    x ->`
	`      // do Something here`
	`}`

See also

The OFBiz installation is replete with hundreds of examples of Groovy code. The best reference is to consult the code.

Pop-up new browser windows

You may embed JavaScript directly in FreeMarker templates to perform interactive actions such as to pop-up new browser windows based on user mouse clicks.

How to do it...

To pop-up a new window on mouse events, follow these steps:

1. Open the FreeMarker template file.

2. Add the following Java script at the beginning of the file:

```
<SCRIPT language="javascript">
  function call_fieldlookup(rootForumId, parentForumId ) {
      var obj_lookupwindow = window.open(
          "addSubSite?rootForumId=" + rootForumId +
          "&parentForumId=" + parentForumId,
          'FieldLookup',
          'width=500,height=250,scrollbars=yes,
          status=no,top='+my+',left='+mx+',
          dependent=yes,alwaysRaised=yes');
      obj_lookupwindow.opener = window;
      obj_lookupwindow.focus();
  }
</script>
```

3. Add the following HTML to call the JavaScript:

```
<a href = "javascript:call_fieldlookup(
               '<@ofbizUrl>LookupFeature</@ofbizUrl>')">
  <img src =
    "<@ofbizContentUrl>/images/fieldlookup.gif</@ofbizContentUrl>"
    width="16" height="16" border="0"
    alt="${uiLabelMap.CommonClickHereForFieldLookup}">
</a>
```

4. Save and close the file.

 Note: all changes to FreeMarker files are immediate. You do not need to restart OFBiz to observe results.

How it works...

FreeMarker supports embedded JavaScripts as shown. Scripts are passed as is within the final HTML document to the browser where they are executed by users as needed.

There's more...

There are a number of JavaScripts packaged with the distribution. Most are found in the `~images/webapp/images` directory.

Also included within OFBiz is the Prototype JavaScript Framework:

`http://www.prototypejs.org/`

And the Dojo JavaScript toolkit:

`http://www.dojotoolkit.org/`

Examples of both are found throughout OFBiz.

Installing an OFBiz Visual Theme

OFBiz "Visual Themes" are like "skins" that allow for a consistent look and feel across all participating OFBiz Applications. A Visual Theme is a collection of files, usually packaged as an OFBiz Component that may include, among other things, FreeMarker templates for:

- A top navigation bar
- A secondary navigation bar
- A HTML web page HEAD element called the "header"
- An HTML web page footer section
- Error messages web page insert

As well as all the CSS, images, and JavaScript necessary to customize the look and feel of one or more OFBiz web applications. Visual Themes provide a way to collect and organize most of the elements necessary to standardize website fonts, typefaces, menu behaviors, and web page presentation layout.

Themes are applied to theme-enabled web pages based on user preferences. A user may switch among available and installed themes at will by selecting the **Visual Themes** link on any out-of-the-box back-office application web page. Users must be logged in to change a theme.

Getting ready

You may either create your own Visual Theme as an OFBiz component in the `themes` directory, or download a theme from the OFBiz theme gallery located at:

`http://cwiki.apache.org/confluence/x/5ABk`

How to do it...

To change a theme, follow these steps:

1. If you have downloaded a theme, unzip it into the `themes` Component directory. This creates a new Component with the same name as the theme.

2. Stop OFBiz if it is running.

3. From the OFBiz install directory, open a command line.

4. Run the following command:

   `ant run-install-seed`

5. Restart OFBiz.

 Note: the above instructions are taken from the official OFBiz Wiki page. Please be aware the `ant run-install-seed` command will rebuild your instance of OFBiz and reload all data marked as seed data, including the new Visual Theme data. If you have any seed data that has changed since the last time the `ant run-install-seed` —for example the default admin user's password—this data will be overwritten with data from unaltered seed data files.

How it works...

Packaging Visual Themes as Components is a convenience that allows for easy installation of new themes and retrieval of theme resources with a minimum amount of work. When you download a Visual Theme to your local OFBiz instance, you are preparing to install an OFBiz Component that includes the OFBiz artifacts necessary to apply a theme to one or more OFBiz web pages. These artifacts have been customized to deliver a unique visual web page presentation or "theme".

Running the ANT script from the OFBiz install directory installs a theme by loading the database with all the necessary information concerning the location of a theme's resources. Once in the database, theme resources are ready to be applied to web pages.

You may also install a theme's seed data directly into the database using the WebTools entity engine **XML Import to DataSource** form. If you load the seed data in this way, there is no need to stop and restart OFBiz.

There's more...

The default installed theme that comes with the download is configured in `~/framework/common/config/general.properties`. In the absence of any other settings such as seed data loaded by an application, this is the theme that is applied until a user changes theme preferences.

 Note: it is possible to have a Visual Theme that is not installed as an OFBiz Component. For example, the OFBiz e-commerce application implements a default theme, `EC_DEFAULT`, using only database values containing pointers to necessary theme resources. If you are curious about how this works, take a look at the following seed data file:

`~/specialpurpose/ecommerce/data/EcommerceTypeData.xml`

Creating an OFBiz Visual Theme

In OFBiz release 9.04, support for Visual Themes has been extended to allow users to define and install themes of their own creation. Creating a new Visual Theme is as straightforward as creating an OFBiz Component.

Getting ready

As with most OFBiz endeavors, it is often easiest to copy an existing theme and then make changes to the copied resources. To get started, use the following theme checklist to determine values for your new Visual Theme:

New theme checklist		
Value	**Example**	**Usage**
Theme To Copy From	`BlueLight`	Select an existing OFBiz 9.04 theme. Themes distributed with the download are found in the `themes` directory located directly beneath the OFBiz installation top-level directory. Any Visual Theme is sufficient to use as a source to copy from.
New Theme Name	`myTheme`	Choose a name for the new theme. Any name—as a combination of 20 ASCII characters or less and no spaces—will work.
New Component Name	`myTheme`	Usually, the new Component name and the new theme name are the same. However, the new Component name may be any value not already taken by another Component. Names must be 20 ASCII characters or less and not contain spaces or blank characters.

New theme checklist		
Value	**Example**	**Usage**

New Webapp Name	`myTheme`	The rules for the webapp name are the same for any OFBiz webapp: 20 characters or less, no spaces or blanks characters allowed. Webapp names must be unique names across the install. The webapp name is set within `ofbiz-component.xml` as shown here:
		
		`<webapp name="myTheme"`
		`        title="myTheme"`
		`        menu-name="secondary"`
		`        server="default-server"`
		`        location="webapp/myTheme"`
		`        mount-point="/myTheme"`
		`        app-bar-display="false"/>`

** Example values will be used in the following process to create a new OFBiz Visual Theme. These are only an example. Your mileage may vary.

How to do it...

To create your own Visual Theme, follow these steps:

1. Create a new Visual Theme as a new OFBiz Component within the `themes` directory. For example, for a new theme called `myTheme`, create a new directory (folder for Windows users) under the `themes` directory called `myTheme`.

2. Copy an existing theme's directory contents to the newly created Component. For example, copy all the directories and files in the `BlueLight` directory to the `myTheme` directory, making sure to preserve the directory structure.

3. Make your planned theme changes (web page layout and styling) to the new theme's artifacts by manipulating the appropriate files or replacing an existing file:

   □ Edit FreeMarker and/or JavaScript files.

   □ Edit Cascading Style Sheet (CSS) files.

   □ Add and/or removing theme images.

   □ Replace the theme logo with another image.

   □ Create a new screenshot and replace the existing `screenshot.jpg` file. (Note: this is optional. This file is used to graphically depict the Visual Theme's appearance).

4. Edit the `ofbiz-component.xml` file for the new theme Component. Refer an existing theme `ofbiz-component.xml` file if necessary. Pay special attention to the many `name` and `location` attributes as they need to be changed to reflect the newly created theme's name and directory location.

5. Modify the theme's seed data file found in the `~/data` directory to reflect any changes you may have made to theme artifacts. You may also need to change the name of this file to reflect any name changes made in the `ofbiz-component.xml` file.

6. Edit the `~/WEB-INF/web.xml` deployment descriptor file using an existing `web.xml` file as an example.

7. Stop OFBiz if it is running.

8. From the OFBiz install directory, run the following ANT script to load the database with new theme information. This theme configuration information is in the seed file modified in step 5:

```
ant run-install-seed
```

9. Restart OFBiz.

10. Test the new theme by navigating to any WebTools page and selecting the **Visual Themes** link. From the list of themes provided, select the newly installed theme and click the **Done** button. If the theme was successfully installed, web page styling and layout for the target application(s) should change to reflect the new theme's settings.

How it works...

The process of creating a new Visual Theme is pretty straightforward. If you use the examples provided in the distribution as your guide, you can't go wrong. Getting a Visual Theme to render your application's web pages as you would like them to be displayed is a different story. To make a Visual Theme behave as you would like requires intimate knowledge of HTML, CSS, possibly JavaScript, and/or other web page building tools. Such guidance is beyond the scope of this book.

However, understanding how OFBiz screen rendering tools use Visual Theme artifacts to dynamically generate web pages based on the user's context may help in mastering this topic. For example, the OFBiz Screen widget rendering engine has a really handy feature that allows screen developers building web pages from widgets to include elements that are applied at runtime. These elements are resolved based on the execution context and the user's preferences. To avail themselves of this capability, the widget developer includes one or more of the appropriate declarations within the `actions` section of a widget's definition.

Note: most of the out-of-the-box OFBiz Application's screen definitions have been set up to support this feature. That means that when you install a new Visual Theme, web pages within these Applications may be able to implement the new theme automatically without further modification to screen definitions.

To take advantage of this dynamic context-driven screen generation capability, Visual Themes as collections of web page artifacts are used. Themes may include any or all of the following:

- Graphical images of any type
- Cascading Style Sheet (CSS) files
- FreeMarker templates
- JavaScript files
- Other, yet to be specified artifacts that go into building dynamic web pages

In practice, Visual Themes are used to dynamically change the look and feel of one or more OFBiz web pages. For OFBiz web applications supporting Visual Themes, there is a default theme defined that is used to create the application's web pages in the absence of any user preferences to the contrary. The user may change this setting at any time and replace the default theme with another available theme. By installing a new theme as described above, you widen the user's choice of theme selections.

 Some OFBiz Applications do not support user selectable themes. For example, the e-commerce application allows for a single application-wide theme setting. The application of a new theme to the e-commerce application may only be performed using the **Catalog Manager** or as a direct result of modifying the appropriate database entities.

To support more than one collection of theme elements in such a way that OFBiz web applications and users may selectively apply themes in real time, OFBiz persists information about available themes and user preferences in the database. When you create a new Visual Theme and run the ANT data loading script, you are installing the necessary configuration information that allows OFBiz screen rendering tools to resolve web page elements at runtime.

There's more...

You may also install a theme's configuration settings (as found in the seed data file) directly into the database using the WebTools entity engine **XML Import to DataSource** form. If you load the seed data in this way, there is no need to stop and restart OFBiz.

See also

For a more complete treatment of the process behind creating new OFBiz Visual Themes, please see:

```
http://cwiki.apache.org/confluence/display/OFBiz/Home
```

Entity Engine by Example

In this chapter, find the following topics discussed:

- ▸ Putting it all together with a data model example
- ▸ Reading data from an OFBiz data source
- ▸ Working with large result sets
- ▸ Removing data from an OFBiz data source
- ▸ Writing data to an OFBiz data source
- ▸ Using the `EntityUtil` utility programmatically
- ▸ The OFBiz automatic sequence generator
- ▸ An entity operator reference

Introduction

In this chapter, we depart from the usual book format to offer useful Entity Engine hints and tips by way of examples. Each example is designed to help you master some aspect of the OFBiz Entity Engine. Intended for Java developers (and Groovy/BeanShell enthusiasts), you will find many details here offered to optimize your use of the OFBiz Entity Engine and add data-driven features to your own OFBiz Applications.

Before we get started, a few ground rules:

The Entity Engine deals with "data sources" and "entities". In many cases, we shall be referring to the concrete instantiation of a "data source" as a database and "entities" as database tables respectively. This is intentional as in the real world you are not likely to encounter a "data source", but rather a database.

Similarly, OFBiz entities only have meaning within the context of OFBiz. For all practical purposes, an OFBiz entity is the model of a relational database table. In a relational database, tables have column names that are referred to here as "fields". Data is stored in database table records. Records and the term "rows" are used interchangeably here.

Putting it all together with a data model example

Since OFBiz comes with over 900 entities and a ready-made database schema defining the relationships of those entities to one another, we would be hard pressed to find a business situation where the existing data model doesn't meet most of our needs. The OFBiz data model includes entities and entity relationship definitions for everything from managing users, whether they be customers, suppliers, vendors, or the system administrator, to selling products and controlling inventory, handling accounting, creating invoices, and even modeling complex workflow scenarios.

Since the goal of this section is to take you from the conception of a new business idea through an implementation using Entity Engine tools and techniques, we shall not use existing entities, but rather devise a new data model. With a little bit of research, we have come up with a use case that is not directly supported by the existing data model. To illustrate how to create new entities and view-entities, read, write, and remove data from an OFBiz data source, we are going to model the business of a bakery.

Sample use case

As a bakery, we manufacture edible products based on recipes mom brought over from the old country. There are many different types of recipes in our collection, including, but not limited to cakes, cookies, pies, bread, and for those dog lovers, dog treats. We should note here that the number of different types of recipes, and thus the goods we plan to bake using these recipes, should remain open ended and not be limited to the initial five identified.

Within each recipe is a sequential list of ingredients. Each ingredient has a value that represents the amount of the ingredient to use in the recipe and a unit of measure indicator. For example, a recipe may have an ingredient of flour, with an amount of "5" and a unit of measure of "cup". To keep things simple, we shall not consider the list of ingredients as steps in the mixing and/or baking process.

Note: the existing data model does support a process-oriented business operation such as a bakery. We have chosen to ignore certain existing data model entities in favor of going at it alone and doing it ourselves, primarily as a vehicle to demonstrate the versatility of the OFBiz Entity Engine. You are free to use existing entities such as "Product", "ProductConfig", and "ProductConfigItem" to model recipes.

Entity diagram

The data model for our additions to OFBiz are graphically depicted in the following figure. We will be adding four new entities: **Recipe**, **Ingredient**, **RecipeType**, and **RecipeIngredient**, each with primary and foreign keys shown here:

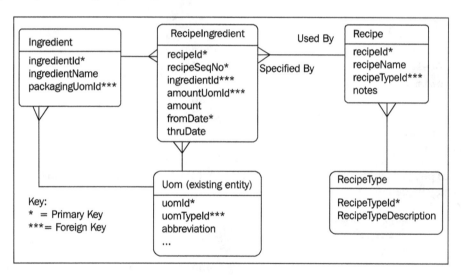

In addition to the four new entities shown in the figure, we shall use the existing **Uom** entity to give our ingredients access to several hundred standardized units of measure (UOM) values already preloaded in the database.

New entity definitions

Based on our business case and data model, we need to create five new entities. Definitions for each of these entities are shown below. We may either create a new entity definition file and update the `component.xml` file with the new entity definition file location, or add these entities to an existing entity definition file. In the interest of time, we shall add these to an existing entity definition file.

In the following entity definitions, notice that we use a package name of `org.ofbiz.bakery`. We are using this name specifically so that we may easily find our entities when using the WebTools **Interactive Entity Reference** utility. As this tool groups together like-named packages, finding a particular entity is made much easier when using a meaningful package name.

The following defines the `Ingredient` entity:

```
<entity entity-name="Ingredient"
        package-name="org.ofbiz.bakery"
        title=
            "One record for each ingredient that makes up a recipe">
    <field name="ingredientId" type="id-ne"></field>
    <field name="ingredientName" type="id"></field>
    <!-- Note: some day make an IngredientType entity -->
    <field name="ingredientType" type="id"></field>
    <field name="packagingUomId" type="id"></field>
    <prim-key field="ingredientId"/>
    <relation type="one" fk-name="REC_ING_UOM" rel-entity-name="Uom">
      <key-map field-name="packagingUomId" rel-field-name="uomId"/>
    </relation>
</entity>
```

The `RecipeType` entity that holds information about the type of recipe (cookies, cakes and so on) may be defined as follows:

```
<entity entity-name="RecipeType"
        package-name="org.ofbiz.bakery"
        title=
            "Recipes come in all shapes and sizes. Keep that info here.">
    <field name="recipeTypeId" type="id-ne"></field>
    <field name="description" type="description"></field>
    <prim-key field="recipeTypeId"/>
</entity>
```

A `Recipe` entity with the unique recipe identifier, a recipe name, and pointers to other related entities (foreign keys) is given here:

```
<entity entity-name="Recipe"
        package-name="org.ofbiz.bakery"
        title="Recipe holds information about our recipes">
  <field name="recipeId" type="id-ne"></field>
  <field name="recipeName" type="id-long"></field>
  <field name="recipeTypeId" type="id"></field>
  <field name="notes" type="very-long"></field>
  <prim-key field="recipeId"/>
  <relation type="one" fk-name="REC_TO_TYPE"
            rel-entity-name="RecipeType">
    <key-map field-name="recipeTypeId"/>
  </relation>
</entity>
```

And finally, the `entity` that ties the recipe with its ingredients is defined here:

```
<entity entity-name="RecipeIngredient"
        package-name="org.ofbiz.bakery"
        title=
          "A recipe is nothing more than a collection of ingredients.
          Here's where the rubber meets the road.">
  <field name="recipeId" type="id-ne"></field>
  <field name="recipeSeqNo" type="numeric"></field>
  <field name="ingredientId" type="id-ne"></field>
  <field name="amountUomId" type="id"></field>
  <field name="amount" type="numeric"></field>
  <field name="fromDate" type="date-time"></field>
  <field name="thruDate" type="date-time"></field>
  <prim-key field="recipeId"/>
  <prim-key field="recipeSeqNumber"/>
  <prim-key field="fromDate"/>

  <relation type="one" fk-name="REC_ING_ING"
            rel-entity-name="Ingredient">
    <key-map field-name="ingredientId"/>
  </relation>
  <relation type="one" fk-name="REC_AMT_UOM" rel-entity-name="Uom">
    <key-map field-name="amountUomId" rel-field-name="uomId"/>
  </relation>
</entity>
```

Once all our new entity definitions are created, the next task is to test these entities to ensure accuracy. An easy and reliable way to begin testing is to first see if the entities are present and viewable using the OFBiz WebTools **Entity Reference - Interactive Version**. To run this test, restart OFBiz, making sure that no obvious entity-related errors are posted to the command-line window and/or primary OFBiz log file (`ofbiz/runtime/ofbiz.log`). If errors are encountered during startup, we need to go back and fix our entity definitions.

If OFBiz startup is successful, we may navigate to the WebTools **Entity Reference - Interactive Version** main web page, and since our new entities were created using the package name `org.ofbiz.bakery`, we may easily scroll down the left side of the web page to locate our package name and link as shown in the following figure:

If you find that your entities are not showing up here, then go back and check each entity definition and or the logfiles. Most definition syntax errors are reported to `~runtime/logs/ofbiz.log` during OFBiz startup.

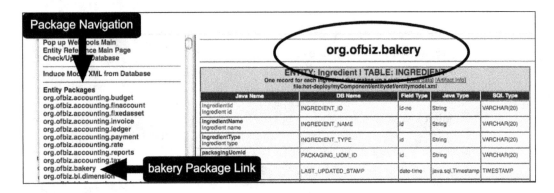

From the WebTools **Entity Reference - Interactive Version**, we may test adding data to our new entities. And so we would, but to speed things up a bit, we shall use the WebTools **XML Data Import** tool to load data a little at a time—so we can view results—from XML documents that we created offline. For example, here we add data to the `RecipeType` entity by copying from a text file and then pasting in the **XML Import to DataSource** tool's HTML form:

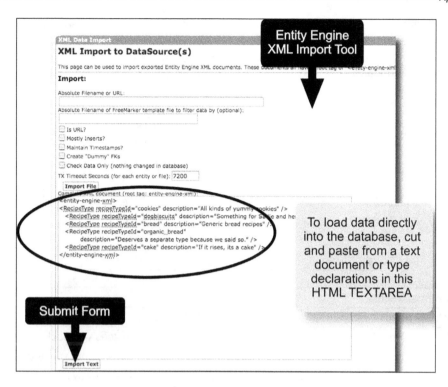

To verify that our data is indeed added to the database, use WebTools and list the **RecipeType** entity as shown here:

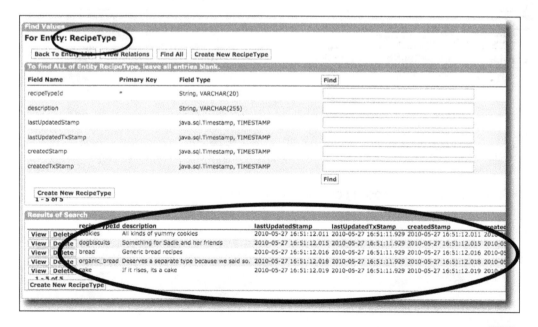

So, it looks like we are on the right track with our entity definitions. In the real world, we would be writing an OFBiz webapp to allow for HTML form-based data entry in addition to loading data directly into the database. For the rest of this chapter, we shall assume that the following data has been preloaded:

Entity name: Ingredient

ingredientId	ingredientName	packagingUomId
10009	eggs	OTH_ea
10001	milk	OTH_ea
10002	pure water	OTH_ea
10003	city water	OTH_ea
10004	wheat flour	OTH_ea
10005	organic wheat flour	OTH_ea
10006	salt	OTH_ea

Entity name: Recipe

recipeId	recipeName	recipeTypeId*	notes
r001	Moms Doggie Delights	dogbiscuits	This one goes way back.
r002	Dont try this one at home!	bread	Same ole stuff but you gotta have it.
r003	Going Nuts, Nut Bread For...	bread	This one goes way back (too).
r004	Moms Goes Green	bread	Green, Healthy Bread. Has spinach to boot!

Entity name: RecipeIngredient

recipeId	recipeSeqNo	ingredientId*	amountUomId*	amount	fromDate
r001	001	10001		1	**
r001	002	10010	VLIQ_qt		**
r001	003	10005	VLIQ_pt		**
r001	004	10002	VLIQ_tsp		**

* Because this field is designated as a foreign key, any values added must already exist in the related table.

** `fromDate` set to "2010-01-01 00:00:00.000" for all records.

2-way SQL join view-entity

A report we want to produce quickly after going live with our new OFBiz bakery and recipe system is a list of all the recipes by type. For example, a list of all the cookie recipes. To create such a list using our existing data model requires that we access more than one entity. To do that, that is, join together data from multiple entities, we create an OFBiz view-entity.

Our first view-entity will merge together data from the `RecipeType` and `Recipe` entity as shown here:

```
<view-entity entity-name="RecipeTypeView"
             package-name="org.ofbiz.bakery"
             title="Show all recipes by type">
   <member-entity entity-alias="REC" entity-name="Recipe"/>
   <member-entity entity-alias="TYP" entity-name="RecipeType"/>
   <alias-all entity-alias="REC"/>
   <alias-all entity-alias="TYP"/>
   <view-link entity-alias="REC" rel-entity-alias="TYP">
     <key-map field-name="recipeTypeId"
              rel-field-name="recipeTypeId"/>
   </view-link>
</view-entity>
```

3-way SQL join view-entity

Not one to gloat over our success so far using the Entity Engine, the next report will draw from three different tables to list all the recipes with ingredients, by type:

```
<view-entity entity-name="RecipeTypeAndIngredientsView"
             package-name="org.ofbiz.bakery"
             title="Show all recipes by type">
   <member-entity entity-alias="REC" entity-name="Recipe"/>
   <member-entity entity-alias="TYP" entity-name="RecipeType"/>
   <member-entity entity-alias="REIN" entity-name="RecipeIngredient"/>
   <alias-all entity-alias="REC"/>
   <alias-all entity-alias="TYP"/>
   <alias-all entity-alias="REIN"/>
   <view-link entity-alias="REC" rel-entity-alias="TYP">
     <key-map field-name="recipeTypeId"
              rel-field-name="recipeTypeId"/>
   </view-link>
   <!-- Note the order of entity-alias here is important.
        Each Recipe record points to one or more
        RecipeIngredient records -->
   <view-link entity-alias="REC" rel-entity-alias="REIN">
```

```
      <key-map field-name="recipeId" />
    </view-link>
    <relation type="many" rel-entity-name="RecipeIngredient">
      <key-map field-name="recipeId"/>
    </relation>
  </view-entity>
```

Writing view-entities is even easier than writing regular entities. Unlike regular entities, where changes to field type definitions or the addition/removal of fields usually requires that you first drop the database table, if you make a mistake with a view-entity, you only need to edit the view-entity definition and restart OFBiz. View-entities are not created or stored as part of the database. Rather, they are used, on demand, to create entity SQL based joins.

View-entity reports

With the view-entities in place, we can easily query the database without constructing complex SQL statements. To test that our new view-entities are doing the job, we can use the OFBiz WebTools **Entity Reference - Interactive Version** to run a quick report as shown here:

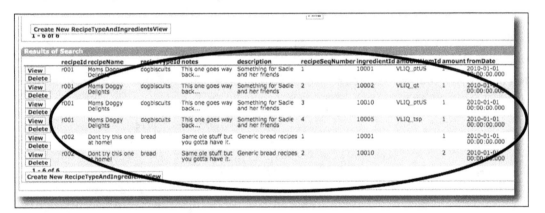

Next steps

That's it. That is how easy it is to augment OFBiz to support additional application data storage needs. Your experiences will be informed by how complex your data model becomes. With OFBiz, you can have your cake and eat it too. You can start by developing a simple prototype as shown in this section, and grow your data management capabilities as your business grows. You can even move your entire database from vendor-to-vendor (tired of Oracle? Ccheckout PostgreSQL, SQL Server, mySQL or just about any database imaginable) without changing a single line of code.

In the next few sections, we shall take a closer look at using some Java application-level tools provided by OFBiz to implement data-driven applications programmatically.

Reading data from an OFBiz data source

Business is booming at the bakery, and we need to move beyond the WebTools Entity Engine interface and start implementing some user-level applications to read from and write to the database. For the remainder of this chapter, we shall assume that we have in place one or more OFBiz Events and/or Services written in Java that will handle the logic of our application's interface to the OFBiz Entity Engine. What remains to be described are specific instances using Entity Engine tools and utilities.

Note: while using the OFBiz Mini-Language and widget tool kit often make reading and writing to an OFBiz data source easier, they are but one option when choosing to use the Entity Engine programmatically. Widgets are discussed elsewhere in this book while the OFBiz Mini-Language is documented on the OFBiz Wiki:

http://cwiki.apache.org/confluence/x/CwFk

To retrieve a single database table row given a table's primary key, follow this example. See the comments within the code for more information. (Note: code is provided for demonstration purposes only. You will need to fill in the gaps in many places to make these code snippets function):

```
import org.ofbiz.entity.GenericDelegator;
import org.ofbiz.entity.GenericEntity;
import org.ofbiz.entity.GenericEntityException;
import org.ofbiz.entity.GenericValue;

// From within a Service, get the GenericDelegator object directly
// from the context
// The object named ctx is passed from the Service Engine as an
// instantiation of the current context
GenericDelegator delegator = ctx.getDelegator();
GenericValue recipe = null;
// All GenericDelegator calls throw GenericEntityException on failure
// So place inside a try/catch block
String recipeId = "r001";          // For demonstration purposes only.
try {
    recipe = delegator.findOne("Recipe",
                    UtilMisc.toMap("recipeId", recipeId), false);
}
```

```
catch (GenericEntityException e) {
    Debug.logWarning(e.getMessage(), module);
}
// recipe is a GenericValue object, so we can access field
// values directly as shown
if(recipe != null) {      // Note: a null GenericValue object is valid
    String recipeName = (String) recipe.get("recipeName");
}
```

To iterate through a list of GenericValue objects as returned by a call to the entity engine, use code similar to the following:

```
// Within an event, get the GenericDelegator from the request
// attribute. As shown here
GenericDelegator delegator =
                (GenericDelegator) request.getAttribute("delegator");
List<GenericValue> recipes = null;
try {
    // The delegator.findList() method returns a Java List or null
    // if no values are found
    recipes = delegator.findList("recipes",
            EntityCondition.makeCondition("recipeId",
            EntityOperator.EQUALS, "r001"), null, null, null, false);
}
catch (GenericEntityException e) {
    return ServiceUtil.returnError(e.getMessage());
}
// recipes contains a list of GenericValue objects. Each object
// represents a single returned record from the data source.
// Loop through this list and extract values as appropriate
if(UtilValidate.isNotEmpty(recipes)) {
    Iterator itr = invoiceItems.iterator();
    while(itr.hasNext()) {
        // Pick off each GenericValue on the list
        GenericValue thisRecipe = (GenericValue) itr.next();
        // Access the thisRecipe GenericValue object just like
        // you would any other
        String recipeId = thisRecipe.getString("recipeId");
        // Do more stuff...
    }
}
```

The following Java code snippets are examples of commonly used OFBiz query constructs.

To return a single database record, that is, a `GenericValue` object, given a primary key value, from the specified table, use the following:

SQL equivalent	`SELECT FROM 'SomeTable' WHERE` `primaryKeyId='SomeValue';`

OFBiz code snippet	<pre>try {
	    GenericValue aValue =
	        delegator.findOne("SomeTable",
	        UtilMisc.toMap("primaryKeyId","SomeVal
	ue"),
	        false);
	}
	catch (GenericEntityException e) {
	    // Process any errors here
	}</pre>

Return all records from the given table. Take all Entity Engine defaults or set required values to `null` as shown here:

SQL equivalent	`SELECT * FROM 'SomeTable';`
OFBiz solution	Use the Entity Engine `GenericDelegator` object's `findList` method to return a list of values. Set all `findList` parameters to `null`.

OFBiz code snippet	<pre>try {
	    List allRecords =
	        delegator.findList("SomeTable",null,null,
	                    null,null,false);
	}
	catch(GenericEntityException ge) {
	    // Process Errors Here
	}</pre>

To select only unique records from a table where a table's column value is equal to some given value, use the following as an example:

SQL equivalent	`SELECT DISTINCT FROM SomeTable WHERE column1='value';`
OFBiz solution	Use the `EntityfindOptions` object to tell OFBiz to find and return only distinct values.

OFBiz code snippet	```// Create an EntityFindOptions object```
	```EntityFindOptions findOptions =```
	``` new EntityFindOptions();```
	```// Set the findOptions to distinct is true```
	```findOptions.setDistinct(true);```
	```EntityCondition findCondition =```
	``` UtilMisc.toList(EntityCondition.```
	```makeCondition(```
	``` 'column1',EntityOperator.EQUALS,```
	``` 'value'));```
	```try {```
	``` List allRecords =```
	``` delegator.findList('SomeTable',```
	``` findCondition, EntityOperator.```
	```AND),```
	``` null,null,findOptions,false);```
	```}```
	```catch(GenericValueException ge) {```
	``` // Process Errors Here```
	```}```

To read data, the following `GenericDelegator` methods are typically used:

GenericDelegator method	Returned result set data type	Usage
`find`	`EntityListIterator`	Used for large data sets.
`findList`	`List<GenericValue>`	Returns a list of one or more `GenericValue` objects, one representing each row returned from the database query.
`findOne`	`GenericValue`	Returns a single `GenericValue` object matching the query conditions.

Note: while there are a fair number of legacy `GenericDelegator` methods to choose from when building queries to read data (available and in use within the OFBiz code), the earlier mentioned methods are the current best practice advice for new code.

To summarize, read requests to the Entity Engine return a result set containing either:

- A single row from the database
- A list of one or more rows
- A null value
- An error

Rows are automatically mapped into `GenericValue` objects based on an entity's model, by the Entity Engine. Because OFBiz does all the low-level data mapping and data type conversions, applications have a much cleaner, consistent view of the data. A single request for data may be run on many different underlying databases without the application developer changing any code.

The OFBiz delegator API contains a rich set of methods to use when accessing the Entity Engine through the Java interface. For more information, please see the **JavaDocs** online at:

`http://ci.apache.org/projects/ofbiz/site/javadocs/`

Working with large result sets (EntityListIterator)

Under normal conditions, the Entity Engine handles all the low-level database access tasks necessary to return a result set to memory for application use. Sometimes, a result set is too large to fit into memory. Under these conditions, a Java **Out of Memory** error will be thrown. To retrieve large result sets that exceed available memory limits, use the Entity Engine `EntityListIterator` object and retrieve partial result sets and process returned values in smaller chunks.

The following code snippet demonstrates the basic use of the `EntityListIterator`. Note: code has been left out to make the snippet readable. To use this code, you will need to add Java statements as appropriate:

```
// Don't forget to import EntityListIterator, EntityExpr,
// EntityCondition and other necessary Java packages
// Create any conditional query expressions
// We know we now have thousands of recipes, so to improve
// performance and conserve memory, we use the EntityListIterator
List<EntityExpr> exprs =
```

```
                    UtilMisc.toList(EntityCondition.makeCondition("notes",
                              EntityOperator.NOT_EQUAL, null),
                    EntityCondition.makeCondition("amount",
                         EntityOperator.GREATER_THAN, Long.valueOf(0))));
// Create a default EntityListIterator object
EntityListIterator eli = null;
try {
    // Use the GenericDelegator method call to return a pointer
    // to data set results. Note we are getting data from a
    // view-entity
    eli = delegator.find("RecipeTypeAndIngredientsView",
            EntityCondition.makeCondition(exprs,EntityOperator.AND),
            null, null, UtilMisc.toList("recipeId"), null);
    List<String> processList = FastList.newInstance();
    if (eli != null) {
        GenericValue value = null;
        // Use EntityListIterator to loop through the result set
        // Each next method call retrieves a GenericValue
        // OFBiz will get more values from the data source
        // automatically
        while (((recipeTypeAndIngredient =
                    (GenericValue) eli.next()) != null)) {
            // Do some processing with this list
        }
    }
}
catch (GenericEntityException e) {
    Debug.logError(e, module);
    // When done, don't forget to close the  EntityListIterator
}
finally {
    if (eli != null) {
        try {
            eli.close();
        }
        catch (GenericEntityException e) {
            Debug.logError(e, module);
        }
    }
}
```

To set scrolling and concurrent read options for a specific query, use the `EntityFindOptions` as shown in the code. Note: these options are valid for any Entity Engine data source query. However, changing scrolling behavior when processing a result set is only valid when using the `EntityListIterator` object as a pointer:

```
// Create a new EntityFindOptions object
EntityFindOptions efo = new EntityFindOptions();
// Set scrolling to INSENSITIVE. This allows forward and backward
// movement, but the result set is NOT sensitive to changes made by
// others. Data may be changed by other users while you are scrolling
// through the set.
// Scroll SENSITIVE instructs the Entity Engine to be aware and
// update the result set if any changes have occurred. Use with care
// as this setting introduces additional processing overhead.
efo.setResultSetType(EntityFindOptions.TYPE_SCROLL_INSENSITIVE);

// set concurrency to CONCUR_READ_ONLY so that a row may only be
// updated by the transaction that selected it.
efo.setResultSetConcurrency(EntityFindOptions.CONCUR_READ_ONLY);

efo.setSpecifyTypeAndConcur(true);
efo.setDistinct(false);
```

Pass the `EntityFindOptions` object as a parameter to the `find` method call.

The following Java code snippet shows direct manipulation of the result set cursor as provided by using `EntityListIterator` object methods:

```
GenericValue genericValue;
if ((genericValue = eli.next()) != null) {
    // Get the last cursor location (end of the result set)
    eli.last();
    // Set the current cursor location as
    int rowIndex = eli.currentIndex();
    // See if we have processed at least 100 rows
    if (rowIndex== 100) {
        // If we have processed as least 100 rows
        // Then get the value pointed to by the previous cursor
        // position
        genericValue = eli.previous();
        // Do some processing here
    }
}
// close
eli.close();
// Don't forget to add finally block here
```

To move within a result set, use the `EnitityListIterator` object's cursor movement methods as shown here:

EntityListIterator method	Usage
`afterLast()`	Sets the cursor position to just after the last result. This makes the `previous()` method call return the last result in the set.
`beforeFirst()`	Sets the cursor position to just before the first result. This makes a call to `next()` return the first result in the set.
`currentIndex()`	Returns the current cursor position.
`first()`	Sets the cursor position to the first result. If the result set is empty, this returns a boolean `false`.
`getPartialList` `(int start, int number)`	Returns a partial list of results starting at the indicated cursor position, containing at most `number` rows.
`last()`	Sets the cursor to the last result in the set.
`first()`	Sets the cursor to the first result in the set.

Removing data from the database (Java)

To remove one or more rows from an Entity Engine-managed database table, use the `GenericDelegator` object and call the appropriate methods as shown in the following code snippet:

Note: the Entity Engine negotiates record removal with the target data source using standard SQL commands constructed from method parameters passed by the calling program. If the target table rows cannot be removed because deletion violates referential integrity, neither OFBiz nor the underlying database will remove the indicated rows. Instead, an error will be thrown and control passed to the calling program.

```java
// Don't forget to add import statements
// First, get a GenericDelegator object from the context
GenericDelegator delegator = ctx.getDelegator();
// Before you can do anything, you must create a model of the
// Recipe table using the makeValue method
GenericValue recipe = delegator.makeValue("Recipe");
// Add the unique, primary key to the model
recipe.set("recipeId", "r001");
try {
    // Use the GenericValue remove method
    recipe.remove();
```

```
    // Or you could use the GenericDelegator remove, but not both at
    // the same time!
    // delegator.removeValue(recipe);
}
catch (GenericEntityException ge) {
    // process errors
}
```

To remove records from a database table using the Entity Engine, use the appropriate `GenericDelegator` method as described below:

GenericDelegator method	Usage
`GenericDelegator.removeValue(GenericValue X)`	Remove a single `GenericValue`. If removing the value causes referencing errors, the operation will fail with a `GenericEntityException` and control returns to the caller.
`GenericDelegator.removeAll(List<GenericValue>)`	Remove a list of `GenericValues`. If any one of the remove operations fail, a `GenericEntityException` will be thrown and all remove requests will be rolled back. No remove requests will be committed unless all requests can proceed successfully.

Please see the `GenericDelegator` Javadocs API for more information:

`http://ci.apache.org/projects/ofbiz/site/javadocs/`

Writing data to the database (Java)

Writing data to the database using the Entity Engine to handle database connections, transactions, data transfers, and data type conversions is preferred over direct SQL calls in almost all situations. To write data to an Entity Engine-managed data source, use the following code snippet as a guide:

```
// To add a row to a database table
// or update an existing table, you must first create a
// GenericValue object
// representing the table as an entity as shown here
GenericValue recipe = delegator.makeValue('Recipe");
// Add any updated fields to the
recipe.set("recipeName", "A new recipe w/raisins an apples");
recipe.set("recipeTypeId", "cake");
// cake better be a valid recipeTypeId or an error is thrown
// This will be an update to the existing row where the
// primary key is r001
```

```
    recipe.set("partyId", "r001");
    try {
        delegator.store(recipe);
    }
    catch {
        // Process errors
    }
```

Other `GenericDelegator` write methods are shown here:

GenericDelegator.method()	Usage
create(GenericValue X)	Creates and stores the `GenericValue`. Will fail if X already exists.
store(GenericValue X)	Stores the `GenericValue`. Will fail if X does NOT already exist.
createOrStore(GenericValue X)	Will create the `GenericValue` if it does not already exist. Values are persistent as either a new table row or an update to an existing table row.
storeAll(List<GenericValue>)	Stores all the `GenericValues` passed in the list.

Please see the `GenericDelegator` Javadocs API for more information:

`http://ci.apache.org/projects/ofbiz/site/javadocs/`

Using the automatic sequence generator

Many modern data-driven applications use automatic sequence generators to create primary keys for new database records. OFBiz provides a handy tool to acquire the next unique sequence identifier for any entity using the `GenericDelegator` object's sequence generator methods.

For example, to add a record with a unique primary key to the `Recipe` table, we could use the OFBiz sequence generator as shown in the following code snippet to find the next `sequenceId` for the `Recipe` entity, and then add a `GenericValue` with that `sequenceId` set as the primary key:

```
String sequenceId = delegator.getNextSeqId("Recipe");
GenericValue genericValue = delegator.makeValue("Recipe",
                        UtilMisc.toMap("recipeId",sequenceId));
// Or we could do it like this:
GenericValue genericValue = delegator.makeValue("Recipe",
        UtilMisc.toMap("recipeId",delegator.getNextSeqId("Recipe")));
// Finish adding field values to genericValue and then store
// it in the database
```

OFBiz keeps track of sequence identifiers, and each time one is requested, it calculates a unique sequence value based on the name of the sequence passed. An easy way to keep sequences unique for entities is to pass the name of the entity as the sequence name. In that way, all calls to the same entity will use the same sequence.

Note: for performance reasons, all primary keys for OFBiz data model entities default to twenty text characters or less. Using the `GenericDelegator` object's `getNextSeqId` method with a target entity ensures that you get a properly formatted Java data types (`String` or otherwise) for use as a primary key for that entity.

You may use the OFBiz sequence generator to return guaranteed unique values, including numeric values, for any purpose. For example, to create a Java `Long` unique sequence value, use a `GenericDelegator` method call similar to the following:

```
Long someSequenceNumber = getNextSeqIdLong('SequenceName');
```

Where `SequenceName` is any sequence name. If the named sequence does not exist, it will be created automatically.

EntityUtil

The `org.ofbiz.entity.util.EntityUtil` has several methods useful for manipulating data returned from an Entity Engine call. This data, referred to as the "result set", is either a single `GenericValue` object, a Java list containing one or more `GenericValue` objects, or a null.

Using the `EntityUtil` works with result sets already in memory. This means that you should use caution when manipulating data in this way as you may run out of memory and/or degrade performance in short order. If you have a choice, it is almost always better to let the Entity Engine and database perform data filtering, ordering, and sorting (by way of conditional `GenericDelegator` find parameters) before bringing a result set into memory.

In this section, we take a look at some handy utilities provided by OFBiz to manipulate result sets.

EntityUtil.getFirst()

There is a data modeling pattern often used within OFBiz where an entity will have three (or more) primary keys. One of the primary keys will uniquely represent a dated value. Using a unique `date` field as a primary key allows for many identical entries, with the only exception being the presence of a unique `date` value. This is great for auditing and tracking updates to a table. (Remember, you can't update a primary key field's value. If you want to change a primary key field's value, you must first remove the row from the database and then rewrite it).

From our bakery example, the `RecipeIngredient` entity uses this technique. By defining the `fromDate` field as a `Timestamp` value and as a primary key, it is possible to have the same ingredient included in the same recipe multiple times during the life of the recipe.

Why would you want to do that? Suppose we want to track the addition or modification of a specific ingredient within a recipe. Only by keeping the old ingredients around can we establish any history with our recipes.

Having multiple primary keys sometimes causes grief when searching for specific data, especially when you know all the primary keys but one. If you know all the primary keys, you may simply query by primary keys and be guaranteed that a single `GenericValue` object (or null) be returned. If you don't know all the primary keys for an entity, you are forced to get a list of values, many of which you may not be interested in.

OFBiz provides a handy utility that lets you easily get the first `GenericValue` off a result set list. In the following example, we first retrieve a list of `GenericValue` objects from the `RecipeIngredient` table (which, if you recall, has three primary keys). From that list, we select the first `GenericValue`.

```
GenericDelegator delegator =
                (GenericDelegator) request.getAttribute("delegator");
List conditions =
        UtilMisc.toList(EntityCondition.makeCondition("recipeId",
                             EntityOperator.NOT_EQUAL, null),
               EntityCondition.makeCondition("recipeSeqNumber",
                                  EntityOperator.NOT_EQUAL,
                                  new Long(0)));
try {
    List listOfEntities = delegator.findList("RecipeIngredient",
        EntityCondition.makeCondition(conditions,EntityOperator.AND),
        null,null,null,false);
    // Get the first GenericValue on the list
    GenericValue someEntity = EntityUtil.getFirst(listOfEntities);
    }
catch(GenericEntityException ge) {
    // Process errors
}
```

This method is often used together with an ordering operator as shown in the following code snippet to first order the return list by date, and then, knowing that the list is in dated order, return the most recent or the oldest dated value:

```
List conditions = UtilMisc.toList(EntityCondition.makeCondition(
                    "recipeId", EntityOperator.NOT_EQUAL, null),
                EntityCondition.makeCondition(
                            "recipeSeqNumber",
                            EntityOperator.NOT_EQUAL,
                            new Long(0)));
try {
    // Return the list where the most recent date in the "fromDate"
    // field is first on the list
    List listOfEntities = delegator.findList("RecipeIngredient",
                    EntityCondition.makeCondition(conditions,
                                EntityOperator.AND),
                null, UtilMisc.toList("-fromDate"),null,
                false);
    GenericValue someEntity = EntityUtil.getFirst(listOfEntities);
    // In this example, return a list where the oldest value in the
    // "fromDate" field is first on the list
    listOfEntities = delegator.findList("RecipeIngredient",
                    EntityCondition.makeCondition(conditions,
                                EntityOperator.AND),
                null, UtilMisc.toList("+fromDate"),null,
                false);
    someEntity = EntityUtil.getFirst(listOfEntities);
}
catch(GenericEntityException ge) {
    // Process Errors
}
```

EntityUtil.filterByDate()

In its simplest form, this method takes a list of `GenericValue` objects and compares each one against the given `moment` value, looking for objects where the default `fromDate` field value is either `null`, before, or equal to the `moment` value and the default `thruDate` field value is either `null` or after the moment `thruDate` value. In other words, the `moment` value falls between the values found in the `fromDate` and `thruDate` fields. This form of the method assumes that the entity has both a `fromDate` and a `thruDate` field defined. It just so happens that the `RecipeIngredient` table has just such fields defined. If our `RecipeIngredient` table has the following records in it:

RecipeIngredient			
recipeId	**ingredientId**	**fromDate**	**thruDate**
r001	10001	2009-01-01 00:00:00.000	2009-01-01 00:00:00.000
r001	10001	2009-03-05 00:00:00.000	2009-09-01 00:00:00.000
r001	10001	2009-09-09 00:00:00.000	2009-09-14 00:00:00.000
r001	10001	2009-09-15 00:00:00.000	
r001	10002	2008-01-01 00:00:00.000	
r001	10010	2010-01-01 00:00:00.000	
r002	10001	2008-01-01 00:00:00.000	2020-01-01 00:00:00.000

```
try {
    // For this example, just get them all
    List recipeIngredients =
    delegator.findList("RecipeIngredient",null,null,null,null,false);
    // First, find all the recipes and ingredients where the "active"
    // ingredient was added to the recipe before January 1, 2009.
    // These ingredients are still active if the thruDate is null
    // (never made inactive) or if the thruDate is after the current
    // date:
    Timestamp moment = Timestamp.valueOf("2009-01-01 00:00:00.0");
    List<GenericValue> alist =
        EntityUtil.filterByDate(recipeIngredients, moment);
    // Do something with the list
}
catch(GenericEntityException ge) {
    // Process Errors
}
```

The code returns a list with the following `GenericValue` objects (where `moment` equals "2009-01-01 00:00:00.0"):

recipeId	ingredientId	fromDate	thruDate
r001	10002	2008-01-01 00:00:00.0	null
r002	10001	2008-01-01 00:00:00.0	2020-01-01 00:00:00.0

This utility provides a convenient mechanism to collect a list of entities filtered by a moment in time. You will see this used frequently in the code where the moment is the current date in `Timestamp` format as shown here:

```
List<GenericValue> newList =
    EntityUtil.filterByDate(allParties, UtilDateTime.nowTimestamp());
```

You may also use this utility and pass the names of the fields that you'd like to use to compare the `moment` value against. For example, if we'd like to retrieve a list of all the rows from the `RecipeIngredients` result set where the value in the `createdStamp` is before a moment value of "2009-01-03 00:00:00.0" and the moment value is before the `lastUpdatedStamp` value, the following code snippet may be used as an example.

```
List recipeIngredients =
    delegator.findList("RecipeIngredient",null,null,null,null,false);
Timestamp moment = Timestamp.valueOf("2009-01-03 00:00:00.0");
// False in this method indicates that all dated values are not the
// same.
try {
    List<GenericValue> alist =
        EntityUtil.filterByDate(recipeIngredients, moment,
                    "createdStamp","lastUpdatedStamp", false);
}
catch(GenericEntityException ge) {
    // Process Errors
}
```

If we have the following three records in the `recipeIngredients` result set and a `moment` value equal to "2009-01-03 00:00:00.0":

recipeId	ingredientId	createdStamp	lastUpdatedStamp
r001	10001	2010-05-27 19:41:40.784	2010-05-28 13:02:14.55
r001	10001	2002-05-27 16:59:22.529	2010-05-28 13:02:15.561
r001	10001	2004-05-27 16:59:22.534	2010-05-28 13:02:33.21

The following two records/rows will be returned:

recipeId	ingredientId	createdStamp	lastUpdatedStamp
r001	10001	2002-05-27 16:59:22.529	2010-05-28 13:02:15.561
r001	10001	2004-05-27 16:59:22.534	2010-05-28 13:02:33.21

EntityUtil.orderBy()

To quickly sort through a list of result sets and return a new list ordered by entity fields that are dated or numeric types, use the `EntityUtil.orderBy()` method. The following Java snippet example orders an existing list as described:

```
// To order the list in descending order where the oldest value is
// first on the list (null values are placed at the beginning of
// the list):
alist = EntityUtil.orderBy(recipeIngredients,
```

```
                                 UtilMisc.toList("thruDate DESC"));

    // Or, if you prefer:
    alist = EntityUtil.orderBy(recipeIngredients,
                               UtilMisc.toList("-thruDate"));

    alist.clear();
    // To order a list in ascending order where the most recent
    // time value is first, followed in ascending order by other values
    // (and null values are all placed at the end of the list):
    alist = EntityUtil.orderBy(recipeIngredients,
                               UtilMisc.toList("thruDate ASC"));

    // Or, if you prefer:
    alist = EntityUtil.orderBy(recipeIngredients,
                               UtilMisc.toList("+thruDate"));
    alist.clear();
    alist = EntityUtil.orderBy(recipeIngredients,
                               UtilMisc.toList("amount","fromDate DESC"));
    // The orderBy method may also be used to order a list by non-dated
    // fields. For example, the following will return a list of
    // GenericValue objects ordered by value in the "amount" field.
    // Amount is a numeric. By default, the final order is by
    // ascending (lowest number first)
    alist = EntityUtil.orderBy(recipeIngredients,
                               UtilMisc.toList("amount"));
    // This call to orderBy will order the return list by the
    // GenericValue with the largest value first on the list
    alist = EntityUtil.orderBy(recipeIngredients,
                               UtilMisc.toList("amount DESC"));
    // You may also order the list by a non-numeric and/or
    // non-dated field:
    alist = EntityUtil.orderBy(recipeIngredients,
                               UtilMisc.toList("ingredientId"));
    // The ordering defaults to ascending (smallest value first).
    // Results may vary if the value in the target orderBy field does
    // not have a collation sequence that makes sorting sense.
```

The following are valid ordering directives supported by the orderBy method:

OrderBy specifier	Sort order
DESC	descending
ASC	ascending
-	descending
+	ascending

EntityUtil.getFieldListFromEntityList()

For a very handy utility to quickly assemble a list of field values from an existing result set, try the `EntityUtil.getFieldListFromEntityList()`. For example, if we have a list of `RecipeIngredient GenericValues` and we quickly want a new list of just the `ingredientIds`, we could do something like the following:

```
GenericDelegator delegator =
          (GenericDelegator) request.getAttribute("delegator");
try {
    // We are just getting started with the Entity Engine Java API
    // So, make the most basic of calls to get all the records/rows
    // from the RecipeIngredient table
    List<GenericValue> recipeIngredients =
    delegator.findList("RecipeIngredient",null,null,null,null,false);
    // Get a list of all the ingredientIds from recipeIngredients
    // Note: true means do not put duplicates in the return list
    // false means put all values in return list
    List<String> alist =
        EntityUtil.getFieldListFromEntityList(recipeIngredients,
                                        "ingredientId", true);
}
catch(GenericEntityException ge) {
    // Process Error
}
```

EntityUtil.getRelated()

Any time you have a list of entities where the entities are part of a one-to-one or one-to-many relationship, you can easily get related entities using the `EntityUtil.getRelated()` method. The following code snippet is an example:

```
GenericDelegator delegator =
          (GenericDelegator) request.getAttribute("delegator");
try {
    List<GenericValue> recipeIngredients =
    delegator.findList("RecipeIngredient",null,null,null,null,false);
     // Since the Ingredient entity is related to the
    // RecipeIngredient entity We can easily get all the entities
    // that are related to this entity using the getRelated()
    // method. We don't need to make another GenericDelegator call.
    // The following returns a list of Ingredient table rows where
    // the ingredientId field is related to the field value in
    // recipeIngredients.
```

```
        List<GenericValue> ingredients =
            EntityUtil.getRelated("Ingredient", recipeIngredients);
}
catch(GenericEntityException ge) {
    // Process Error
}
```

EntityUtil.filterByCondition()

As our data extraction needs get more sophisticated, we can avail ourselves of ever more precise filtering by using the EntityCondition object to create "condition" statements that further filter the values we are looking for. For example, if we wish to find recipes that have a specific set of ingredients, we could use:

```
try {
    // We are just getting started with the Entity Engine Java API
    // So, make the most basic of calls to get all the records/rows
    // from the RecipeIngredient table
    List<GenericValue> recipeIngredients =
    delegator.findList("RecipeIngredient",null,null,null,null,false);
    // Make up a list of arbitrary ingredients just to show how
    // this works
    List<String> arbitraryIngredients =
                UtilMisc.toList("10001", "11121", "10020", "1005");
    // This condition method returns all the GenericValue objects
    // from the recipeIngredient list where the value in
    // RecipeIngredient.ingredientId = any of the values in the
    // arbitraryIngredients list
    List<GenericValue> aList =
                    EntityUtil.filterByCondition(recipeIngredients,
                        EntityCondition.makeCondition("ingredientId",
                            EntityOperator.IN, arbitraryIngredients));
    // This call will only return values NOT in the
    // arbitraryIngredients list
    List<GenericValue> bList =
                    EntityUtil.filterOutByCondition(recipeIngredients,
                        EntityCondition.makeCondition("ingredientId",
                            EntityOperator.IN, arbitraryIngredients));
}
catch(GenericEntityException ge) {
    // Process Errors
}
```

There are all sorts of variations on the `filterByCondition()` method, limited only by your imagination in making up condition statements. We leave it as an exercise to the reader to experiment and come up with more ways.

EntityOperator reference

OFBiz "entity operators" are equivalent to SQL comparison operators. They allow for optimum flexibility in building entity condition statements. Entity operators are listed in the following table:

operator/operation	EntityOperator
and	EntityOperator.AND
between	EntityOperator.BETWEEN
equals	EntityOperator.EQUALS
greater than	EntityOperator.GREATER_THAN
greater than equal to	EntityOperator.GREATER_THAN_EQUAL_TO
in	EntityOperator.IN
not in	EntityOperator.NOT_IN
less than	EntityOperator.LESS_THAN
less than equal to	EntityOperator.GREATER_THAN_EQUAL_TO
like	EntityOperator.LIKE
not like	EntityOperator.NOT_LIKE
not	EntityOperator.NOT
not equal	EntityOperator.NOT_EQUAL
or	EntityOperator.OR

Index

Thank you for buying
Apache OfBiz Cookbook

About Packt Publishing

Packt, pronounced 'packed', published its first book "*Mastering phpMyAdmin for Effective MySQL Management*" in April 2004 and subsequently continued to specialize in publishing highly focused books on specific technologies and solutions.

Our books and publications share the experiences of your fellow IT professionals in adapting and customizing today's systems, applications, and frameworks. Our solution based books give you the knowledge and power to customize the software and technologies you're using to get the job done. Packt books are more specific and less general than the IT books you have seen in the past. Our unique business model allows us to bring you more focused information, giving you more of what you need to know, and less of what you don't.

Packt is a modern, yet unique publishing company, which focuses on producing quality, cutting-edge books for communities of developers, administrators, and newbies alike. For more information, please visit our website: www.packtpub.com.

About Packt Open Source

In 2010, Packt launched two new brands, Packt Open Source and Packt Enterprise, in order to continue its focus on specialization. This book is part of the Packt Open Source brand, home to books published on software built around Open Source licences, and offering information to anybody from advanced developers to budding web designers. The Open Source brand also runs Packt's Open Source Royalty Scheme, by which Packt gives a royalty to each Open Source project about whose software a book is sold.

Writing for Packt

We welcome all inquiries from people who are interested in authoring. Book proposals should be sent to author@packtpub.com. If your book idea is still at an early stage and you would like to discuss it first before writing a formal book proposal, contact us; one of our commissioning editors will get in touch with you.

We're not just looking for published authors; if you have strong technical skills but no writing experience, our experienced editors can help you develop a writing career, or simply get some additional reward for your expertise.

Apache Maven 2 Effective Implementation

ISBN: 978-1-847194-54-1 Paperback: 456 pages

Build and Manage Applications with Maven, Continuum, and Archiva

1. Follow a sample application which will help you to get started quickly with Apache Maven

2. Learn how to use Apache Archiva - an extensible repository manager - with Maven to take care of your build artifact repository

3. Leverage the power of Continuum - Apache's continuous integration and build server - to improve the quality and maintain the consistency of your build

4. Guidance on how to use Maven in a team environment to maximise its potential

Apache OFBiz Development: The Beginner's Tutorial

ISBN: 978-1-847194-00-8 Paperback: 472 pages

Using Services, Entities, and Widgets to build custom ERP and CRM systems

1. Understand how OFBiz is put together

2. Learn to create and customize business applications with OFBiz

3. Gain valuable development and performance hints

4. A fully illustrated tutorial with functional step-by-step examples

Please check **www.PacktPub.com** for information on our titles

Apache MyFaces 1.2 Web Application Development

ISBN: 978-1-847193-25-4   Paperback: 408 pages

Building next-generation web applications with JSF and Facelets

1. Build powerful and robust web applications with Apache MyFaces

2. Reduce coding by using sub-projects of MyFaces like Trinidad, Tobago, and Tomahawk

3. Update the content of your site daily with ease by using Facelets

4. Step-by-step and practical tutorial with lots of examples

Apache JMeter

ISBN: 978-1-847192-95-0   Paperback: 140 pages

A practical beginner's guide to automated testing and performance measurement for your websites

1. Test your website and measure its performance

2. Master the JMeter environment and learn all its features

3. Build test plan for measuring the performance

4. Step-by-step instructions and careful explanations

Please check **www.PacktPub.com** for information on our titles

Drupal 6 Panels Cookbook

ISBN: 978-1-849511-18-6   Paperback: 220 pages

Over 40 recipes to harness the power of Panels for building attractive Drupal websites

1. Build complex site layouts quickly with panels

2. Combine Panels with other Drupal modules to create dynamic social media websites

3. Get solutions to the most common 'Panels' problems

4. A practical approach packed with real-world examples to enrich understanding

5. Part of Packt's Cookbook series—each recipe is a carefully organized sequence of instructions to complete the task as efficiently as possible

Magento 1.3 Sales Tactics Cookbook

ISBN: 978-1-849510-12-7   Paperback: 292 pages

Solve real-world Magento sales problems with a collection of simple but effective recipes

1. Build a professional Magento sales web site, with the help of easy-to-follow steps and ample screenshots, to solve real-world business needs and requirements

2. Develop your web site by using your creativity and exploiting the sales techniques that suit your needs

3. Provide visitors with attractive and innovative features to make your site sell

Please check **www.PacktPub.com** for information on our titles

open source
community experience distilled

JSF 2.0 Cookbook

ISBN: 978-1-847199-52-2   Paperback: 396 pages

Over 100 simple but incredibly effective recipes for taking control of your JSF applications

1. Discover JSF 2.0 features through complete examples

2. Put in action important JSF frameworks, such as Apache MyFaces Core, Trinidad, Tomahawk, RichFaces Core, Sandbox and so on

3. Develop JSF projects under NetBeans/Glassfish v3 Prelude and Eclipse/JBoss AS

4. Part of Packt's Cookbook series: Each recipe is a carefully organized sequence of instructions to complete the task as efficiently as possible

Ext JS 3.0 Cookbook

ISBN: 978-1-847198-70-9   Paperback: 376 pages

Clear step-by-step recipes for building impressive rich internet applications using the Ext JS JavaScript library

1. Master the Ext JS widgets and learn to create custom components to suit your needs

2. Build striking native and custom layouts, forms, grids, listviews, treeviews, charts, tab panels, menus, toolbars and much more for your real-world user interfaces

3. Packed with easy-to-follow examples to exercise all of the features of the Ext JS library

Please check **www.PacktPub.com** for information on our titles